Unmasked:
The **Gonzales** Family Killer

Unmasked:
The **Gonzales** Family Killer

Kara Lawrence

HarperCollins*Publishers*

Excerpts from transcripts of the committal hearing (August 2003) and murder trial (April to May 2004) of Sef Gonzales and from the sentencing report of Justice Bruce James (17 September 2004) reproduced with permission from the New South Wales Attorney General's Department: April 2006.

Excerpt from *Gaculais and Minister for Immigration and Multicultural Affairs* [2000] AATA 959 (25 August 2000) copyright Commonwealth of Australia. Reproduced by permission.

If any copyright holders have not been acknowledged, the author would be grateful if they could contact her care of the publishers.

HarperCollins*Publishers*

First published in Australia in 2006
by HarperCollins*Publishers* Australia Pty Limited
ABN 36 009 913 517
www.harpercollins.com.au

Copyright © Kara Lawrence 2006

HarperCollins*Publishers*
25 Ryde Road, Pymble, Sydney NSW 2073, Australia
31 View Road, Glenfield, Auckland 10, New Zealand
77–85 Fulham Palace Road, London W6 8JB, United Kingdom
2 Bloor Street East, 20th floor, Toronto, Ontario M4W 1A8, Canada
10 East 53rd Street, New York NY 10022, USA

National Library of Australia Cataloguing-in-publication data:

Lawrence, Kara.
 Unmasked: the Gonzales family killer.
 ISBN 0 7322 7903 8.
 1. Gonzales, Sef – Trials, litigation, etc. 2. Gonzales,
 Sef – Family. 3. Gonzales family. 4. Murder –
 Investigation – New South Wales – Sydney. 5. Trials
 (Murder) – New South Wales – Sydney. I. Title.
364.1523

Cover photographs courtesy News Limited. *Top:* Sef Gonzales in May 2002, at his family members' graves. *Bottom:* The young Gonzales family shortly after their move to Sydney from the Philippines.
Typeset in 11.5/15pt Bembo by Kirby Jones
Printed and bound in Australia by Griffin Press on 79gsm Bulky Paperback White

5 4 3 2 1   06 07 08 09

For the Claridades family, in memory of
Teddy, Loiva and Clodine Gonzales

Contents

PART 2

PART 3

'O, what a tangled web we weave,
When first we practise to deceive!'
— Sir Walter Scott

Prologue

000 call received by New South Wales Ambulance Service operator at 11.48 pm, Tuesday, 10 July 2001

OPERATOR: Ambulance service, ambulance service.

CALLER: Please come, someone has — someone is at my parents, killed my family!

OPERATOR: Sorry?

CALLER: Someone has shot my parents, please come!

OPERATOR: What's — someone's what?

CALLER: Someone has shot my parents, I think. They're all bleeding there on the floor.

OPERATOR: What suburb are you in?

CALLER: They're not breathing, what do I do?

OPERATOR: What suburb are you in?

CALLER: North Ryde.

OPERATOR: North Ryde?

CALLER: Yes.

OPERATOR: What's your street address?

CALLER: Number 6.

OPERATOR: Number 6.

CALLER: Collins Street.

OPERATOR: Which one?

CALLER: Collins.

OPERATOR: Collins, C–O–L–L–I–N–S?

CALLER: Yes.

OPERATOR: What's your nearest cross street, do you know?

CALLER: Wicks Road.

OPERATOR: Weeks Road?

CALLER: Yes. I can't find my sister!

OPERATOR: What's, what's your phone number there?

CALLER: My, my phone line has been disconnected. I've been trying to use the phone. I'm on the mobile phone now.

OPERATOR: Yes. What, what's your, what's your mobile phone number? 0–4–1–6?

CALLER: 3–0–6–2–0–6.

OPERATOR: 3–0–6–2–0–6.

CALLER: Yes. Please hurry!

OPERATOR: And your parents are both —

CALLER: They're not moving.

OPERATOR: They've both been shot, have they?

CALLER: I don't know, there's a lot of blood everywhere.

OPERATOR: Okay. Have you rung, have you rung the police yet?

CALLER: No, I haven't rung.

OPERATOR: Do you think they've been shot?

CALLER: I don't know. There's a lot of blood. My mother —

OPERATOR: Hmm-mm.

CALLER: I can't find my sister!

OPERATOR: Okay. Well you just, you just, we'll get the police out there straightaway.

CALLER: On the way home —

OPERATOR: Right.

CALLER: *[Short burst of loud music in the background.]*
I think they've just been murdered. Help me!

OPERATOR: Just hold on. Yes, we will, we will, we're sending an ambulance now.

CALLER: Help me, help me, help me! When will they come?

OPERATOR: Okay, if you just stand, if you just stay there, just stay inside, right, don't go outside and the ambulance is on the way and I'll call the police, okay? Okay then?

CALLER: Yes.

OPERATOR: All right then, I'll call the police straightaway.

CALLER: Thanks.

OPERATOR: Okay then.

Call ends.

PART 1

Chapter 1

Three bodies

'Help me! Help me! John, John!'

Shane Hanley was watching a videotaped episode of the television comedy *Friends* inside his home at 5 Collins Street, North Ryde, when he heard the urgent cry.

Shane, a 44-year-old plumber, enjoyed his quiet, ordinary life with his mother in their old fibro home in Sydney's leafy northern suburbs. Collins Street was peaceful, despite being short and intersecting a main thoroughfare, Wicks Road. The street was lined mostly with homes very much like the Hanleys', perched on small blocks with neatly manicured lawns. Nothing much out of the ordinary ever really occurred in Collins Street, and on that cold winter's day — Tuesday, 10 July 2001 — things appeared no different.

Shane had worked all day and been out to a friend's house that night, returning home about 10 pm. The clouds overhead were heavy and ominous. It had already rained lightly that day, but then the rain had broken, and Shane counted himself lucky to have got home before it started bucketing down.

It was after 11.30 pm. Shane's mother was already asleep and Shane had been contemplating retiring himself. He didn't need to watch the end of the taped episode. That was one of the good things about *Friends*: you didn't need to watch the beginning, or the ending, to pick up the plot and get a good laugh out of it. You could just switch it off when your eyelids started getting heavy.

Shane thought the screaming was coming from next door, 7 Collins Street, where John and Sue Atamian lived. The couple were getting on in years; although Shane didn't know them very well, he judged John to be in his seventies.

The voice appealing for help had sounded high-pitched, like a woman's. Shane assumed the voice belonged to Sue, and that John was in some kind of strife. His first thought was 'heart attack'. His mother had suffered one two years earlier, and had survived because she got prompt medical treatment. Shane had first-aid training; maybe he could help. He yanked on his Adidas sneakers and ran out the door.

In the light spilling from his next-door neighbours' front verandah, Shane saw two figures standing in the Atamians' front yard. John was one of them, but the small figure with him — the source of the cries — wasn't Sue. Vaguely, Shane recognised the son of the Filipino couple who lived directly across the road from the Atamians. Sef Gonzales, a baby-faced, diminutive twenty-year-old, was dressed in jeans, hiking boots and a blue-grey jumper.

Sef's father (Teddy) was a lawyer, who had moved with his wife and two children into the newly built home across the street seven months before. Shane knew this because Ted had been thoughtful enough to bring over a stack of small plates as a gift for the Hanleys the previous Christmas, when he had introduced himself as the new neighbour. Shane knew him simply as 'Ted'.

The young man was in a state of panic, and barely coherent.

'They're all dead, they're all dead, they've all been shot!' he wailed. 'My whole family's been shot, they're all gone!'

Sef was telling Shane and John something about chasing people from his home and down towards Ryrie Street, where Collins Street ended in a T-intersection. Shane heard what Sef was saying, but his mind could not fathom it. A murder in his quiet street? He struggled to accept it.

Meanwhile, John was trying to shake off the fog of sleep after being abruptly roused when Sef banged on the outside wall of his front bedroom. His wife, Sue, wasn't home; she was staying the night at her mother's house. John had come to the front door and there stood Sef, yelling that his family had been killed.

Shane hadn't yet arrived when Sef grabbed John's hand and tried to pull him towards the house across the road, urging him to come and see what had been done to his family. John resisted. No way was he going in there. John's father had always told him not to get himself involved in other people's business. It was advice John had heeded well all his life.

That was when Shane had arrived and taken charge. He and John tried to ascertain if Sef had called emergency services, but couldn't make out his answer. Shane directed John to go back inside his house and ring for an ambulance. As John explained the situation on the phone to the operator, he was informed someone had already called to report the same emergency. Help was on the way.

At this point, Shane was trying as best he could to comfort and support the distraught young man, whom he barely knew. Shane could not seem to come up with the words he wanted; how do you comfort someone who has just lost their family? So Shane walked Sef back and forth across the street, his wiry frame supporting that of the young man, who was sobbing and falling all over the place. All of a sudden, it seemed to Shane, they were standing on the driveway of the Gonzales home.

Turning his attention towards the house, Shane saw that one of the roller doors to the double garage was open, the garage dark inside. There was, however, a light on inside the house itself. The clouds still hung heavy in the sky. All was silent and still, as if the rest of the street were indifferent to this unfolding nightmare. Shane had seen enough newspaper and television reports to know that if what Sef was saying was true, this was a major crime scene. Where were the sirens? The flashing lights of emergency vehicles?

Shane squatted beside Sef, who had all but collapsed onto the driveway. Sef was making terrible sobbing noises, but as Shane ran his hands over Sef's face, trying to comfort him, he felt no moisture there. In the panic of the moment, this barely registered with Shane; it was only much later that it would strike him as peculiar.

Then Sef jumped to his feet and said something that made Shane think there was still hope for the Gonzales family, that they might still be alive.

'I know CPR, I know CPR!' Sef said, and ran in through the garage door.

Shane felt a flash of anger at that point. 'Then what the hell are we doing standing out here?' he immediately thought. 'Jeez, don't tell me they're still alive!'

Sef darted towards the house, with Shane in tow. His heart pounding, Shane vaguely noted a big white vehicle parked in the garage: Teddy's four-wheel drive. (Beside it was a white sedan, which John didn't have time to notice.)

'Daddy, Daddy, Daddy!' Sef cried.

They passed through the doorway that connected the garage to the ground-floor study area of the house. Then the pair entered the tiled foyer to the right.

What followed — the images that Shane saw that night — would plague his sleep for a long time. He had seen dead bodies

— car accident victims — before, but had never witnessed the results of murder. It seemed that after that night, every time he closed his eyes he would see those horrible visions, and his mind would tick over with unanswered questions. Despite time and trauma counselling, the terrible scene would never quite be erased from Shane's mind. Aside from Sef and the trained emergency personnel who later attended the scene, he would be the only person to witness first-hand the full force of the violence that claimed the lives of three people.

TEDDY GONZALES LAY face up in the foyer, on a white rug just inside the front door. The poor bugger hadn't had a chance, Shane thought.

The 46-year-old immigration lawyer was dressed in a dark business suit and still had his glasses on. His arms were angled slightly away from his body, his head towards the dining-room entrance, and his feet, clad in black shoes, stretched towards the front door, one of them resting on it. His grey metallic briefcase lay open to the right of his body, and papers spilled out of it onto the tiles.

At first Shane thought Teddy was wearing a red vest under his suit, then realised his mistake. The white business shirt was stained red with blood, and there was a huge hole in Teddy's chest. Shane initially decided it was a bullet wound that must have been inflicted at almost point-blank range. On seeing him, Shane immediately reassessed his earlier thought that Teddy might be saved. He was still with death.

Sef ran to his father, straddling him and grasping him by the shoulders. He gently shook him, as if trying to lift him, sobbing, 'Papa, Papa, Papa!' Shane felt his heart go out to the young man. The scene was pitiful.

Shane dragged Sef off his father's body, and it was then that he noticed a silver mobile phone lying about a metre to the right of Teddy's body. The screen was lit up a bright blue, as if the phone had just been in use. (This was Sef's phone, used to call 000, and was later seized by crime-scene officers for testing.)

Sef then snapped back into action, yelling, 'Mummy, Mummy, Mummy!', running past his father's body and into the formal lounge–dining room adjoining the foyer. While the foyer had been brightly lit, the dining-room area was gloomy. Shane could make out a figure lying behind a small glass coffee table topped with a colourful flower arrangement. It was the body of Teddy's 43-year-old wife, Loiva. She was lying in an awkward position on her side, one leg bent. It struck Shane, from the position of her body, that she had been trying to flee her attacker by running towards the front door when she was caught and flung down.

Loiva was dressed in jeans, a dark-coloured jumper and black lace-up shoes. There were dark bloody patches on her neck and shoulders, and to Shane they also looked like bullet holes.

Sef repeated what he had just done with his father, pulling at his mother's shoulders and wailing 'Mummy!' over and over again.

While Shane kneeled by Loiva, he had a chilling thought. What if the killers were still in the house? 'Jeez, I hope they're not still here,' he thought. 'I don't want to look up and see a pair of eyes up there.'

As before, Shane dragged Sef from his mother's body, and Sef ran back to his father, flinging himself onto him again. 'Papa, Papa, Papa!' he cried.

Shane followed him. He immediately noticed that the mobile phone screen he had seen lit up only moments before was now dark, and he wondered if Sef, for some reason, had quickly turned it off. He wondered why Sef would bother doing that, having just discovered his parents' bodies. It was at that point, as Shane led Sef from the house, that he began to become suspicious of the young man's behaviour.

From what Shane had observed, the rest of the ground floor had been orderly and undisturbed. He didn't go upstairs, where a third body lay. But Shane's clear impression from what Sef had told him was that Sef's sister was dead too.

While the scene inside the house had been horrific, the overwhelming feeling Shane experienced was immense sadness. Not just one life lost, but a whole family. And they had seemed such proud, happy people, so loving. To Shane, the only blessing was that Teddy, who Shane assumed was attacked just after entering the house, probably had not had the chance to discover his wife's and daughter's bodies before he died.

In all, Shane figured he and Sef had been inside the house for about ten minutes. In reality it was less than two, but time often seems to stretch into slow motion in such circumstances. Outside, there was still no sign of emergency vehicles.

Shane remembered that the Gonzales family owned some yappy little dogs, but there had been no noise from the dogs that night, not even when he and Sef had entered the house.

Looking across the road towards the corner of Collins and Ryrie Streets, where an elderly female relative of the Gonzales family lived, Shane noticed there were no lights on or signs of movement there.

Shane's gut instinct told him there was more to this scene than met the eye. The dogs, and the relative across the road. Where were they? He decided it was time he called the police. He was assuming this was a family 'hit', so the relative across the road could be dead too.

As he and Sef emerged from the house, John was coming up the driveway. Shane asked John whom he had called, and John replied he had rung for an ambulance.

'Well, I've got to go and make a phone call,' Shane told John. He did not want to mention the word 'police' in front of Sef. Already he was entertaining suspicions about Sef's possible involvement in the murders.

Shane left Sef in John's care, warning him not to go into the house. The elderly man may not have had the heart to take it, he thought; Shane did not want to risk John's health on top of everything else.

Shane crossed the road to his house and thought at first of ringing the nearest police station, which was three suburbs away at Gladesville. Stuff it, he thought, dialling 000.

The 000 operator asked which service he required.

'Definitely police, homicide if possible,' Shane told the man.

Shane told the operator that the dogs were not in the Gonzales house, and mentioned his concerns for the safety of a female relative of the Gonzales family nearby. Although Shane, at that time, was not aware of exactly what the woman's relationship was to the Gonzales family, he was referring to Loiva's mother and Sef's grandmother, Amelita Claridades. (Police later discovered that she was in Melbourne, visiting relatives.)

Then Shane heard sirens and was flooded with relief. The responsibility was now out of his hands. When he went outside next, the dog squad had arrived and emergency vehicles clogged the street. And it had begun to rain again.

Shane approached a constable and told the officer he had been inside the house. The officer asked him to go back inside his home, and told him that he would be spoken to later.

Hours afterwards, when police had secured the crime scene, Shane would be interviewed at Gladesville police station about the events of that night. He would hand over the clothes and shoes he had worn into the house to police for forensic analysis, as they tried to ascertain if he had any involvement in the crime. Shane was eliminated from involvement when his description of his movements inside the house tallied with the evidence of his clothing and shoes. There was one spot of blood on one knee of his pants, and blood on both soles. Sole imprints from his shoes were taken and found to be consistent with some sole smudges left inside the house, but most of the imprints were left by another type of shoe.

Shane, the ordinary bloke from an ordinary street, had been dragged into what would become a major investigation, and he would become an important witness in the case. He took an avid interest in its progress. He would go over and over what he had done that night, feeling that he had 'stuffed up': that he should have felt for a pulse on the victims, that he hadn't done enough to help those poor people. His feelings battled with rational thought: it had just been too late to make a difference.

Chapter 2

Teddy

A world away from Sydney's middle-class northern suburbs is the town of Baguio, on the northern tip of the Philippines, where Teddy Chua Gonzales came into the world on 2 October 1954.

The residents of Baguio, in the Cordillera Mountains region, are blessed with spectacular tree-topped mountain scenery and soothing temperatures offered by the city's position 1511 metres above sea level. For these reasons, their city is known as the summer holiday capital of the Philippines, and also as the City of Pines. When summer temperatures in the Philippines capital, Manila, soar, city-slickers embark on the seven-hour drive north along treacherous winding roads to Baguio to seek relief from the oppressive humidity.

When the United States began its almost 50-year occupation of the Philippines at the end of the nineteenth century, the US military was quick to see the benefits of developing the lush Baguio area, and set up a base there. Now this military base has been converted into a golf course, where Filipino doctors, lawyers and other professionals spend their weekends perfecting their swings.

These people work hard for their successes. In the Philippines poverty still abounds; you can see it on Baguio's outskirts, where squatters live in shanties perched precariously on hillsides surrounding the congested business district, and freshly washed laundry flutters from the balconies of cramped concrete apartment buildings.

Adding to the financial pressures for Filipinos is the fact that a lot of families have many mouths to feed. In this strongly Roman Catholic country, birth control is not freely exercised in many areas. Plus, family is central to Filipino culture. Without the love and respect of a close-knit family, you are very poor indeed.

TEDDY GONZALES WAS not born into the lap of luxury. A millionaire when he died, he clawed his way up the financial ladder during his 46 years, with a powerful work ethic fuelled by ambition. He was a self-made man.

Teddy was born into a typically large Filipino family. He was the youngest child of William and Belen Gonzales. From his parents he inherited some Filipino blood, but there was also a strong dash of Chinese, particularly on his father's side. Belen bore William four children: Mercy, Freddie, Annie and then Teddy.

Teddy and his siblings grew up in a modest rented house in Baguio. They were a tight-knit bunch, the Gonzales clan, with William and Belen emphasising the value of family and striving hard for success. The children certainly went without the luxuries many Western children in the 21st century demand as their right. Nevertheless, Freddie would always remember it as a normal, happy childhood. Freddie and Teddy forged a bond, one in which Freddie was his little brother's protector, confidant and, later, business partner.

Like most Filipino children raised in the 1950s, the Gonzales children were taught to respect and obey their parents. According to Freddie, the husband is the undisputed head of the Filipino family, and his wife is expected to defer to her husband's wishes. The children look up to their parents. They do not question their parent's decisions, unless they wish to feel the sharp sting of a parent's hand. One of the commonly spoken Filipino languages, Tagalog, which the Gonzales family spoke, has a term, *po*. It indicates respect and is spoken at the end of a sentence. Filipino children use it all the time to address their parents, says Freddie.

'Of course we're all very family-orientated and since we were not born with a silver platter, it was also implanted in us to strive hard to be successful,' says Freddie.

Teddy had this work ethic in spades. From an early age, his ambition became obvious. So did his organisational and planning skills.

'He established goals and really tried to obtain his goals,' says Freddie.

What the Gonzales children lacked in material possessions was more than made up for by formal education. Perhaps this was why they went on to become so successful in later life. Freddie qualified as an engineer and established his own hotel in Baguio, the Forest Inn. Annie Gonzales-Tesoro is a lawyer who rose to a senior management position within the Securities Exchange Commission's office in Bagiuo. Mercy married and had children, becoming a housewife.

Teddy began his education at St Theresa's College, a Baguio school run by Belgian nuns. He progressed through high school, performing well academically, then went on to study political science and economics at St Louis University in Baguio. Teddy graduated with outstanding grades in 1974.

Like his sister Annie Gonzales-Tesoro, Teddy decided to pursue law. It fitted in with his idealistic views and his sense of justice, says Freddie. In 1975 Teddy began the four-year law course in a class of about 35 students at Baguio Colleges Foundation. It quickly became apparent that he had a natural aptitude for law.

One of his fellow students, lawyer and federal agent Bensheen Apolinar, recalls Teddy as a 'brilliant' student and a 'just' and fair person.

'He graduated *magna cum laude*, he was one of our top achievers,' says Apolinar. 'I think he placed thirteenth in the 1979 bar examination [for the whole of the Philippines].'

Teddy's fellow students saw a different side of him from that seen by his family. To those close to Teddy, he could be light-hearted and hilarious, revelling in being the centre of attention, using his razor-sharp wit to crack jokes at family gatherings. His fellow students saw the flip side of his personality. The young man, dressed in a suit and tie, was intense, incredibly focused and mature for his age, with no time for the frivolous extracurricular activities of university life.

Apolinar remembers Teddy as a quiet man who did not drink, smoke or have any other apparent vice. He certainly didn't go out drinking with the other students. Apolinar got the impression that Teddy was already wealthy and socialised with important people in the community. Though this could have easily have been interpreted as snobbishness, Apolinar remembers Teddy as being on friendly terms with the other students.

He recalls Teddy placing a ten-peso wager against him on a boxing match between Muhammad Ali, the self-proclaimed 'greatest', and Joe Frazier. It was not a large bet, but the reason why Teddy made it amused Apolinar. 'I don't like Muhammad Ali. He talks too much,' Teddy said. Soon afterwards, Apolinar collected his ten pesos from Teddy, who was unperturbed. After all, he'd made the bet on principle.

Apolinar thought this was just like Teddy — a quiet achiever who put little faith in flashy talk. It was dedication, hard slog and results that mattered to Teddy.

As well as studying law at night, he worked to support himself. By day he was selling real estate in the Baguio area. He was making a pretty good living out of it, enough to buy himself a battered brown four-door sedan to get around in. Later, while still studying, he and Freddie became partners in a taxi company. In addition, Teddy was involved in a business selling gas cylinders.

Teddy did not want to wait until graduation to have something to his name, something he could offer to the right woman, when she came along. So it was that two years into his law degree, in early 1977, he met the woman he would love and dote on for as long as they both would live. Her name was Mary Josephine Loiva Siochi Claridades. While Mary was her Christian name, to those close to her, she was Loiva (pronounced 'Loy-va').

Chapter 3

Sirens, lights

10 July 2001, 11.55 pm

Collins Street was dark and still as ambulance officers Greg Jones and Darren Hosking roared in. The pair, the first emergency personnel to arrive at the triple murder scene, pulled into the street exactly seven minutes after Sef Gonzales telephoned 000.

All the pair had been told as they were sent out to Collins Street that night was that there had been a shooting reported. The tableau that confronted them on the driveway of number 6 only heightened Jones's concern for his own safety and that of his partner.

In the dim illumination of street lights and the vague light emanating from inside the house, Jones saw two people. One figure was stooped on the ground, while the second figure stood over it.

Quickly Jones assessed the scene, drawing on his thirteen years of experience as an ambulance officer. He had planned to wait until the police turned up, as the ambulance officers had no weapons to protect themselves if a gunman was still nearby. Dashing in heedlessly would go against all his training.

Yet the figure stooped on the ground could well have been shot and in need of urgent medical care. Jones and Hosking quickly decided on their course of action. They would pull into the driveway, place the wounded man on a stretcher and into the ambulance, then get the hell out of there.

Hosking ventured out of the ambulance first, approaching the figure on the ground — Sef. The person standing over him was John Atamian. As per Shane Hanley's instructions, John was watching over Sef. Hosking quickly discovered Sef was physically unharmed but in a state of great distress. Together, Hosking and Jones decided to radio in to base and ask for back-up. They reported that so far there was one patient at the scene.

The next step was to ascertain whether the area was safe. Jones approached Sef, still concerned. 'He told me his family had been stabbed, murdered, they were lying inside and they needed help … I believe that he did say that it was his mother and his father and his sister upstairs, because he wanted us to go upstairs as well,' Jones says.

Sef told Jones he had disturbed people inside the house and chased them away, pointing down the street to a T-intersection. Jones resisted Sef's urgent pleas that he go inside the house and help his family members. He wasn't willing to stake his life on what this young man, a complete stranger, was telling him.

11 July 2001, 12.02 am

A LIGHT RAIN was falling as Constables Luke Mulligan and David Peters radioed in that they had arrived at 6 Collins Street. The rookie officers were on the night shift at nearby Gladesville police station, so their response had been prompt.

The uniformed officers got out of their marked police car. The ambulance officers, Hosking and Jones, had moved Sef and John Atamian into the double garage that jutted out from the house.

Sef was sitting on the garage floor, crying and shaking. Despite his miserable state, he was quick to notice the arrival of the men in blue. As the police officers walked up the driveway, Sef stood up and approached them, grasping Peters around his waist.

'You must help me!' Sef implored the young, clean-cut officer. 'My mother, father and sister have been killed inside and you must help me!'

Mulligan, meanwhile, only recalled that Sef mentioned finding the bodies of his mother and father, after returning home from a night out.

Sef then described chasing people from his home.

'I followed them and then I came back in and they [my family] were bleeding everywhere,' Sef told Mulligan, pointing in the direction of the intersection of Collins Street and Ryrie Street, about 20 metres away.

Returning to the subject of his parents' injuries, Sef told Mulligan he had tried to start his mum's and dad's hearts, mimicking the CPR motion of two hands pumping. Both officers noticed a marked lack of blood on both Sef's hands and clothing. Sef tried to persuade them to come inside, as he had done with the ambulance officers. 'They're bleeding everywhere, help them please!'

Mulligan tried to pin Sef down on how many attackers the police should be casting a net for.

'One or two, I can't remember,' Sef said.

'Were they in a car?' Mulligan probed further. This detail was extremely important; it would make all the difference to how far they could have travelled since the emergency call was made at 11.48 pm, and the descriptions to be issued to police.

'No, no car,' Sef replied.

Who exactly was inside the house? Mulligan asked Sef.

'My mother and father, please help me!'

At this point, Mulligan left Sef and spoke to one of the ambulance officers, who said he believed there were three bodies inside. At this point, no emergency personnel had been inside the house. They were relying on the scrambled and contradictory information supplied by an obviously distressed young man.

Peters decided to investigate further. Entering the garage, he walked past the two white vehicles parked inside, Teddy's four-wheel drive Mitsubishi Pajero and Loiva's Toyota Celica sedan, and stepped onto the internal access stairs to the study.

Poking his head through the doorway and looking to the right, he saw what Shane Hanley had earlier observed. An Asian man lay on the floor of the foyer with blood around him. Peters didn't venture in any further, but radioed this information back to his supervisors.

Peters then returned to Sef. The young man confided that he had been studying medicine but had changed his studies to law, a fact he severely regretted now. If only he had a greater knowledge of medicine, he perhaps could have saved his family, he lamented.

Sef then told Peters of a road rage incident that would become the subject of great speculation later on. Sef said that the incident had occurred the evening before, when he'd been driving his family home from dinner. Another vehicle had passed him, the occupants angrily yelling out, 'Bloody Asians!' The young man seemed to think that some traffic argy-bargy — not at all uncommon on Sydney's congested roads — could be relevant to the triple murder of his family.

11 July 2001, 12.04 am

GLADESVILLE STATION'S Senior Sergeant Bob Betts, a cop with 31 years in the police force, arrived sixteen minutes after Sef's emergency call. He had seen his fair share of murder scenes and bodies in various stages of decomposition, but what he was about to see would strike him particularly hard, plaguing his thoughts for a long time. As with Shane Hanley, it wasn't just that the victims had been so savagely attacked, it was the fact that this savagery had wiped out almost an entire family. Betts, along with senior paramedic Jeff Gilchrist, who arrived within two minutes of the first ambulance crew, would be the first emergency personnel to properly enter the Gonzales home that night.

When he arrived at the scene, Betts found Sef sitting against the garage wall. At first, Betts didn't speak much to Sef, except to ascertain if the attackers were still inside the house. From what Sef told him, Betts got the impression that one attacker had run out of the house and that another might still be upstairs.

Gilchrist and Betts entered the house through the internal garage door, Betts leading the way. At the sight of Teddy's body in the foyer, Betts motioned to Gilchrist to check for signs of life. Then he pulled out his service pistol and kept it drawn. As Betts stood on lookout, Gilchrist devoted his attention to Teddy. But Teddy's pulse had given up several hours ago. Rigor mortis — a stiffening of the muscles after death — had begun on Teddy's face, head and neck. His skin was cold.

Betts's gun remained cocked as he ventured further into the house. He kept one eye out for victims but most of his attention was focused on detecting a noise, a movement, any sign that an attacker was still in the house. His heart was racing at a million miles an hour, but his training kicked in as he went about 'clearing' each room he passed through. Aside from the darkened formal lounge–dining room on the ground floor, both floors of the house were pretty well lit, but the pair took a torch with them nevertheless.

In the neat modern kitchen at the back of the ground floor, the window above the sink was open, though the blind was drawn. Betts then ventured to the laundry at the left of the ground floor. As he opened the door, he heard a scuffling noise and his heart jumped to his throat. He almost let loose a shot, but there was only a little white dog, surrounded by new pups, cowering behind the door.

Urging himself to keep calm, he crossed to the darkened formal lounge–dining room, and the light of the torch illuminated the body of Loiva Gonzales. Betts saw a large amount of blood on and around the body.

Gilchrist went to work again. Like Teddy, Loiva's skin was cold, indicating she had been dead for some time. She also had stiffness in her upper body and neck. Again, no signs of life.

Betts headed up the curving wooden staircase to the upper storey, finding all the lights on except that in the main bathroom. After a brief pause he called down to Gilchrist that he had found a third body. Betts had not been expecting this; he was under the impression it was only Sef's parents who had been killed. The body was in the bedroom to the left of the landing, 18-year-old Clodine Gonzales' room. The pitiful sight of the young girl's body struck at Betts's heart.

As Gilchrist followed Betts, he noted there was a cordless black telephone lying on the wooden floor of the landing at the top of the stairs, and he stepped around it on his way in to Clodine's bedroom.

Clodine's body was curled up in the fetal position, lying sideways on the floor, her arms across her chest. Her chin was tucked downwards, her head pressed against the wall behind her. An arc of blood smeared behind her towards the floor, indicating she must have rested her back against the wall and remained upright at some stage before sliding to the floor. There was a large amount of coagulating blood under her head, and drying blood on the floor nearby. A red jumper lay draped across her body.

Gilchrist performed the formalities — for that was all they were — feeling for the carotid arteries in her neck, those all-important, life-sustaining vessels. No pulse. Clodine, too, had been dead for some time.

Betts noticed the wardrobe doors and drawers in Clodine's bedroom were open. In fact, they were open in all three of the four upstairs bedrooms he was able to check — Sef's bedroom, Clodine's and the spare bedroom at the front of the house. He tried the door to Teddy's and Loiva's bedroom, also at the front of the house. It was locked. This was Teddy's and Loiva's practice when they were both not home. Behind the door, another dog's yapping could be heard.

When the pair re-emerged into the garage, Sef was still sitting on the floor, being attended to by ambulance officers. Sef told Gilchrist he had tried to resuscitate his parents. Still sobbing, he asked Betts for some rosary beads, saying he wanted to pray for his mother and father. He did not mention his sister at all.

Sef told Betts his father was a lawyer, and handed him a business card for his father's practice. He told Betts he had worked that day at his father's office at Blacktown, trying to fix a computer, and then told Betts about the road rage incident.

Later, about 2 am, Betts had a further conversation with Sef. Until that point, Betts had felt very sorry for the young man, imagining the shock of being a family member stumbling into such a horrific scene. Then Sef asked Betts: 'Can I tell you something in confidence?'

The first thought to cross Betts's mind was that he had been wrong about Sef and that the young man was about to confess to killing his family. Briefly, Betts considered warning

Sef about the legal ramifications of a confession, before deciding against it.

'Sef, no worries, yep,' Betts replied.

Sef then said something so out of context it altered Betts's opinion of him dramatically. He told Betts he had some pornography, a video, in the dresser drawer of his upstairs bedroom. Possession of such material by a young man was far from unusual, but Sef was obviously embarrassed about its potential discovery by police.

Betts couldn't believe what he was hearing and was immediately suspicious of Sef. Why would Sef bring that up when he had just found the bodies of his family? 'If I was in that situation, it wouldn't even cross my mind,' Betts thought.

11 July 2001, 12.13 am

SENIOR CONSTABLE PAUL CORNALE had cop written all over him. A fit man who had been part of the elite State Protection Group's dog squad for five years, he was familiar with the adrenalin rush of chasing suspected criminals over fences and through bushes. His German shepherd sniffer dog, Tyson, arrived with him that night at 6 Collins Street. The dog had a sense of smell 17,000 times stronger than a human's, and was also capable of detecting scents up to two hours old.

The conditions for tracking that night were optimum. There was virtually no breeze, and far from washing away any scent clinging to the ground, the light rain that had fallen had the capacity to enhance smells on bitumen or grass, drawing them to the surface for detection by the dog's eager nose. Of course, sniffer dogs are not infallible. They are animals, and all animals are capable of making mistakes.

Dog-squad officers have a set of preformatted questions to ask when they arrive at a crime scene. Cornale asked the ambulance and police officers where they had walked, so the dog would not be confused by their tracks. He also conferred with Sef and asked him in which direction the attackers had escaped. Sef pointed to a 40-kilometre speed-limit sign across the road.

'How many did you chase?' Cornale asked.

'I know I chased one for sure, maybe two or three, I'm not sure, but one, yes,' Sef replied.

There was no vehicle that they escaped in, Sef told Cornale. So the dog-squad officer began his work. He covered all bases, searching for a good hour. He carefully walked down both directions of the street from the house, jumped fences into adjacent yards, painstakingly checking every possible path of escape. The dog simply did not tell him anything. It could not pick up a trail in any direction. In the end, Cornale was forced to give up.

Chapter 4

Loiva

Mary Josephine Loiva Siochi Claridades was eighteen years old and a university student when she met Teddy Gonzales. Teddy, who was almost four years older than Loiva, fell for her delicate beauty and quiet poise instantly. With the determination he applied to his other goals, Teddy set about making her his wife.

At the time, Loiva was living at home with her mother, Amelita Claridades, and her father, Spanish-born dentist Simeon Claridades. Amelita had a passion for developing and selling real estate. When she decided to put her Baguio house on the market, Teddy paid a visit to the Claridades home. Amelita held a high regard for the responsible young man. He was a competent estate agent and charged at a reasonable rate.

Emily Luna, Loiva's younger sister, was aged eleven at the time and was vicariously interested in the possibility of a blooming love affair in her sister's life. She remembers Teddy's reaction to Loiva when he came to their home.

'Teddy was actually selling our house at that time and he brought in an uncle of his, I think, who was interested in buying our house, and at that time our family was at home. The first time he laid eyes on my sister he didn't let go. My dad would talk to him and he'd be staring at my sister.'

Freddie Gonzales, too, recalls that Teddy was taken by Loiva. Freddie accompanied his brother to a family dinner at the Claridades home around that time.

'I was married then already, so I said, that's a nice lady. I started telling him it's about time [you settled down]. He did say yes, that's a pretty lady,' Freddie says.

In Freddie's view, Loiva had qualities that made her wife material: 'She was very prim, proper, nice, like somebody ideal for a family, to be a wife and mother.'

Teddy's courtship of Loiva was old-fashioned. The ground rules were set by Loiva's parents: Teddy visited Loiva at her home, or if they wanted to go out on a date, they were to be chaperoned by Amelita.

There was no kissing allowed, but Teddy was permitted to hold Loiva's hand. This hand-holding would become a loving habit of theirs for the rest of their lives. Many people would comment on how rare it was to see a long-married couple remain so affectionate.

Perhaps it was because of the restrictions imposed on them in their courtship that they valued this simple act of affection. While these rules may seem outdated now, in the 1970s in the Philippines, when many women married the first man they dated, such restrictions were not altogether unusual, explains Emily.

Another of Loiva's sisters, Annie Paraan, recalls that Teddy became a frequent visitor to the Claridades home long after his prospective buyer decided against purchasing it.

'My sister was at home then, that's when he saw my sister and according to him he fell in love. He started to come over to the house even if there were no buyers.'

The Claridades family nicknamed Teddy after the cartoon character 'Speedy Gonzales', as he would call to say he would come over, then arrive two minutes later, eager to see Loiva.

Emily would meet him at the front gate, holding onto his arm and chatting as she led him to the house. She liked Teddy, who had a wicked sense of humour and enjoyed teasing her. 'He would be really welcome in the family, he was funny and warm as well,' she says.

Annie Paraan describes the couple's courtship as a 'whirlwind affair', lasting two or three months before he proposed marriage.

Teddy had to overcome reluctance on the part of Loiva's father, as Loiva was so young and only in her first semester at St Louis University. However, Amelita's fondness for Teddy and the fact he was making such a success of himself early in life won over Simeon Claridades.

So on 12 June 1977, Teddy and Loiva married in the chapel in the grounds of St Louis University. It was a small, simple wedding, just family and some of Teddy's close friends. The ceremony was conducted by an elderly Catholic priest, Father Desmet James, one of Teddy's friends.

Annie Paraan remembers Teddy being extremely excited. Loiva was obviously happy, but, with a sister's insight, Annie saw she was also nervous. 'Loiva was very shy, especially as that was her first kiss. My parents were very conservative when they were dating, so her first kiss was at her wedding.'

Emily recalls that when the time came for the groom to kiss the bride, Loiva nervously pulled back for a moment, eliciting a chuckle from the onlookers.

With the vows said, the wedding party moved on to the reception at the five-star Hyatt Terraces in Baguio. The young couple honeymooned at La Union, a resort town west of Baguio, perched on the South China Sea.

Teddy's and Loiva's marriage was, if not one of equals, close to it, which was unusual in conservative Filipino society. They appeared to have tremendous respect for one another. Annie

Paraan recalls, for example, that if the usually shy Loiva strongly voiced opposition to a decision of Teddy's, he would sometimes give in to her will. 'And, if my sister would come in conflict with Teddy's mother, Teddy would side with Loiva. This would make his mother sometimes hurt,' she says.

Another example of Teddy's devotion to his wife was his tolerance of her pets. Teddy was not a pet person, whereas Loiva loved animals, especially cats, says Freddie. 'She would have one or two and pamper them like babies, which was the opposite of Teddy, he didn't like pets. But of course he did his best to like them too.'

Annie Paraan says there was a streak of independence in Loiva that showed itself from time to time. 'I see her as a timid person, although sometimes she could be difficult. I think she showed that kind of personality when she believed she was right and she was the type that when she won't be able to get her way she would rather not talk.'

This behaviour perhaps had its roots in Loiva's childhood, particularly the first nine years of her life.

Unlike Teddy, Loiva was raised not in Baguio but in Malabon, a suburb of Manila. She was the first of six children. Next came Annie, then Edmund and Joseph, then Emily and, finally, Liza.

'When my parents got married and my mother was carrying Loiva, they didn't have a house yet, they were living with my maternal grandparents in Malabon,' says Annie.

When Loiva was about three years old, Amelita and Simeon moved to a house in Cala'ocon City, about 30 minutes' drive from Malabon. However, Loiva's grandmother became very sickly and offered part of her land in Malabon to her daughter and son-in-law to build a house, so they moved back.

While the rest of the Claridades children were raised in their parents' house, their grandmother, who doted on Loiva as the eldest, prevailed upon Amelita to let Loiva sleep in her house. So while Loiva played with her younger brothers and sisters during the day, she was in effect living apart from them.

It appears the younger children were aware of her special status. Annie says Loiva was spoiled by her grandmother as a young girl, and was given her choice of new, imported dolls to play with. Annie still recalls a big glass cabinet in her grandmother's house that displayed Loiva's extensive doll collection. Once, Annie, who was fascinated by the blonde hair on a particular doll, asked if she could touch it.

'I asked if I could touch the hair to feel the difference between the doll's hair and mine, because I'd only ever felt black hair. She said, "Okay, I will allow you to touch", but there was always something she would ask me to do for her [in return].'

WHILE THIS SPECIAL treatment could have seemed like a dream to a young child, there is some doubt whether this was actually the case for Loiva.

At that time Manila was torn with violence in the lead-up to President Ferdinand Marcos's declaration of martial law. There were numerous protests in the Plaza Miranda, close to where Loiva and Annie attended St Theresa's College in San Marcelino. Amelita would keep tuned to the radio for the increasingly frequent announcements of the school closing so the children could be brought home to safety.

In 1969, Loiva's grandmother's health declined, and her death, as well as the increasing unrest in Manila, led Amelita and Simeon to move north to Baguio.

Initally the family moved into a house belonging to a friend of Amelita's. Then Simeon and Amelita bought a small parcel of land and built a house, into which the family moved.

Amelita converted the basement into a sewing and clothes repair shop, encouraging the children to help out. Loiva was not very keen on sewing and preferred watching TV, Annie Paraan remembers, but she showed artistic flair in her school art assignments.

'I felt she had problems adjusting to us because when she moved in she had gotten used to getting her way, now when she moved to us my parents were not that well off [and] there were four of us children home,' says Annie.

Annie Gonzales-Tesoro, Teddy's sister, remembers Loiva breaking down in tears years later as she confessed to some unhappiness in her childhood.

'The first nine years of her life she was raised by her grandmother, then her grandmother died and she went to live with the rest of her brothers and sisters,' says Annie. 'She told me that when she moved in with them she had to sleep on the floor because there wasn't enough room for her.'

The family had a maid — typical of many households in the Philippines — but after a year she left the job and the children had to do the household chores. Loiva was not used to it, and like many children would shirk washing the dishes if she could get away with it.

In Baguio, Loiva was enrolled in the Holy Family Academy and she continued there throughout high school before attending St Louis University, enrolling in a business course.

However, when she married, family responsibilities took over, and she left university.

Chapter 5

Sheehy

11 July 2001, 1 am

Detective Senior Constable Mick Sheehy of the New South Wales Homicide Squad was on call the night of the Gonzales murders. He was woken from his sleep by a telephone call summoning him to Collins Street, North Ryde. Being on call means that you must be available to attend a crime scene at any hour over a seven-day period. Every homicide officer has his or her turn. Sometimes, you can go a whole week without a murder; other times you are run off your feet. It was Sheehy's last night on call for the week, and until then he had not been called out once.

The married father of two young children, Mick had recently scored a promotion within Homicide, but he was a few months off officially becoming a Detective Sergeant. Two years before he had joined the Homicide Squad after a ten-year stint in drugs investigation, at the end of which he felt his career had begun to stagnate. The Homicide Squad was generally viewed as the elite of the New South Wales Police Force, the place to be, and Sheehy wanted a new challenge.

Sheehy had kind of fallen into becoming a cop. Leaving school at the age of sixteen, he got a job as an aircraft maintenance engineer, in which he worked alongside some tough nuts. He also worked in bars as a doorman. During this period Sheehy learned to get on with people from all walks of life. His first love was rugby union, and by the time he decided to enter the force, he was a second rower with the Dirty Reds, a first-grade team in Drummoyne, in Sydney's Inner West. He was 22, and extremely fit, with a big build. At almost two metres, or six feet five inches, Sheehy cut an imposing figure.

He had got to know serving police officers through footy, and the lifestyle seemed attractive. Every day was a new adventure — you never knew what you would be confronted with — and there was a lot of travel involved. Plus, the force was encouraging entry by sports-minded people, and he could keep playing his beloved rugby.

Sheehy's attitude to policing was that it was 80 per cent common sense, and 20 per cent legislation. If you had the ability to talk to people, and could develop a rapport with them, you'd be a good cop. This theory was reinforced by his training in negotiation and undercover work. He found he did not often have to use confrontation, as his physical stature meant not many crooks wanted to tangle with him. In fact, he found that most criminals, whether they were drug importers or armed robbers, responded better to praise than menacing. You just needed to pat them on the back, tell them what good crooks they were, and they couldn't help but brag.

In short, Sheehy believed you caught more flies with honey.

All Sheehy was told in that 1 am phone call was that he would be attending the scene of a family murder. Also attending would be Detective Sergeant Mick Ashwood and Detective Senior Constable Darren Sly. They were to be coordinated by their team leader, Detective Inspector Kim McKay.

Of all these officers, Sheehy lived closest to the scene. He was the first to arrive, pulling up at 1.35 am. The ambulance officers were still milling around, as were the uniformed police. Sheehy got a quick rundown from the 'locals' before organising for the area to be sealed off with crime-scene tape.

As the other homicide officers started to arrive, Ashwood was placed in charge of crime-scene management. This meant ensuring no unauthorised person trespassed into the sealed-off area, as well as coordinating the roles of those who would search for evidence. Lighting had to be rigged up so the coroner's staff could examine the bodies and the forensics team could do their work, scouring the house for clues and spreading black fingerprinting dust on surfaces to try to determine the killer's identity.

Sly was assigned the role of canvassing witnesses outside the crime scene. He ran the doorknock of neighbours in the immediate vicinity that night to find out if anyone had noticed something amiss that evening, and also recorded the registration numbers of all the vehicles in the area. While this might not be immediately useful, it could prove essential at a later stage if a suspect emerged and vehicle registration checks showed the suspect had been near the murder scene that night.

As Sheehy walked to the Gonzales' garage, he met up with Bob Betts. At first Sheehy was not aware of the small figure sitting against the garage wall, a blanket over his head. Betts informed him that Sef was the son who had discovered the murder victims. Sef was extremely emotional, but quiet.

Sheehy tried to draw him out, to get a rapport going. He needed to find out where Sef had been that night and what time he had arrived home. He was not trying to get Sef's alibi at this stage, just ascertain the basic facts.

Sheehy thought it was strange that Sef was able to focus and pull himself together to give organised answers after finding his family members murdered. One of the uniformed officers, Constable Scott Tozer, had mentioned that Sef had talked about how the attackers had brushed past him as they fled the house, and Sheehy had the ambulance officers check Sef for injury. Physically, Sef was unharmed.

Sheehy took Sef out to his car and sat him in the passenger seat, asking whom police should contact to inform relatives. Sef suggested his aunt, Emily Luna, his mother's sister. However, he could not remember Aunt Emily's number, so Cecile Ferrer, Emily's cousin on her mother's side of the family, was contacted. She would be able to alert Emily.

At this stage, Sheehy was treating Sef as a victim of crime. Even though Sef's demeanour at the scene seemed suspicious, Sheehy didn't allow himself to dwell on it, striving to be open-minded.

For other homicide officers, also, suspicions were building, fuelled by the fact that Sef had found the bodies and was the only surviving family member. At one point, Sheehy walked past Darren Sly, out of Sef's earshot. 'He did it,' Sly told his colleague, indicating Sef.

Sheehy wanted to pin Sef down to his version of what had happened that night, and as quickly as possible. Sef could have information that would be vital to the investigation.

At Gladesville police station, the incident room was being set up by Kim McKay. About 3 am, Sheehy drove Sef there to make his statement, having never actually entered the Gonzales house that night.

Chapter 6

Emily

In the hour between midnight and 1 am on Wednesday, 11 July 2001, Loiva's younger sister Emily Luna slept. Beside her was her husband, and in another room in their home in Lane Cove Road, North Ryde, slept the apple of her eye, her bright eight-year-old son Gerard.

Being a mother meant everything to Emily; she loved children. A youthful-looking 35, Emily retained some childlike elements herself: a free and contagious giggle and a girlish sense of humour. Like the impeccably fashionable outfits that draped her petite frame, these qualities masked, to the casual observer, her great heart.

Emily, a devout Catholic like Loiva, was extremely sensitive and felt deeply for the suffering of others. Once, she had thought she would make a good child psychologist, and had even trained for it in the Philippines before moving to Australia in 1987. But she decided hearing day after day about other people's pain — especially that of children — would be too much for her. Instead, Emily took a series of jobs in multi-national corporations, working her way up to become personal assistant to the managing director of a large company based in Sydney's north. It was a job that utilised her people skills in a different way. It was demanding but rewarding work, and Emily enjoyed it, even if it meant she received phone calls at odd hours.

The previous day, 10 July 2001, Emily had gone to work as usual, then at 6 pm had picked up her son at his day-care centre at North Ryde. From there, it was a five-minute trip to Loiva's house in Collins Street, and Emily decided to drop in. She was Clodine's godmother, her *ninang*, and Clodine was up on a holiday break from Melbourne, where she went to school. She lived there with Emily's younger sister, Liza Carroll, and Liza's husband. Clodine had arrived in Sydney in the last week of June, and was due to fly back to Melbourne on Thursday, 12 July.

Emily adored her brother-in-law Teddy, but her special bond was with Loiva and Clodine. She and Loiva were best friends, and she called Loiva her 'twin'. Loiva, eight years older, had been her protective mother hen in the days of growing up in a household of six children. Loiva would call her at home almost every morning at 8.30 am as Emily applied her make-up and dressed for work, just to chat. It had become a ritual, like their shopping trips together, and Emily's visits to Loiva's house for lunch on a Saturday, after they both attended the Holy Spirit Church at North Ryde, with their families. There was next to nothing that was taboo in their conversations, including sensitive family and health problems.

However, Emily and Loiva were opposites in many regards, particularly in mannerisms. While Emily admired her sister's tireless grace, she became a touch impatient whenever they walked anywhere, their arms linked. Loiva would take dainty, decorous steps, while Emily would just want to get to their destination as quickly as possible. Loiva would laugh delicately and speak softly, while Emily quite frankly didn't really care if her chuckle or her voice were too loud.

In Clodine, Emily had a soulmate. Clodine, a bit of a tomboy and vivacious, was more like a younger female friend than a niece. Clodine also got along famously with Emily's son, and during their frequent trips to the beach in summer, Clodine and Gerard would chat animatedly the whole way in the back seat, bringing a smile to Emily's face as she listened.

Clodine was so unlike her brother Sef, who was quiet, reserved and very smart. That was not to say Emily and Sef did not have a good relationship. Sef was family, her own blood, and she loved him deeply and unconditionally. She was always there to encourage him if he had a problem. Nevertheless, Sef remained a bit of an enigma to her.

Emily was two weeks out of hospital, having had abdominal surgery, and was still sore when she arrived at 6 Collins Street just after 6 pm on 10 July. It was dark and drizzling very lightly as she pulled up outside the imposing two-storey brick home. She saw a light on in the ground floor inside, and a quick movement, travelling right to left, behind the frosted glass panel to the left of the front door. It caught her eye as she parked at the curb. Emily decided she didn't need an umbrella as she and Gerard walked up the driveway to the front door. As they walked, Emily noticed Sef's green Ford Festiva parked in the carport. Oh good, Sef is home, she thought.

As they reached the door, Emily pressed the doorbell, as Gerard stood beside her. Once, no answer. Again and again, no answer. She was puzzled by the lack of response. Behind the left pane of frosted glass, Emily saw a figure, standing a bit higher than her 160 centimetres (five feet three inches) on the slightly elevated foyer floor inside. Sef was the same height as Emily. Putting a hand up to each side of her face, she pressed against the glass for a better look.

'I think that's a man,' she told her son.

'Mum, it's just a coatstand,' Gerard said. That was all, but in that instant, she dismissed the figure from her mind.

Emily decided to head left past the carport, and through the side gate to a rear sliding door at the back of the house, to see if anyone was home. From the front door, she walked past the closed double garage door and reached the carport, stopping at the rear of Sef's car. There was no light on inside the car, and she detected no movement.

'Maybe I'll just call them when I get home.' The thought came, unbidden, into her mind, but it was a powerful one. She turned back to her son, who was waiting by the front passenger door of her car. Then Emily left Collins Street with Gerard. She had no inkling that two bodies already lay inside the silent house, or of the danger she, too, could have faced if she had investigated further. Therefore, it would be at least another six hours before her whole world, her safe, secure life, crumbled.

EMILY HAD TRIED calling the Gonzales home that night at 9.30 pm but got a busy signal. She tried a few more times before deciding someone was on the Internet. Before going to bed at 11 pm, she called Clodine's mobile telephone, but it was switched off.

Emily was awoken by a phone call from Cecile Ferrer.

'There's been a shooting in North Ryde. Clodine has been taken to hospital,' Cecile told Emily.

Immediately, Emily was besieged by shooting pains cramping her abdomen, from the recent operation. Her thoughts whirled. Cecile told Emily that Sef needed a change of clothes brought to Collins Street. Cecile was scared; she didn't want to go. Could Emily do it instead?

Emily asked her husband to do it. She, too, could not face going there. Her husband gathered together some of his own clothes and left for the quick drive to 6 Collins Street, which by that stage was sealed off by blue-and-white checked police tape. It seemed, to Emily, just a matter of minutes before he was back.

Gently, he broke the news to his wife. Teddy and Loiva were both dead, and Clodine was in hospital, seriously wounded.

Emily became hysterical. With all her force, she pounded her fists against her husband's chest. 'Why? Why? Why?' she screamed. It was all she was capable of saying, of even thinking.

'Calm down, Emily, calm down. Your blood pressure!' Her husband was concerned for her. She suffered from high blood pressure, like her sister Loiva.

The Lunas wanted to inform other family members, before they heard about the tragedy on the news. It presented some difficulties, though. Emily's brother Joseph was reached at his North Sydney home, and Edmund at his Gold Coast home in Queensland. But Amelita, Sef's maternal grandmother, was staying with Emily's younger sister, Liza Carroll, in Melbourne. Frustrating things, answering machines, and that was all they got as they dialled Liza's number. Such devastating news could not be left on an answering machine. Victorian police would be sent to Liza's house to inform them in person early that morning. The family members on Teddy's side were all in the Philippines.

Police wanted the Gonzales' relatives to come to Gladesville police station to comfort Sef. Emily told Joseph over the phone that she was incapable of driving in her state. Could Joseph come and pick her up?

As Joseph drove Emily to Gladesville, she clung to a slim hope. She told her older brother she hoped Clodine would survive. Clodine was the only witness who could explain what had happened.

Emily didn't know then that Clodine was not in hospital. She was never taken there. Emily's eighteen-year-old niece was dead, just like the girl's mother and father. How the news became so garbled could only be explained by the confusion of that night.

In her distress, it didn't register with Emily that she had become probably the most important witness in the case. But it would hit her with full force as soon as she saw her nephew at Gladesville about 2 am on 11 July 2001.

NEVER BEFORE HAD Emily known white-hot rage. The heat started at the top of her head, burned her face and travelled down through her body like molten lava. She felt it as soon as she laid eyes on Sef.

Sef was sitting in a room at the police station, hunched over, clutching a blanket around his shoulders. Cecile and her husband were already there comforting him, and Joseph had walked in before Emily. Soon to arrive was a twenty-year-old man by the name of Sam Dacillo, one of Sef's closest friends, whose parents were friends of Teddy and Loiva. Sam and Sef had gone out to dinner only a few hours earlier. Sam would be accompanied to the station by his father, Sammy Dacillo.

Cecile got up from the seat next to Sef, making a space so Emily could sit down. Emily didn't want to, instantly recoiling at the thought, but forced herself. Sef was making crying noises, and they immediately struck Emily as false. Emily leaned forward to see his face. As she'd suspected, there were no tears. But in the hairline above his forehead, she noticed a single spot of blood. She didn't comment on it to the police until later, and they told her they hadn't seen it.

When she sat down next to her nephew Emily didn't beat around the bush. Because of what she had seen at 6 Collins

Street the previous night, she felt that Sef had something to do with the murders. The first thing that flew out of her mouth was directed squarely at Sef, and it went over like a tonne of bricks with those assembled in the room. 'I was at the house at six o'clock. Why didn't you answer the door?'

'Emily!' Her brother Joseph, who was trying to stay level-headed and neutral, admonished her for her insensitivity towards their nephew. He was interrupted by the sudden presence of police, who divided everyone up to be interviewed separately by detectives.

The question Emily had posed was the only one she wanted — needed — to be answered satisfactorily, to allay her suspicions. She would not have long to wait to hear Sef's explanation.

Chapter 7

Sef gives his statement

Mick Sheehy began taking Sef's statement at 3.15 am. Preparation of the nine-page document, signed by Sef as a true and correct version of events, lasted almost five hours. It was a long night for all involved.

Sef told Sheehy he had woken the day before about 8 am, at which point his mother and sister were both at home. His father, an early riser, had already left the house. Teddy worked long hours at his law practice, T Gonzales & Associates, in the working-class suburb of Blacktown in Sydney's west. Normally, he left the house around 7.30 am and did not get home until about 7 pm. Loiva, who worked as Teddy's office manager, routinely left the house later than Teddy and arrived home earlier, between 5 pm and 6 pm.

Sef told police that after waking up he quickly began preparing to leave for Macquarie University, located near North Ryde, where he was studying law. His mother departed around the same time as he did. He did not know his sister's plans for the day.

Clodine, a Year Twelve student who attended school in Melbourne, was home for the school holidays. She had been sent to Melbourne because she had been dating a man named Chris, an Australian aged about nineteen. Sef's family was 'very conservative', he explained, and had wanted Clodine to break up with Chris. Chris had been a bad influence on Clodine, resulting in an 'exchange of words' between the Gonzales family and Chris about a year before, Sef said. After Clodine moved to Melbourne, Chris sent her gifts, such as a formal dress, which she sent back to him.

Jumping back to the events of 10 July 2001, Sef told police, 'I returned from university about 12.30 pm to 1 pm. I had a quick lunch because my father had arrange [*sic*] for me to go to his office straight after lunch.'

He said when he went home for lunch, his sister was still there but there was no real conversation between them. He said he got to his father's Blacktown office between 1 pm and 2 pm to identify a computer problem his father's secretary was having. He couldn't find or fix the problem. Soon after his arrival, the work started to pour in and Sef said he helped out by answering telephone calls.

'At my father's company I spoke with my father and mother. The night before I had sought permission from my mother not to eat dinner at home and had arranged to go out with Sam Dacillo. It was his birthday the previous week but I was sick and busy with university. We postponed dinner until this date.'

Sef told police that when he left his father's office he 'wasn't really focusing on the time' but definitely departed before the secretary left, about 4.30 pm to 5 pm.

He said he was on his way to meet up with Sam, who lived four blocks from his house in North Ryde, when he received a text message on his mobile from Sam.

'He said that there was a change of plans, he had a basketball game. It was a bit unclear what he meant. I then tried to call my mother on her mobile to ensure she was aware that I was going out for dinner. I can't remember if it was out of range or turned off but I did not speak to my mum. I decided to call home, as I assumed my sister was still there. Nobody answered the phone, it just continued to ring.'

By that time, Sef explained, he was near home so he decided to drop by and check that no-one was there. Sef said he got there about 6 pm and there was a light on in the kitchen area at the back of the house, which he could see through the front door.

After parking his green Ford Festiva with its vanity plates 'SEF–80G' in the carport, Sef got a call from Sam. During a three-minute conversation, the pair arranged to meet at 8 pm at Sam's house.

'I stayed in the car when I spoke with Sam, I didn't get out because it was raining,' Sef said.

The sight of his pet chihuahua, Snoopy, tied up confirmed to him that no-one was home. He said he tried calling the house from his car, and still the phone went unanswered. He was in the carport for about five to ten minutes in all, he said, before driving off, believing nothing to be amiss. There was simply nobody home, he thought.

Left with two hours until his meeting with Sam, Sef said he decided to visit a friend of his, Raf De Leon, at the house he had recently moved into at Kingsgrove. (Police later determined Raf actually lived in a suburb near Blacktown, Kings Ridge.) Sef had never been to Raf's new home and decided he would have time to pop in and say hello, he told the police.

Driving to the Kingsgrove area through peak-hour traffic via Victoria Road, one of Sydney's main thoroughfares, Sef looked for Raf's address in his street directory. 'I have an old street directory and couldn't find it on the map. By this time it was already past 7 pm. As I had not made any commitment to Raf, I decided to return and meet Sam.'

Driving straight to Sam's house, he was welcomed inside by Sam's family. Sam was not ready yet so Sef waited almost twenty minutes for his friend.

Sef farewelled the Dacillos about 8.15 pm and drove Sam into the city, where they decided to have dinner at Planet Hollywood in the George Street entertainment strip. Entering the restaurant about 8.45 pm, they had to wait fifteen minutes for a table.

During this period, Sam got a phone call from his younger sister, Michelle, a good friend of Clodine's. 'Sam asked me where Clodine was, as Michelle had been ringing and no-one answered the phone. When she tried again, the phone was then busy.' Sef said he tried himself to telephone home during dinner, and again the phone was busy. He assumed someone was on the Internet at home.

After they finished their meal, Sef and Sam played a game of pool at Planet Hollywood, before going to Galaxy World amusement parlour next door and playing video games. About 10.30 pm, they started to head home.

The traffic was light, and after dropping Sam at his house, Sef drove into Collins Street shortly after 11 pm.

'The first thing I noticed was the light in the guest room was on, from the front of the house it is the first-floor room to your right ... I drove into the carport and heard both dogs barking and thought that was unusual, as they don't bark when I arrive home.'

Getting out, Sef noticed his chihuahua still tied up outside the laundry door. He wondered about this, as he believed someone was awake inside. Putting his key into the laundry door, he entered the house. The white poodle that Betts had noticed, Angela, usually did not get out of her bed in the laundry, but she was up and barking at Sef. Opening the internal laundry door, he went into the house and saw his father lying in the foyer. Sef described the dramatic scene to police.

'There was blood everywhere and there were papers scattered around him. My father was lying on his back and there was a lot of blood on his white shirt. I rushed over and started calling out to my mum to come and help. I was thinking that Mum was asleep, as the lights upstairs were off,' he said. This conflicted with his earlier statement that the guest-room light upstairs was on.

'I noticed holes in the chest and stomach area, I thought these were shots. I tried to cover up where it was bleeding using only my hands. I tried to lift his head to wake him up. I was hugging him and when I put him back down I tried to give him CPR.'

He went for the portable phone in the study to the left of the foyer, and tried dialling 000. There was no dial tone, so he used his mobile telephone to ring the emergency operator. As he spoke, he walked back towards Teddy and then noticed his mother in the living room.

He said he could not recall exactly what he said to the operator, but stayed on the phone as he went to his mother.

'I was hugging her whilst I was on the phone. My mother was lying on the floor in the living room.' Sef said his mother was on her back and there were large amounts of blood. As he hugged her, he put down the phone for 'a little while', and when he picked it up again the operator was still on the line.

Suddenly, he thought he should look for his sister. Running upstairs, still carrying the phone, he noticed that the door to his room was open and the light on, as it was in the guest room and his sister's room. He opened the door to Clodine's room.

'As I opened the door, I think her leg was in the way. I opened it slowly and [there] was my sister lying on her side in an awkward position. There was blood everywhere. I grabbed her, trying to wake her up, and there was blood gushing out from her side. I tried to stop it using my hands. I checked for a pulse but I couldn't really tell. I assumed her heart was still beating, as there was blood gushing out.'

At this point, he said, he heard a noise downstairs and thought his mother or father was recovering. With no idea where he had put the phone, he ran down the staircase, and as he did this, heard the side gate behind the carport close. Going for the front door, he found his father was in the way, so he rushed into the garage and pressed the remote door control. The door was painfully slow going up, so he crawled under it as it rose. As he straightened up, he saw someone running towards Ryrie Street, across the street to the right.

'I'm not sure if I saw two people or one person and a shadow. I chased after them shouting something. I am assuming it was a male person, as I recall short hair and the way the person ran was like a male.'

He said he chased them until he reached the second house from the corner of Ryrie Street before thinking again of his sister, possibly still alive and needing help. He went to John's house across the road to raise the alarm, crying. When he went back inside with a neighbour, he closed his father's eyes and did the same for his mother.

Sef said he did not know of anyone who felt ill will towards his family. The only thing he could think of that might be relevant to his family's murder was an incident on Monday, 9 July, the night before the killings. It was Clodine's birthday and the family went out for dinner to celebrate. As Sef was driving his family home in his Festiva, doing about 70 kilometres an hour along Victoria Road, an old white four-wheel drive behind his car started to blow its horn. As the car, driven by a man and containing three or four people, passed, a male passenger yelled out, 'Bloody Asians.'

'He yelled this before he could see who was in the car, all our windows were closed. The car then pulled in front of us, cutting us off. Then he stopped suddenly and we had to stop behind him.'

Sef said he drove past the car and thought he had lost it, until he turned into Wicks Road in North Ryde, near his home. He stopped near the Shell service station because he saw the four-wheel drive in his rear-view mirror. The vehicle stopped a few metres behind his Festiva.

'My father and I were going to get out of the car to see what was going on and my mother convinced us to stay in the car. The four-wheel drive then sped off. There was nothing distinguishing about this car but it may have been a Toyota, like a Land Cruiser.'

And so his statement ended. Having listened to his story, Sheehy thought the young man's alibi was filled with details, times and locations that police would have no trouble confirming or ruling out. For example, the calls and SMS messages that Sef had referred to making or receiving could easily be checked. If he wasn't telling the truth, he must have next to no knowledge of police investigative capabilities. To Sheehy, Sef seemed more intelligent than that. He would tell fellow officers of this belief at a briefing that morning.

AFTER THE INTERVIEW, Sheehy took Sef's clothes and shoes so they could be sent for forensic analysis. Sef also underwent gunshot residue tests at the station that morning, as police were still under the impression a gun had been used in the murders.

The unfortunate Sam Dacillo, dragged into this whole messy affair due to the fact he was with Sef during what was meant to be a pleasant night out, was also under suspicion. He, too, had gunshot residue analysis done on his hands. Sam was Sef's best mate, and the only one who could back up his alibi for a large part of the evening. Fortunately for Sam, his movements on the afternoon and evening of the murders checked out, and he was quickly eliminated as a suspect.

Obtaining CCTV footage of George Street that night, police confirmed Sam and Sef had indeed been there around 11 pm, and had left at 11.11 pm. Sam gave his own brief statement to police. Contrary to what his mate had told them, Sam said their 8 pm meeting time for the night of Tuesday, 10 July had been arranged the night before, Monday night. He made no mention of a telephone conversation with Sef around 6 pm on 10 July.

EMILY LUNA'S FIRST statement to police that night lacked a fair amount of pertinent detail. She outlined the family's history before telling police about her visit to Collins Street at 6 pm. She told police she had seen Sef's car in the carport, and a light on somewhere on the ground floor. She said she had rung the doorbell probably four times and got no response. Emily also told police she saw no movement inside the house whatsoever.

'I then thought that there was nobody home so I left with my son.'

Emily wasn't volunteering anything but the basic details to the police about her visit. In fact, she was holding back information that might have indicated a physical presence inside the house at the time when Sef's car was in the carport. She was holding this back because Sef was her blood relative, and she wanted to give him an opportunity to explain himself before she got him into trouble with the police.

At one stage that night, she was allowed to sit in with Sef as he answered police questions, preparing to make his own formal statement. Emily was excused from the room after a period, while Joseph was allowed to stay.

While she was in there, Sef clutched her hand. Emily noted Sef's mention of the fact it was raining at 6 pm as the reason he had not got out of the car. It jarred with her. Emily remembered not even needing an umbrella to approach the front door when she arrived.

On hearing her nephew's version, Emily immediately let go of his hand. Her suspicions about his involvement in the murders had only been increased by this little detail.

Chapter 8

Love and marriage

After his marriage to Loiva, Teddy continued his quest to become a wealthy man. It was a year after the wedding, in 1978, that he learned that the accumulation of assets is not always a smooth ride. For when you win something, there is almost invariably someone else who loses out. People can become angry and resentful. For Teddy, it was a near-fatal lesson.

Colourfully worded Baguio court documents outline what happened on 6 July 1978. At 8 am, Loiva was inside a house occupied by the Gonzales family, at 12 Legarda Road. Loiva was doing some paperwork for the taxi business that Teddy and Freddie were operating at the time.

Next door, at 14 Legarda Road, lived Peter Ng and his family. The Gonzales family had recently purchased the house the Ngs were renting.

Peter Ng states he was walking along Legarda Road with four men when Freddie Gonzales called out to him. He alleges Freddie crossed the street towards him, demanding Ng immediately pay outstanding rent on the house. According to the colourfully worded court papers:

> *Freddie Gonzales informed Peter Ng that he had bought*
> *the house from the former owners, but Peter Ng countered*

that he would not pay because he did not receive any notice from the former owners. There was an exchange of words as they both hurled derogatory remarks against each other. As they were thus arguing, Teddy Gonzales, the brother of the accused, emerged from their house in a bellicose mood and went near them. After further heated altercation, Teddy Gonzales hit Peter Ng near the left eye. An exchange of blows followed. In the scuffle, Teddy Gonzales was wounded on his chest and fell to the ground, hence Freddie Gonzales chased Peter Ng as the latter ran towards their house. As he [Ng] was trying to open their gate, Freddie Gonzales caught up with him and the two exchanged blows. William Gonzales, the father of the Gonzales brothers, also came out of their house, and hit Peter Ng with a dustpan.

Freddie Gonzales maintained it was Ng who had started the fight with Teddy and that Freddie merely watched the initial incident, only fighting Ng after Ng hit him first. According to the court papers:

In the midst of their argument, Peter Ng challenged Teddy Gonzales to a fistfight. Peter Ng suddenly hit Teddy Gonzales. Provoked, Teddy Gonzales removed his eyeglasses and hit back. The two exchanged blows and grappled ... Freddie Gonzales saw his brother Teddy Gonzales fall to the ground bleeding on his chest.

Loiva had emerged from the house and saw her husband prostrate on the ground, bleeding from a 'gaping wound' in his chest. He also had injuries to his right arm, abdomen and ear. She rushed him to Baguio's Notre Dame de Lourdes Hospital for treatment.

The court acquitted Freddie of assault, causing 'slight physical injuries'. Meanwhile, Ng was initially charged with 'frustrated homicide', but the charge was reduced to a lesser one of causing physical injuries.

To this day, Ng, who is a hotel owner in the Philippines, holds a grudge against the Gonzales family. He remembers wanting to buy the property he was renting next door to the Gonzales, and says he was surprised and disappointed when he was told the property had been sold out from under him.

'We wanted to buy it. I asked him [the previous landlord] how much, if we can afford to buy, but the previous owner said they were not going to sell it,' he says.

Ng, who had rented the house for ten years, remembers having to move because of the bitterness between him and the Gonzales family after Teddy's stabbing. 'They feel that they are better than other people, that's my impression, because by then they have the money, they can buy lots of things.'

Ng maintains he acted in self-defence against the Gonzales brothers and their father. 'I have [sic] a small knife so I stabbed Teddy many times. I have to protect myself,' he says.

Teddy recovered and continued his law studies, travelling with Loiva in 1979 to Manila, where he undertook a six-month review to take the bar test, which enabled him to practise as a lawyer. He officially passed the bar exams in 1980. Later, he would return to Baguio Colleges Foundation to lecture in law.

THE NEW LAWYER and his wife did not waste much time before starting a family. Towards the end of 1979, Loiva fell pregnant with her first child.

Freddie Gonzales remembers that Teddy and Loiva had carefully worked out the number of children they would have, as Teddy wanted to make sure he could provide for them both financially and emotionally.

'Obviously they just planned two, a typical American family,' says Freddie. 'Teddy took responsibility of fatherhood very seriously, perhaps this is why he only had two. [Teddy believed] that it's very hard to be responsible for the future of people . . . you cannot guarantee their happiness.'

Sef Gonzales entered the world after a difficult labour on 16 September, 1980. He was born at the Notre Dame de Lourdes Hospital and weighed five pounds, thirteen ounces. Loiva was aged 22, Teddy 26. Aside from the fact this was Loiva's first child, the labour was complicated by Loiva's sickness. She had suffered vomiting and nausea during the entire pregnancy, and was throwing up as she went through labour. Her doctor had prescribed medication to quell the sickness early on in the pregnancy. Loiva worried it would harm her unborn baby, but the doctor had assured her it was safe.

Teddy was an extremely proud father. Having a boy as a first child was exceptionally good fortune for someone of his Chinese heritage. 'I will name him Sef,' Teddy declared, but did not explain where he had got the name. He planned for the secret of the name to be a gift to his son on Sef's 21st birthday.

Sef as an infant was a real cutie, with his father's dimples. One day, Teddy took an impromptu photo of his son, fresh from a bath and dressed only in a nappy. The Gonzales sent it in to a baby photograph competition, run by a baby care product manufacturing company. It didn't win, but the point was how proud they were of their little boy.

For Teddy, having a child was an inspiration to work even harder, to become more industrious. Around this time, he set up a real estate agency at Legarda Road. He named it Telov Realty, a combination of his and his wife's names. Freddie says the agency really took off, as the economy was good. Together Teddy and Loiva would also set up a video shop and a pharmacy. They would often prevail on Emily to help out by working at these two businesses.

On 9 July 1983, Loiva gave birth to a second child, a girl. The couple named her Clodine.

Teddy and Loiva raised their children in the typical Filipino way, in which children are taught discipline at an early age. From the start, they were strict parents. Loiva would give her children an allotted time to play with their toys — of course, not as much time as they would have liked — before she made them pack the toys away.

When Sef was particularly naughty — cursing at his mother or striking Clodine — and Teddy found out, he would strap Sef with a belt, says Annie Gonzales-Tesoro.

Emily saw Teddy strike Sef once, when he was going through the 'terrible twos'. Teddy had had a long day at work and arrived home tired and tense. Emily had visited Loiva for lunch and Sef was throwing screaming tantrums. 'Sef has been very naughty today,' Loiva told Teddy as soon as he got in the door. From infant Clodine's room upstairs, Emily saw Teddy wrap a belt buckle around his fist and strap Sef twice. Sef was curled up on the ground, his body forming a little semicircular shape. He was crying in Tagalog that he didn't want the strap any more.

Emily felt sorry for Sef, and told her father Simeon, who had a chat with Loiva. He advised her that she should not dump her problems with the children on Teddy when he'd had a long day at work. Emily never saw Sef being strapped again.

Annie Gonzales-Tesoro says Sef was strapped only for serious instances of disrespect. From the point of view of Filipinos, this discipline was not classified as abuse, as it may be nowadays in the United States or Australia, Annie explains. 'He [Sef] was not a battered child.'

However, a lawyer friend of Teddy's in Sydney, Bernado David, tells a different story. He says a mutual friend, a real estate agent, invited Teddy and his family to his Jervis Bay holiday home, on the New South Wales South Coast, some time in 1998.

The real estate agent later told David that his son and Sef had gone to the beach together without asking Teddy's permission, provoking Teddy's rage. 'When the boy [Sef] came back [from the beach] he was beaten black and blue by Teddy,' says David.

According to David, the real estate agent could hear Sef being bashed against a wall in another room. The real estate agent complained to David that Teddy had violated the laws of hospitality, beating his son when he was a guest in the agent's home.

IN THE EARLY 1980s, Teddy and Loiva built a house in Crystal Cave, near Baguio, moving from Legarda Road. Teddy's parents lived in a house at the back of the Legarda Road property which Teddy had built them. Later he also built some apartments on the land.

Meanwhile Teddy became a Rotarian and developed a close circle of friends.

'He was very active in the community, that's what got him into government,' says Freddie.

Teddy's stint in government began in 1986. According to Freddie, Teddy worked as secretary to the Mayor of Baguio City. He was then poached to work as assistant to the Minister of Agriculture and Food, Ramon Mitra, who later ran unsuccessfully for President of the Philippines. Then in October 1987 Teddy was appointed to the President's Committee on Ethics and Accountability, again at the Agriculture Department.

Freddie says Teddy was just too honest for politics. He was a go-getter, but he was also an intellectual and had a strong moral code. He could not abide the system of politics he came across while working for the anti–graft section of a government department. There is some suggestion Teddy was offered a bribe during this period as an anti-corruption campaigner, and that he received death threats as a result of his refusal to take it.

Freddie remembers advising Teddy that politics was not necessarily about morals. He told Teddy he was either in, or he was out. Teddy, deciding he couldn't change the system, quit government for good. 'He was too idealistic, there was no room for him in government,' says Freddie.

In 1988, Teddy took a break with his family, travelling to Australia for Expo '88. Loiva in particular really enjoyed Australia, especially Sydney. Loiva's mother Amelita had moved to Australia with her children Edmund and Liza in 1987 and Emily had joined them later in the year. Loiva's other brother Joseph had arrived not long afterwards.

Amelita suggested it would be wonderful if Teddy and Loiva moved to Australia too. They could all be together.

However, Teddy had many ties to Baguio. And he had an ambition to be a hotelier. He poured his accumulated wealth into building a new hotel on the site of the house once occupied by Peter Ng.

The hotel was a modern, light-coloured concrete construction, four storeys high, with around 40 rooms. It had a restaurant and music lounge to cater for the Filipino passion for music. Teddy named it the Queen Victoria Hotel, after Sydney's Queen Victoria Building, which the couple had admired during their Australian visit. When it opened in late 1989, Teddy was extremely proud. This was what he had worked so hard for. But his happiness wasn't to last.

Chapter 9

Tawas

After an arduous night, Sef and his Uncle Joseph went back to Joseph's North Sydney home on the morning of 11 July 2001 to get a few hours' sleep. They would need it for the ordeal they would face that afternoon, when they were to attend Glebe morgue, in Sydney's Inner West, to formally identify the bodies of Teddy, Loiva and Clodine. Joseph had agreed to be the relative to conduct the formal identification, and Sef had also asked to be present. That was no problem for Sheehy, as he could organise for one of the morgue's counsellors to speak to Sef.

The identification would prove to be a relatively quick, clinical procedure. Neither Sef nor Joseph would visibly break down, although it must have been traumatising as they were shown the bodies of their loved ones through a viewing window. Joseph would simply be asked, 'Is this the body of Teddy Gonzales ... Mary Gonzales ... Clodine Gonzales?' and be requested to sign documents formally identifying each of them, which he did.

At 9 am that morning, at Gladesville police station, McKay, Sheehy, Ashwood and Sly held a briefing with some of the local police officers. It soon became obvious to Sheehy that a good many of them had already formed the same opinion:

that Sef Gonzales was the killer. Sheehy made a comment that would earn him a fair bit of ribbing from his colleagues down the track. He argued they should be focusing on a wider group of possible suspects. He stated his belief that Sef's statement to him early that morning had been so precise about times and locations of events that he held some doubt as to whether Sef was the killer. They should also be considering other possible suspects, Sheehy felt. He thought about the mobile telephone calls and SMS messages Sef had referred to in his statement, and was convinced that young kids today knew all about how mobile phones worked, so it was unlikely he would have made that up.

The media were clamouring for more details of the triple murder, and the pressure to solve the case was already on, from the then New South Wales Police Commissioner, Peter Ryan, down. Strike Force Tawas, a name generated at random by the police computer, was quickly formed, and the officers who were to comprise it would meet McKay and Sheehy at the murder scene later that morning.

The New South Wales Homicide Squad, like most police agencies, was overburdened with active investigations. So police from other detective squads were also allocated to Tawas. From the Violent and Major Offenders Unit — since renamed the Robbery and Serious Crime Squad — came Detective Sergeant Tony Polito, who had previous homicide experience, and Detective Senior Constable Paul Auglys.

The South East Asian Crime Squad also provided two officers: Detective Senior Constables Shaun Ryan and Brian O'Donoghue. For all anyone knew at the time, this could have been an Asian organised-crime hit. At this early stage, no-one really knew much about Teddy Gonzales' business dealings, or whether Sef was tied up with an Asian crime gang.

Mick Sheehy and Detective Senior Constable Ritchie Sim, from Homicide, were also allocated to Strike Force Tawas. Both were supposedly there for the short term.

Detective Inspector Geoff Leonard, a seasoned homicide investigator, was appointed commander, giving him managerial oversight of each line of investigation.

The investigation started big. At first, it was all hands on deck as a mass of leads that needed to be checked out were identified. Over time, other serious crimes occurred, and some officers were pulled onto other jobs, and new faces would take their place.

Of the original team, Detectives Sheehy and Auglys would be there from start to finish. Leonard would also be there at the finish, but he would miss about a year of what would become a three-year investigation, as he recovered from a serious illness.

In those first few frantic days, when investigators worked up to eighteen hours a day before collapsing into bed for a few hours' sleep, crucial information — much of it damning towards Sef Gonzales — would come to light. It was safe to say he became one of a tiny number of suspects.

Much of the evidence came from the painstaking work of crime-scene analysts, who were crawling over the Gonzales house from the early hours of 11 July. These analysts formed the view that the crime scene had been staged to indicate that there had been an intruder in the house, whereas other evidence at the scene pointed to items in the house being used to commit the murders. Why, it was asked from this early stage, would an intruder intent on triple murder come to the scene of the crime so ill prepared as to grab any available object from within the home to use as a weapon?

An example of this contradictory evidence was that a flyscreen had been removed from the kitchen window above the sink, cut in several places, and placed against a brick wall at the back of the house. The window itself was open, but there were no pry marks on the frame or latch to indicate a serious attempt to break in through a locked window. There were no shoe prints on the sink or kitchen benchtop.

In the study, the phone landline connection cable had been cut in a rather amateurish way. On one side of the cable there was a sharp, clean cut, but it didn't go all the way through the cable. The other side of the cable sported a jagged tear, as if the person doing the cutting had decided mid-task just to yank the cable apart.

Also, in the family room adjoining the open-plan kitchen at the rear of the ground floor a racist slur had been scrawled in blue spray paint on the pale Gyprock wall. Officers were confronted by capital letters that screamed 'FUCK OFF ASIANS'. Underneath, right above the floor, squeezed into the right-hand corner in smaller capitals, was 'KKK', an apparent reference to white supremacist group the Ku Klux Klan.

To the left of this obscenity, a glass sliding door stood open at the rear of the side of the house behind the external laundry door. It would have allowed anyone who decided to come around to the back of the house to investigate why the Gonzales were not answering their phone or doorbell to be confronted with the writing straightaway, and their suspicions to be aroused.

As well, Teddy was carrying close to $700 cash and Loiva had $300. It was untouched, as were the various expensive pieces of jewellery and electronic equipment in the house. Robbery by an intruder was ruled out as a motive.

Near Teddy's body, his briefcase lay open, spilling papers, in what appeared to be an organised state of disarray. There was blood underneath his briefcase. The contents of Loiva's handbag — keys, tissues and other paraphernalia — had been similarly spilled onto the ground near her body. There was blood underneath these items too. Surely, if Loiva and Teddy had been attacked and forced to drop their belongings as they struggled with her assailant, the blood would be on top of the items, not underneath. To crime scene officers, it was apparent that Teddy's briefcase and Loiva's handbag had been placed on the ground and emptied after the blood was shed.

Around all three bodies, as well as in the ground-floor hallway leading to the family room–kitchen area and on the spiral staircase to the upstairs floor, were the tracks of bloodied shoe prints. Crime-scene officers used chemicals to enhance the shoe prints to a deep purple colour. Upstairs in Sef's bedroom — immaculately tidy apart from the open doors and drawers — officers checked his collection of shoes. Their attention was drawn to a cardboard shoebox containing his hair clippers. The box was for a Human brand, Rhythm model shoe, size UK 7/US 8. The label read 'Insport' — a sporting goods shop — and carried a pricing label of $79.95. Tawas officers rushed out to track down a pair of the laceless running shoes to check the sole impression they left. Bingo! There was a perfect match between shoe print impressions left in blood near the bodies and the sole of a Human brand, Rhythm model shoe, size UK 7/US 8. But as the search of the house continued, the pair of shoes that had left the prints would elude them. They were nowhere to be found at the scene. Were they used by the killer and later discarded, along with the clothes the killer had worn, because they were bloody? It seemed a likely scenario.

On the Gyprock wall above where Clodine's body had been found in her upstairs bedroom was a series of curious impressions — elongated semicircles. Crime-scene analyst Detective Sergeant Robert Gibbs, conducting an experiment on another piece of Gyprock, bashed it with numerous objects to see which one left the most similar impressions. He used chair legs, table legs, an axe, a spade handle and a number of baseball and T-ball bats. A black-painted aluminium T-ball bat, slightly smaller than a baseball bat, left the most similar impression.

In a corner of the kitchen, near a spice rack and small potted plant, stood a cylindrical metallic block built to contain six Global brand knives. The two largest knives, the largest non-serrated and the second-largest serrated, were missing from the set. Were they the murder weapons? As with the Human brand shoes, Tawas officers would purchase an identical set of Global knives so that they could be measured against the wounds on the bodies.

FORENSIC PATHOLOGIST Dr Allan Cala performed the postmortems of Teddy, Loiva and Clodine at Glebe morgue on 12 and 13 July 2001.

Postmortem examinations are crucial to determining the cause of death and can also give an approximation of the time of death. Needless to say, this information was vital to Tawas investigators. According to Sef, he had located the bodies approximately between 11 pm and midnight on 10 July, and Clodine had still been gushing blood. Sef's statement had also suggested the killers had been in the house when he arrived home after dinner with Sam Dacillo.

The postmortems ruled out shooting in the case of all three victims. Instead, they painted a grim picture of a knife, or possibly knives, being wielded with great ferocity, and all three victims fighting in vain to ward off their attacker.

Dr Cala began with Teddy at 9 am on 12 July.

Teddy stood about five feet six inches and was stocky in a fit way, but the force used on him was vastly greater than that necessary to inflict death. He had been stabbed five times in the neck, one of the blows passing through the jugular vein (which drains blood from the head back towards the heart) and the carotid artery (which supplies blood to the head). He had been stabbed seven times in the chest, the wounds penetrating his right lung and his heart. Teddy had also been stabbed twice in the back, and one blow had partially severed his spinal cord. The wound would not have caused Teddy to lose consciousness but it may well have caused paraplegia of his lower body and a loss of sensation down one side. After that particular blow had been inflicted, Teddy Gonzales had probably been rendered unable to fight back, or his struggles would have weakened considerably.

But Teddy, a martial arts devotee who had trained with Sef in the family garage, had struggled quite hard at some point during the attack. His left arm bore three stab wounds and there were four cuts to his left fingers. He also bore four cuts to his right hand and fingers. Teddy had used his hands to try to ward off the blows.

Dr Cala reached the conclusion Teddy had died some time between 3 pm and 10 pm on 10 July 2001, due to multiple stab wounds.

Loiva Gonzales' postmortem began at 2 pm that same day. Her face had been cut, and on her neck were multiple stab wounds which had severed her trachea. Her throat had also been slit.

The attacker had stabbed Loiva in the back, the left chest, the central chest, the right breast, the lower chest, the abdomen and the right groin area. Her right elbow was cut, as were her right fingers; these were defence wounds. The attack had been a frenzy, an overkill. Given the location of some of the wounds, one or two would have dealt a fatal blow.

Dr Cala decided Loiva had died some time between 1 pm and 6 pm of multiple stab wounds.

It was not until 9 am the next day that Dr Cala began his analysis of Clodine Gonzales' injuries. They were more complex than those of her parents. She had been bashed, stabbed and choked, and it was a combination of all three actions that had killed her. The eighteen-year-old had suffered.

At least six blows to Clodine's head, however, had caused massive injuries. On the left side of Clodine's head above her ear were a skull fracture and bruising to the scalp. Her brain had bled, shaken around her skull by the trauma. These blows may have rendered her unconscious, but they also may not have. In Dr Cala's opinion, the blows were not caused by a sharp object such as a knife or broken glass, or even by someone's fist. To his mind, the attacker had used a blunt object, something like a piece of timber or a brick. Other possibilities were a cricket bat or baseball bat.

Clodine also had two stab wounds to the right side of her lower chest. They had caused massive damage, passing through the liver into her diaphragm, penetrating her stomach, right kidney and aorta as well as the inferior vena cava, the large vein that sits next to the aorta and carries blood back to the heart.

There were tiny pinprick haemorrhages on Clodine's eyelids and cheeks, and bruising to her neck and jaw, indicating her throat had been compressed, depriving her of oxygen. Due to the absence of any ligature marks, it was likely to have been done by someone's hands. Her neck also bore five serious and six superficial stab wounds which had injured her larynx. Her cheek and the areas around her ears and the back of her neck and head also bore cuts and stab wounds.

There were also signs of defence wounds on Clodine's hands and wrists, in particular, a cut to her right thumb. Dr Cala was leaning towards the theory that Clodine's neck was compressed first, then the head injuries inflicted, before the attacker started his grisly work with the knife.

Analysis of Clodine's clotted blood at the scene by bloodspatter expert Dr Tony Raymond also gave a good insight into the timeframe of the injuries. The arc of blood smeared from the wall to the floor, where Clodine's head came to rest, suggested she had been sitting upright, or leaning upright against the wall, before being moved at least a couple of minutes, and perhaps many minutes, after the assault to her head. After that, as she lay with her face to the ground, she was still breathing, albeit in a tortured way. This was deduced from the bubbles in the clotted blood on the floor, beneath her nose. There was a distinct lack of blood, however, on Clodine's red jumper, which lay over her body. Curiously, it appeared to have been draped over her after the attacker had finished. It covered her stab wounds.

Clodine had died within a similar timeframe to her mother: between 1 pm and 6 pm.

Comparing his measurements of the stab wounds with an identical knife provided to him by police, Dr Cala concluded the missing knife could have been the murder weapon. In Dr Cala's opinion, the knife used by the killer was non-serrated. A serrated-edge blade — like the second-largest Global knife — would have left serration marks on the wounds. Of all the stab wounds inflicted that night at 6 Collins Street, only a single one on Loiva showed some form of serration. That could have been explained, however, by her skin being pulled as that particular wound was inflicted.

Dr Cala's conclusion about the murder weapon assisted Tawas investigators from the point of view that the largest missing Global knife could have been used, but many other readily available brands of knives also could have inflicted the same wounds.

The times of death were of more assistance, as they pinned down the periods of time police had to focus on when they considered a suspect's alibi. The crucial time period was 1 pm to 10 pm.

OF COURSE THE police quickly tried to narrow down the timeframe, using the telephone records of all three victims.

It had already been established that both Teddy and Loiva went to work at Teddy's law practice, T Gonzales & Associates, on the morning of 10 July. Loiva was Teddy's office manager at the practice, which specialised in immigration law.

Clodine Gonzales had been at 6 Collins Street in the afternoon. The family had celebrated her eighteenth birthday the night before.

At 4.04 pm, Clodine had sent an SMS text message from her mobile telephone to that of a schoolfriend, Vanessa O'Mera, along the lines of 'Hey, how are you, how was Muriel's party?' As far as police could determine, this was the last confirmed communication Clodine had with anyone — except her killer, of course.

At 4.50 pm the same day, Loiva had left her husband's office on Kildare Road, Blacktown, with Teddy's office receptionist, Patricia Tonel, in Loiva's car. Loiva dropped Tonel off at Blacktown post office before heading home. Tonel would be the last known person to have any contact with Loiva — again, aside from her killer.

Teddy Gonzales' mobile telephone had made two calls to his home phone, at 6.20 pm and 6.23 pm. Both these calls lasted three seconds. From telephone records, police determined Teddy was somewhere in the Wentworthville area, a short drive from his Blacktown office, when he made these calls, which went unanswered. This was the last time Teddy tried to telephone anyone.

Police began to work on the theory that Clodine had been killed first, probably attacked in her bedroom while studying at her desk, where her books lay open. She had probably been killed around 4.30 pm. Loiva was next, as she arrived home about 5.30 pm. And Teddy was killed last, as he got home close to 7 pm.

This gave the investigators something else to consider about the nature of the crime. The killer was calculating, and had the stomach to wait inside the house, risking discovery, with the bodies of his victims until the next one came home. Of course, according to Sef's statement, that killer or killers, with nerves of steel, had waited some four hours inside the house, only to flee when Sef came home. It didn't make sense.

Chapter 10

The quake

Time and pressure are the forces that create an earthquake. You can build your home, your family, your life, on a geographical fault line and be ignorant of what is building beneath the surface. Then one day, without warning, the life you worked so hard to build is torn down.

Such was the case for the young Gonzales family on Monday, 16 July 1990, in the city of Baguio. The giant tremor that struck that day came like a bolt out of the blue. The earthquake killed or claimed as missing more than 1000 people out of Baguio's population of around 120,000.

The main quake began at exactly 4.26 pm, measuring 7.7 on the Richter scale. It lasted only 45 seconds, but this was all the time it needed to tear down massive concrete office buildings and hotels. This quake was followed by at least 600 aftershocks over the next two days.

Teddy and Loiva were at their hotel when the ground started shaking. As the hotel began to collapse, everyone ran out of the front entrance onto Legarda Road. Everyone, that was, except for nine-year-old Sef. According to his Aunt Emily, Sef ran out the rear entrance into the back yard, where he discovered he was alone. Turning round, he ventured back into the hotel. The small boy was hit by a falling beam, which pinned his lower right leg to the ground. He couldn't hope to free himself.

Teddy Gonzales noticed his son was not outside the hotel. Gathering his courage, he went back in to look for Sef. Inside the collapsed hotel it was dark and smoky.

'Teddy actually had to crawl through the debris looking for him,' says Emily.

Attracted by his son's cries of pain and panic, Teddy pulled Sef from the wreckage, then turned his attention to getting his son medical help.

Dr Amado Dizon, an orthopaedic surgeon, was having a coffee in Baguio's main street, Session Road, when the earthquake hit. He watched in disbelief as the earth began to open and close like some ghastly, giant mouth, devouring all in its path. Shattered glass rained down from tall buildings, and people were running everywhere, shouting and crying. 'I thought it was the end of the world,' he remembers.

Dr Dizon remained calm. His wife, also a doctor, was uninjured at her clinic in central Baguio, but his two-year-old son was at home with his nanny. He had to make sure they were safe. He drove in the direction of home, hiking the last 800 metres due to a blocked road, and collected his son and nanny.

Once his family's safety was assured, his next thought was to help others who were not as fortunate. At about 6 pm, he arrived at Notre Dame de Lourdes Hospital. The quake and subsequent aftershocks had made the hospital buildings unsafe, and staff grabbed the medical supplies they needed from inside before setting up a work area in the hospital's carpark.

It was raining and getting dark as Teddy and Loiva arrived with their injured son. 'I think the mother was crying. He [Teddy] was a little bit calm, and asked me if I could do anything to help,' recalls Dr Dizon. 'The thought [they had] was that the kid was about to have an amputation.'

Inspecting Sef's injured leg, Dr Dizon saw there was a massive crushing injury, but no broken bones. However, the skin had been smashed off, exposing the muscle underneath, and the child was losing blood. It was not a life-threatening injury, but one of the 30 or 40 serious injuries Dr Dizon had to treat that night. The biggest risk was infection.

He assured Teddy that Sef's leg could be saved.

'So first, because it was getting dark, I just gave emergency treatment. I packed the wound, and gave fluid and antibiotic,' says Dr Dizon.

Over the course of the next two days, aid began flooding into Baguio. Tents were set up in the parking lot of the hospital for use as operating theatres.

Sef would undergo a number of operations in the makeshift surgeries. He was given anaesthetic for the painful procedure of cleaning the wound. Dr Dizon used an electrical apparatus to 'harvest' skin from Sef's uninjured left leg. This skin was stitched onto Sef's wounds, then covered with a pressure bandage to ensure it grafted properly.

Within a fortnight, Sef was released from hospital, and Teddy could not express enough gratitude to the doctor who saved his son's leg. He presented Dr Dizon with a glass cocktail set as a thank-you present. After all, Teddy had made a momentous decision, and that decision meant he did not need the glasses himself any more.

'He told me he was planning to emigrate to Australia. Of course, his business, the hotel, was gone,' Dr Dizon says.

Teddy's family remember his devastation at the time.

Freddie Gonzales was not in Baguio when the earthquake occurred. He came back a month later and saw what had happened to his brother's hotel. Freddie's hotel next door, miraculously, was saved, and Freddie felt for his brother. 'It was a total collapse, it was not repairable, it was a total loss,' he says.

Teddy was in tears as he showed his brother the wreckage in Legarda Road. 'The first thing when he saw me, he embraced me and cried right along [the] sidewalk ... He cried and said why did this have to happen? I said it's okay, you're young, you can start again.'

Teddy was grateful he had not lost any family members, but the financial loss — and the fact he had to fork out for the demolition of his hotel's remains — made him extremely bitter, says Freddie. 'He felt very depressed with the material loss. It was years of hard work. He felt devastated, he was disgusted.'

Despite attempts by Freddie and his parents to persuade Teddy to stay in Baguio, Teddy believed his future was in Australia. It was an opportunity for a new beginning. He liked the lifestyle he'd had a taste of during his 1988 visit to Australia — the government, the people and the availability of land, the fact it was not overcrowded like the Philippines. He saw the opportunity there of returning to the practice of law, and prospering. And his family would be close to his wife's relatives in Sydney.

Ironically, it was their losses in the Philippines that would reaffirm Teddy and Loiva's faith in God. Already Catholic, they became more devout after the earthquake. They believed God, through the quake, had granted them a chance to make a fresh start in another country.

'So it was a new life for them and the first thing [Teddy] told me [when he arrived in Australia], which I cannot forget, is "You know, God always has something better in store",' Freddie recalls.

'He saw the tragedy in the Philippines as a blessing. Something good came out by becoming residents of Australia.'

Chapter 11

Auglys

Detective Senior Constable Paul Auglys quickly became the chief point of liaison with key family members and witnesses. That first night at Gladesville, the officers doing the original police statements really had not known what questions they should be asking. It was only in the ensuing days and weeks, when the forensic evidence was returned and witness statements were compared, that the questions the police should really be asking became apparent.

Auglys was tall, dark and handsome, with a direct kind of charm that assisted him in his dealings with people. He had been in the police force for twelve years. He got into the force not through a burning desire to save the world, but simply because his parents wanted him to get a job, and the police force seemed attractive.

Auglys started off doing general duties at Bankstown, in the days when it was one of southwest Sydney's major crime hotspots. After eight years he became a detective, working around the Bankstown, Bass Hill and Auburn areas, before hitting the big league in 1998: Crime Agencies, the central New South Wales detectives agency based in Sydney, since renamed the State Crime Command. Auglys primarily worked on serious violent crimes such as armed robberies.

He'd worked on his fair share of homicides, but had never been posted to Homicide, as such.

Auglys loved being a detective, loved the thrill of thinking of ways to crack cases. Watching the pieces of the puzzle fall into place was incredibly rewarding. Paperwork he could do without, but of course it was necessary.

If Sheehy was the good guy as far as Sef was concerned, Auglys in particular would become the bad guy. He didn't mind; in fact he enjoyed the thrill of working in the background, being Sef's faceless nemesis. From the start, Auglys would be kept away from Sef. Indeed, he would not meet him face to face for a good eleven months, but Sheehy and Auglys constantly consulted on investigation strategy.

It quickly became obvious to detectives of Tawas that the Gonzales family would be difficult to crack. In Auglys's mind, they were the key to solving the whole thing, but there were numerous barriers to getting them to talk. First, there was the cultural barrier, the fact that where they came from there was a view that police could not be trusted. But there was also the fact that most of the family did not want to believe they had a killer among them, did not want to face the fact that Sef might be guilty.

Auglys immediately picked Emily out as being different. It was obvious she was the strong one in the family, and due to her presence at the house at 6 pm that evening she was a crucial witness. Reviewing her first statement, taken at Gladesville station on the night of the murders, Auglys observed the major holes, the paucity of information regarding what she had seen that night. On 13 July, he called her in to Gladesville police station to clarify her statement.

Auglys realised Emily was holding back information. It was frustrating, the way she would only give details if they were specifically requested. Sometimes, she would tell him there was more, but that she wasn't ready to tell him yet what it was. At other times, she would start to tell him something new, realise she had said too much, and rein herself in.

Auglys knew that Emily was scared of Sef, and that if any information she told police that was adverse to her nephew got back to him she could be in danger. He felt her fear was justified. If only he could gain her trust.

Little did he know at the time that Emily wanted desperately to trust the police. She came to feel her family was not supporting her whenever she raised the question of Sef's possible involvement in the murders. So she simply stopped talking to them about it. She felt very alone. Eventually, she would realise the police were her last card to play if she wanted justice, but it would be a long and gradual process before she would tell them everything.

That day, 13 July, two days after her first statement, Emily elaborated a little on her visit to the Gonzales home at 6 pm on 10 July. She told Auglys that what she saw that evening had led her to believe that someone was indeed at home when she arrived. This, she said, was confirmed by seeing Sef's car in its usual location, the carport. She told him in this statement that she had said to her son, 'Oh, *kuya* Sef is home.' (*Kuya* is a Tagalog term for a respected elder brother.)

'I thought this for one reason, that being that his car was in the carport and to my knowledge Sef does not leave the house without his car,' Emily told Auglys.

She said the light she had seen on the ground floor was coming from the kitchen, confirming someone was home, as she visited her sister's home regularly and had often seen this particular light on through the frosted windows on either side of the front door.

Emily told Auglys that Sef's car lights were off but she didn't see anyone inside the car. She said she wasn't looking for anyone there, however. Nor was the engine of Sef's car running, as she would have noticed smoke coming from the exhaust pipe.

She said that as she got out of the car she commented to her son Gerard that they would not need an umbrella, as it was only drizzling very lightly. She said that after ringing the doorbell and waiting a minute for an answer, she tried again, asking her son to listen for the doorbell ringing within the house. Her son heard it ring as she pressed the doorbell again. She said that after they got no answer she thought of walking around to the side of the house and looking through the rear glass sliding door to the family–kitchen area to see if anyone was home. Something stopped her from doing this.

Emily told Auglys that she thought maybe the family had gone out but that her knowledge of the family convinced her otherwise. Teddy would not have arrived home from work yet, but her sister always arrived home before 6 pm to prepare dinner.

Emily added that Loiva, upon arriving home, usually parked in the garage, walked into the front foyer and placed her handbag on the small table in the hallway. Then she would remove her shoes and place them under the stairs. She would never wear her shoes in the rest of the house unless she was planning to go out again very soon. Loiva had been wearing her shoes when she was killed and her handbag was on the floor of the formal lounge–dining room, near her body.

'I cannot think of any reason or of any time when Mary [the police prosecution team would always refer to Loiva by her Christian name, Mary] would come home and take her bag into the formal lounge–living area of the house. This area was for guests of the house and the family never used this area of the house on their own,' she said.

Then Emily hinted at her belief that Sef was involved in the murders.

'Since the incident I have constantly wondered if Sef was home when I came to visit about 6 pm on Tuesday, 10 July 2001. I have also wondered, if he was, why he didn't answer the door. I have been told by other relatives that Sef may have been in the car on the phone when I was at the house so this does explain somewhat why he did not hear me at the house. I have also spoken to Sam Dacillo about his movements with Sef.'

Emily told Auglys what had happened when she arrived at Gladesville police station the night of the murders, and described her anger. She said she had asked Sef: 'Why didn't you come to the door, I was there at six o'clock, your car was there.'

It didn't take much reading between the lines that day for Auglys to realise that Emily suspected her nephew, but he had his work cut out to actually commit what she knew to paper. He needed her evidence.

SAM DACILLO WAS another loose end waiting to be followed up. Auglys did this on 15 July, two days after getting a fresh statement from Emily Luna.

Sam expanded on his arrangements with Sef for the night of 10 July 2001. He said that he had arranged with Sef on the afternoon of Monday, 9 July, to meet up the next day. Sef had rung him at home and asked if he wanted to lift weights in the afternoon, then go to dinner afterwards. They arranged to meet at 6 pm, but at that stage Sam had forgotten he had a basketball game organised for the following evening. Late on Monday night, Sam called Sef on his mobile phone and rescheduled their meeting for 8 pm.

About 11 am the next day, Sam got a text message from Sef asking if he was going to be home during the day, but did not reply to it. While playing basketball — the game began at 7 pm — he had a missed call from Sef. Around 7.45 pm, after finishing the game, he called Sef back and Sef asked him if they were still on for that night. Sam said yes, and asked if they were still going to lift weights, but Sef said no, they would just go out for dinner. They arranged to meet at Sam's house at 8 pm, and Sam told Sef he would call him when he got home. Sam arrived home at about 7.50 pm and called Sef again, just to confirm arrangements, and they decided they would go into the city for dinner.

In this statement, Sam Dacillo had clarified that there was no 6 pm conversation between Sef and him. Sef had known since the previous evening that they were meeting at 8 pm, not 6 pm. He would have known he would have time to kill his family, clean up and go out with Sam for dinner. It fitted in, then, when Sam mentioned that Sef barely touched his dinner at Planet Hollywood — a cheeseburger with mushrooms — claiming he and his mother had suffered food poisoning the previous week.

Sam told police that on the way into the city Sef had mentioned driving out to find Raf De Leon's place, and on the way home spoke of the road rage incident of the night before.

Sam also told police that as they were driving home along Wicks Road and approaching the intersection of Collins Street, Sef had slowed his car and looked up Collins Street towards his house. Sam also looked up the street; the house was in darkness. Sam asked his mate if he wanted to stop at his home before dropping Sam off at his house, but Sef said no.

It made the police think, why was Sef slowing down? Was he looking for emergency vehicles? A sign his family's bodies had already been discovered?

Sam also mentioned another item of interest, considering the marks on the wall above Clodine Gonzales' body.

'I would say that Sef thinks that he can stand up for himself. I say that because he had bragged to me in the past how people have stopped in a similar manner to the road rage incident he described to me ... On these occasions, Sef has told me he had gotten out of his car and taken a baseball bat out of the boot and scared them off.'

So Sef owned, or had owned, a baseball bat. Could this be the weapon used to bludgeon Clodine? police wondered.

POLICE HAD OBTAINED the 000 call transcript within 24 hours of the murders. The story it told did not tally with Sef's first statement. Sef said he had discovered only his father's body when he made the call, yet he told the operator someone had killed his family. There was no mention of Sef finding his mother during the phone call, or putting the phone down for a period to try to assist her.

The clothing Sef had worn that night during the discovery of the bodies had gone through an early analysis. There was blood on the back of the right sleeve, but other than that, no blood on the jumper. There was blood staining on the front of the right leg of his jeans, and there were a few spots of blood on the tops and sides of his boots, but none on the soles.

Most fascinating was an area of blue discolouration on the inside left lower sleeve of Sef's jumper. Later it would be sent for analysis and found to be blue paint.

Most damning at this stage, however, were Sef's statements about the calls he had made on the afternoon and early evening of 10 July, the period police now knew was the most likely time of the murders.

On 17 July, Detective Senior Constable Shaun Ryan got working on the phone records. He drove out to the

Westmead crime laboratories, where Sef's mobile phone, seized by police, was being stored. Police had not yet had a response to their request for call records from the phone service providers, but there was nothing to stop them from checking Sef's phone and recording all the numbers and calls and SMS messages made and received from the handset itself.

It was quickly discovered Sef had not been telling the truth about the calls he made and received on the afternoon and evening of 10 July 2001. There was no record of a call from Sam Dacillo about 6 pm, or an SMS about a basketball game shortly before that. And he had not tried to call either his mother's mobile telephone or his home phone in that same time period, during which he claimed he was sitting inside his car in the carport. The official phone company records for both Sef's and Sam Dacillo's mobile telephones would tell the same story.

Sef's alibi was fast unravelling. Of course, this might not mean he was guilty — the statement had been made while he was in a traumatised state. But it did mean that Sef had some clarifying to do with police.

Phone records also revealed a tantalising detail that puzzled the police. They knew Sef had arrived at his father's law firm at 1.14 pm because he had called on approach to be let into the secure car parking. At 1.22 pm, a call had been made from the Collins Street home phone — presumably Clodine was the caller — to her parents' work. Then, at 1.38 pm, Loiva had rung Clodine from her mobile telephone. Just twelve minutes later, a call was made from Teddy's office to the switchboard of Cumberland Psychiatric Hospital in Sydney's west. Try as they might, though, police could not locate anyone at the hospital who remembered receiving the call.

The only person who could help reconstruct what happened between Sef and his parents at the office that day was the young secretary Patricia Tonel. She thought Sef may have had a closed–door discussion with his parents shortly after arriving at the office, but her memory was pretty hazy. This could have been the time when that call was made to Cumberland Hospital, but times also were difficult for her to recall. In the end, it was information too vague for the cops to rely on.

Chapter 12

An orphan's appeal and a reconstruction

For the first week after the murders, Sef stayed with his Uncle Joseph, then at the North Ryde home of Cecile Ferrer.

Even though the grief was raw for the relatives, police knew the urgency of conducting a public appeal for anyone who might have any information about the murders to come forward. The way to reach the widest audience was an appeal through the media.

Of course, the police had already asked for witnesses to come forward and had issued a photograph of the Gonzales family, dressed to the nines for the wedding of Loiva's younger sister Liza to her husband Steve Carroll, with Sef's face blanked out from the photo. However, the police appreciated that an appeal is strongest when it comes from a relative of the victims. Only those close to the victims can truly convey the agony and outrage of the crime, and describe the victims properly.

Sheehy asked Joseph Claridades if he would be willing to make an appeal. Asking Sef, the only surviving member of the immediate family, indeed the one who found the bodies, was not really contemplated. It was assumed it would be too difficult for him to address the media.

When Sef learned from his Uncle Joseph about the request, he surprised everyone by offering to issue the appeal himself.

Sef carefully prepared the statement, and on the night of 12 July, two days after his family's murder, showed what he had written to Sheehy for approval. The statement was fine. In fact, it was extremely well written.

So on Friday, 13 July, the media turned out in droves to listen to and report on Sef's statement, issued in the media briefing room at the old New South Wales Police Headquarters at College Street in central Sydney.

Sef wore a dark blue suit. For moral support, his Uncle Joseph stood by his side. Sef read from his statement in a dignified voice, maintaining his composure.

As the cameras clicked in quick succession and the television cameras rolled, this is what Sef Gonzales said:

> *Most of you are probably aware of the tragedy that my family has experienced this week. I would like to speak briefly about my family.*
>
> *The best way I could possibly describe my father is that he was my hero and role model. He believed that there was no limit to what he could do for his family, friends or those less fortunate.*
>
> *I admired him in every way possible and my greatest aim in life was to one day become at least half the man that he was. I'd always said that if I was ever to have a son, I would name him after my father.*
>
> *My mother was the heart of my family. She was the heart of her friends and anyone who knew her. She had a very strong, passionate character and always stood up for what she believed was right. We have always confided in each other as*

best of friends and she made it seem that nothing was impossible. No problem seemed unsolvable. She had given life meaning through sharing her strong faith in God.

My sister was the life in the family. She was an expert on smiling and made us all believe that life should be taken lightly. She had always told me she believed that I was more talented than her and that she looked up to me. I had always replied to that with a smile. I never got the chance to tell her that I looked up to her. She had so many qualities that many people, including myself, envied. But she would always be my baby sister.

It is difficult to explain the love and ties in my family but if you were to picture the four corners of the world, in my world we were the four. We had so many plans and we had just started to bring our dreams to life. Unfortunately on Tuesday night, they were all taken away.

The other three corners of my world are now gone.

My father never got the chance to see a grandchild named after him. My mother won't be able to give any more meaning to the unsolvable, and my sister, who had just turned eighteen on Monday night, was just beginning to bloom.

My family, friends and myself would like to ask anyone out there to please help us and provide any information that could possibly help find who took them away in Tuesday night's senseless act. I would also like to take this opportunity to ask those concerned to please join us in prayers for my family.

So many of my family and friends are in mourning. I would like to ask the media to please respect our privacy and leave us in peace as we mourn. We would like to thank those who have shown concern and helped us so far.

Thank you.

Shortly afterwards, Sef was led from the room.

ON 16 JULY, Sef Gonzales participated in a video reconstruction of his movements at the Gonzales house on the afternoon and evening of 10 July 2001. The police wanted to tie him to a comprehensive version of his movements.

Sef arrived at the house accompanied by two of his uncles, Joseph and Edmund. They were there to give him moral support.

The video began with Sef and Mick Sheehy standing outside the house on the paved driveway. Both were dressed in blue forensic jumpsuits and white booties. On video, Sef looked half the size of Sheehy, who towered over him. They looked strange, almost comical, standing together, dressed identically, as Sheehy began to talk seriously for the camera, introducing Sef and his two uncles.

He told Sef that at any time the recording could be suspended so he could speak to his uncles. 'As I said to you before, I want you to understand that you're not obliged to say or do anything unless you wish to do so, as your activities and anything you say will be recorded on camera and form part of the evidence. Do you understand that?'

'Yes,' Sef replied.

Sheehy was extremely conscious of his height and the possibility it could be seen as physically intimidating to the small-framed man. He had decided from the outset to keep his distance from Sef as the video camera operated, and if he needed to be near Sef for the purposes of the reconstruction, he crouched down. He would continually be alert for signs that Sef was becoming upset, and at those points would offer Sef the opportunity to take a break from filming.

Sef pretty much stuck to his former version of events, confirming the phone calls in the car at 6 pm and then explaining how he had come home later that night and discovered his parents and sister. He kneeled down and mimed hugging their bodies. At times during the re-enactment Sef would start to breathe in a distressed fashion and Sheehy would give him the opportunity to stop, but Sef insisted he was okay to continue. Then he would be off again, unprompted, telling police what he had done next. It was the same behaviour Sheehy had observed the night of the murders: Sef had the ability to throw off his upset and organise his thoughts remarkably well.

By this stage, Sheehy's original opinion that Sef was not likely to be the killer had virtually gone down the drain. The re-enactment reinforced his suspicions of Sef, but he never let them show, except at one point during the reconstruction. As Sef led him to the corner of Ryrie Street, describing the point where he had stopped chasing the running figure, Sef became distressed. Again, though, he did not wish to stop or take a break. As Sef turned and began describing how he had headed back to his house to see if he could help Clodine, Sheehy for once looked directly into the camera. It was only a quick glance, but his face conveyed a bemused disbelief more than words could have.

BY THIS STAGE, there had been heated debate amongst Tawas detectives about how Sef should be interviewed from now on. It was the view of Auglys and Tony Polito that police should be applying a lot of pressure to Sef; that if they put the inconsistencies in his alibi to him, Sef would crack and confess.

Sheehy, Shaun Ryan and a few of the others, including Detective Senior Constable Paul Sullivan, a trained psychologist who had joined Tawas, disagreed. From their observations of Sef's behaviour, he was never going to confess, so they had to have Sef commit himself so strongly to a version of events that he could not back out. Let him talk, and then follow it up. It could be proven wrong afterwards, but the main thing should be that Sef thought police believed him. This was the tactic they would adopt.

Sheehy's instincts told him he was taking the right approach. He and Sef had developed a rapport. Sef saw him as an officer who could be trusted, the one who would 'save' him. If Sheehy told Sef he did not believe what he was saying, Sef would clam up and stop talking. Sheehy thought if police were patient, gave Sef enough rope, he would end up incriminating himself beyond doubt.

Chapter 13

A new life

The Gonzales family arrived in Australia in 1991 on visitors' visas. Amelita, thrilled to have her eldest daughter in Sydney, let the family stay in one half of a duplex she owned along Lane Cove Road, Ryde. Teddy, Loiva and their two children stayed in the three-bedroom part, while Loiva's sister Emily and her husband resided in the two-bedroom section.

Teddy and Loiva chose Our Lady of Dolours Primary School at Chatswood, an upmarket suburb in Sydney's north, for their children. They would get the same good Catholic education Teddy and Loiva had had. Every morning and afternoon, Sef and Clodine would hop on the school bus, with Sef as big brother entrusted with ensuring Clodine's safety. Through the Chatswood Catholic parish, Loiva and Teddy met Father Rex Curry and invited him to their home several times for dinner.

'They were very private people, and because of their association with the church, they just invited me to their house and showed me a high level of trust and respect, but there was very little [personal] information traded as such,' he recalls.

While Loiva got a part-time job working in a Chatswood bridal shop, Teddy set about making enquiries to gain permanent residency.

Loiva, in particular, was glad to be close to her family, says Freddie. 'Because her mother, brother and sister were already there it was something good for all of them. Both children were admitted to school, they were able to find a house so they adjusted very fast,' he says.

Through Amelita, Teddy met Jess Diaz, a cheerful, diminutive Filipino lawyer who ran an immigration law practice in the city. Diaz had arranged residency for virtually all the Claridades family members who lived in Australia.

Teddy could not gain permanent residency either for being married to an Australian citizen or having any dependent relatives living in Australia. Those options were out. However, there was a way he could stay in Australia, at least for a short period. That was if he made a refugee application.

Essentially, to qualify as a refugee, you had to prove you had left your own country because you were being persecuted because of your political or religious beliefs, your race, or your membership of a particular social group. Diaz advised Teddy that this application was unlikely to be successful, even though events had taken a very unfortunate turn for him in the Philippines with the earthquake.

However, Teddy forged ahead with the refugee application. He asked Diaz to read through his application. It was lengthy and very well written. Basically, the application revolved around Teddy losing his livelihood when his hotel collapsed in the earthquake, and detailed Sef's injuries. It was supported by photographs of the injured Sef.

Refugee applications could take several years to process in the early 1990s, says Diaz. Until their cases were reviewed, Teddy and his family would be allowed to stay in Australia on bridging visas.

Diaz advised Teddy, in the meantime, to do something about qualifying as a skilled migrant, which was a far better option to allow them to live in Australia permanently. For this, Teddy would have to satisfy a points test, which took into account qualifications, age, language skills and sponsorship.

Teddy enrolled in a University of Sydney law extension course run by the Solicitors Admission Board, which would take about two years, and Diaz gave Teddy a job as a paralegal at his law firm.

'He appeared to me to be a very honest person and well qualified and trustworthy,' Diaz recalls. 'He wrote very well. I had him do some research work, which was quite satisfactory.'

Teddy told Diaz he wanted a shift in his life direction after his work in the Philippines. He told Diaz that his father had had ambitions for him to run for the position of mayor of Baguio, but he was no longer interested in politics.

'He told me he could not stand corruption back in the Philippines. He had exposure to being subjected to a big bribe, which he refused,' recalls Diaz.

Simply put, Teddy wanted a quiet life in Australia, to spend time with his family and to create financial security for them. To this end, he took a keen interest in the share market.

'He also has many times asked me how to do property investment, in terms of developing properties. I know he had made a lot of studies, I don't know if he ever did it,' says Diaz.

Teddy studied hard at law. Juggling a job and the course would have been tough, let alone family as well. His two young children occasionally turned up at Diaz's office, and with Diaz's children they would browse through the shops in the city.

Teddy had such high expectations of himself that he became bitterly disappointed when he did poorly in one subject, recalls Diaz. 'I don't think he could take any failure, he wanted to go back [to Baguio] and give up on Australia.'

Ultimately, Teddy weathered the difficulties and decided to stay. He graduated from his law course and qualified to practise in Australia.

Towards the end of 1992, Teddy, Loiva and their two children went back to Baguio, where they would stay at least six months as Teddy prepared the paperwork for his skilled migrant application. Unlike a refugee applicant, a skilled migrant applicant has to make the application from their country of origin.

Freddie recalls that at that time it was necessary to give up Filipino citizenship when you became a resident of another country. 'It was discussed with my father and me because before, you had to relinquish your citizenship, so that was a big thing for him.'

To Teddy and Loiva, the sacrifice was worth it. They had fallen in love with the Australian lifestyle and the Australian people.

WHEN THE GONZALES family successfully migrated to Australia in mid-1993, they returned to the duplex at Lane Cove Road, Ryde. Yet Teddy and Loiva were keen to establish their own roots in their new country.

Teddy, ever the planner, saw an opportunity at Blacktown. The area had a large Filipino population, and Teddy saw it as a good place to set up an immigration practice.

The family bought a modest single-storey brick home at 6 Ashgrove Crescent, Blacktown. Around June 1995, that was where Teddy opened his sole practice, T Gonzales & Associates. Later, he purchased a commercial space at 15–17 Kildare Road, Blacktown, where he moved his practice.

Freddie remembers Teddy complaining he felt discriminated against in his practice. He felt judges would give him a more 'difficult time' than they gave Caucasian lawyers.

'From the outset everything was okay, but when he got to be a little successful, when he was doing well with his profession, that was the time he felt discriminated [against] … but I told him that's something you have to live with, it's part of a cultural system,' Freddie says.

The Gonzales family lived in the Blacktown house until early 2000. Loiva kept it spotless, neighbours recall. The Gonzales were friendly neighbours, and Sef and Clodine played with the other young children in the street.

The house was located just around the corner from St Michael's Catholic church. The Gonzales family quickly became members of the Catholic community. St Michael's had about 2000 regular parishioners, many of whom were Filipino, Maltese or Croatian.

Parish priest Father Kevin Dadswell recalls Teddy Gonzales coming to the 8 am Mass almost every day on his way to work, and Loiva would sometimes accompany him. So would Sef and Clodine.

'Not too many people come to Mass that regularly — devout, devoted people with a very strong faith. They were very pleasant people, very nice people, but fairly private,' he says.

Teddy and Loiva forged a few close friendships. They were very choosy with their friends, but once you were friends with Teddy and Loiva, there was nothing they would not do for you. They were caring and generous, and Teddy would refuse to accept payment for conveyancing work he did as a favour for his close friends.

Chapter 14

Aftershocks

On the first three days and nights after the murders, Emily Luna did not sleep, eat, or leave her home.

Wearing the same pair of pyjamas, Emily sat on her couch, staring into space. Her thoughts kept returning to the visit she had paid to the Gonzales home on the night of the murders and the fact she had seen Sef's car outside. She thought of the veiled accusation she had made to Sef at the police station that night. She wondered whether visiting the house that evening, becoming a witness, meant she had endangered her safety and that of her immediate family.

All she was concerned about was the safety of her husband and child. It was all right if they slept, as long as she was awake to watch over them.

Her eight-year-old son could not understand the depth of her fear. Occasionally, he would give her a hug, trying to comfort her with words of childish innocence: 'Everything will turn out okay, Mum.'

Emily did not think anything would be okay, ever again.

On the night of 11 July, the night after the bodies were discovered, Emily got up to search for a photograph of Teddy, Loiva and Clodine. She could only find one, an old one from a family get-together. Placing it on an altar in the living room, she lit some candles and said a prayer for the souls of her family. Then, summoning up her courage, she made a promise to her three dead family members that she would fight until their killers were brought to account.

'I promised the three of them I will not stop until justice is served, basically even if I had to risk my own life, I will not stop until justice is served.'

It was easier said than done, though. Emily did not trust the police not to repeat anything she said to them about her nephew back to him, and put her at greater risk.

That was the main thing playing on her mind, the risk. She made sure the burglar alarm at her house was armed 24 hours a day, regardless of whether she was home or not. She thought about how her house was raised off the ground, how easy it would be for her nephew to crawl underneath and up into the house, and be waiting for her when she got home. She stopped going to the Holy Spirit Church in North Ryde, keen to avoid the media, that were sniffing around in the hope of speaking to relatives of the murder victims.

Most of all, she didn't want to speak to her nephew, or even lay eyes on him. It occurred to her that if he had murdered his immediate family, if her suspicions were true, then he would have no compunction about harming his other relatives.

Later, when she allowed herself some sleep, she dreamed of Loiva and Clodine. They were terrifying, vivid dreams, full of violence. In one, Clodine was explaining to Emily where she had been stabbed, and as she pointed to each wound, Emily would feel the knife go into her own body.

In another, Loiva was lying in a coffin, then she stood up holding a knife, and began chasing Emily with it. This dream made Emily fully understand the terror her sister must have experienced before her death. 'I just felt how she would have, when she had been chased by someone with a knife,' says Emily.

TEDDY'S AND LOIVA'S relatives in Baguio had received news of the murders within hours. Annie Paraan, Sef's aunt, received the news via SMS text message from her brother Edmund about 6 am in the Philippines (8 am Australian time) on the day after the murders. At first she thought the message was some kind of cruel joke, then she asked her husband, Dr Ronnie Paraan, to read it over for her, just to make sure it was real.

Later that day the news flashes about the murders began airing on Annie's television. They were repeated frequently, and showed the scene from Sydney the night before. Annie says the local TV stations were reporting that Australian police wanted the Filipino relatives of the dead family to 'let themselves be known'.

Annie had a soft heart by nature, and was quite emotional. She was also close to her sister Loiva and brother-in-law Teddy. She would speak to Loiva maybe twice a month and exchange SMS messages in between. She watched the television footage and saw her nephew curled up in a foetal position outside the family's garage. He was an orphan now, she realised, and with Loiva dead she was the eldest of the Claridades siblings. Annie was struck with a strong sense of responsibility for Sef, heightened by the fact she was his godmother.

'My heart really felt for him and I said I wanted to do something for him because he's alone there … when I first saw him on TV, my initial reaction was to go there and help wherever I can, and also find out why this thing happened to them, what is the reason?'

Annie began making immediate plans for some time off from her manager's position at a major Baguio bank, so she could go and assist Sef in Sydney. Her husband Ronnie didn't want her to go, but Annie insisted. She had visited Sydney in

May that year, and her one-year tourist visa was still current. She could leave as soon as she got her luggage in order and arranged some time off from the bank. That weekend, she flew out of Manila, Sydney-bound.

Freddie Gonzales, his daughter Monica and his sister Annie Gonzales-Tesoro also made arrangements to catch a flight to Sydney. Their elderly parents stayed behind. Evelyn Gonzales was not in good health.

On Friday, 13 July, the Gonzales and Claridades family members from interstate and overseas arrived in Sydney. Amelita Claridades returned from Melbourne with her daughter Liza. Edmund Claridades arrived from the Gold Coast. Freddie and Monica Gonzales, Annie Gonzales-Tesoro and Annie Paraan arrived from the Philippines.

Police forensics officers had arrived at Amelita's house on the night after the murders to search for signs that the killer had washed up in her yard. They found no evidence, but Amelita was not comfortable returning home.

She and her daughters Annie and Liza stayed at the Ryde home of Cecile Ferrer, who had taken the first call from police on the night of the murders. The Gonzales side of the family stayed with close family friends at Turramurra, on Sydney's North Shore. Edmund stayed at Emily's home in North Ryde.

That Friday evening, Joseph rang Emily and said, 'I think there's something you have to clarify with Sef.' Joseph asked her to come to the Ferrer residence, where Sef was being comforted by relatives. Emily agreed to go.

The first thing Sef said to her when she arrived was: 'Aunty Emily, it was raining very heavily that night, wasn't it?'

Emily put up a good front. Not wishing to upset family members or further provoke Sef, she agreed. She realised she had been too confrontational that night at Gladesville police station. She wanted Sef to think she believed the explanation he had given police for why she had seen his car in the carport of Collins Street at 6 pm that Tuesday.

'I told him that I was sorry I scolded you that evening, and sorry that I didn't realise that you were in the car when you were making a phone call,' she says.

Sef seemed appeased. He told his aunt it was all right, that he understood. Emily made herself give her nephew a hug.

Emily wasn't the only family member to question Sef about the subject of his guilt or innocence. After his arrival in Sydney Freddie Gonzales also tried to confront him.

Freddie recalls giving his nephew a hug and telling him, 'You can be honest with me, whatever happened.' He says Sef paused, then replied, 'No, what I said happened, happened.'

Freddie felt a deep disappointment. He thought Sef was evading him. Later, Freddie would puzzle over the fact that all Sef had to do was ask for help, financial or otherwise, from his uncle, and he would give it to him. He was a wealthy man. So why wasn't Sef asking for help? Was it an admission of his guilt? He did not know that during that period Sef was telling Sam Dacillo that Freddie probably wanted to get his hands on Teddy's 'millions'.

Annie Paraan also remembers comforting Sef, who appeared to be sobbing. 'I can't be 100 per cent sure because every time [there was] the action of sobbing, but I can't remember seeing tears falling.'

It was inevitable in that stressful time that tempers would begin to fray. Freddie remembers a spat occurring about two nights into his stay in Sydney, when a lot of relatives and friends were assembled. He recalls that Emily and a couple of others stated their belief that Sef was guilty, and that the family should not extend help to him. However, the rest of the family took the attitude that of course the family should help Sef.

Emily recalls that an argument erupted when Freddie was talking to Sammy Dacillo, Sam Dacillo's father, about the circumstances surrounding the timing of the events on the night of the murders. There was a discrepancy between what Dacillo was telling Freddie, and what Sef had told Freddie that afternoon, and Freddie commented on it. Annie Paraan got upset. She felt that her godson was being unfairly accused of having something to do with the murders.

Difficult though it was, the extended family was forced to push these issues aside and prepare for the burial of their loved ones.

THE FUNERAL WAS scheduled for 20 July, ten days after the murders. A viewing of the bodies in open caskets was arranged for family members by the funeral home, several days before the funeral.

At the viewing, Sef kneeled beside Teddy's coffin and held his father's hand. He stayed there a good five minutes, with his head bowed. He repeated this with Clodine and Loiva.

The family members observed the shocking injuries to Teddy, Loiva and Clodine, which, despite the best efforts of the funeral home, were still visible. Freddie and Annie Gonzales-Tesoro noticed Teddy had stitching across his hands and wrists. They thought this was because he had tried to defend himself, Freddie says. Emily observed that Sef appeared to be praying beside each family member and she wondered: was he asking God for forgiveness? but she didn't notice any sign of tears on Sef's face. However, Annie Paraan says the viewing was the first time she saw Sef lose control of his emotions. 'When the bodies were released to us, it was then I saw him really sob.'

The relatives wanted a burial, but Sef told the family that he recalled Teddy mentioning to him that he wanted to be cremated after death. However, it was pointed out to him that as there was an ongoing police investigation into the murders it would be wiser not to cremate the bodies in case further forensic tests were needed. Sef agreed.

But he would not bend on the issue of who was to give the eulogy for his father. Freddie wanted to speak about his brother at the funeral, but Sef was adamant, Emily recalls. Sef wanted to do it, and he wanted to be the only one to do it. It was agreed that if Sef got too emotional at the funeral then Freddie would take over reading the eulogy. Annie Paraan volunteered to say the eulogy for Loiva, and Liza Carroll agreed to say Clodine's. She was extremely fond of her lively niece, who had lived with her in Melbourne for the year before her death.

SEF HAD EXPRESSED fears for his own safety, saying that his family's killers would come after him next. On the morning of 18 July, two days before the funeral, the police checked him into a motel on Victoria Road, Ryde. Later that day, they helped Sef change the personalised numberplates of his car.

The room Sef was first checked into was quickly changed. Sheehy told Sef he had hand-picked the second room because it provided better security. But safety wasn't the real reason for the choice, unbeknownst to Sef. Covert police surveillance of Sef Gonzales was about to start. It was a low-key way to determine whether Sef really was an innocent victim or was just playing the part. Sheehy knew the room he had chosen would best allow the surveillance officers to follow Sef's comings and goings. But Sef would only stay at the hotel for a couple of nights, with his family paying the bill.

SEF WAS EATING very little, telling his relatives he was not hungry. Emily suggested he should try some soup, and went and bought it for him to take back to the hotel.

One night — when he had just got his car back from police — Sef told his relatives he just wanted some time alone, to go for a drive. He had an appointment at a family friend's house to get a haircut before the funeral. The appointment was for midnight, but Sef failed to show up. When the friend telephoned the family to let them know Sef had not arrived, there was panic and the family telephoned police to say they had 'lost' him.

Sef later said he had gone to a park in West Ryde to contemplate all that had happened. Emily would soon hear that he had been spotted around that time tucking into a meal at a Lane Cove steakhouse, alone.

After he moved out of the hotel, Sef was scheduled to stay at the Ferrers', and the next night at the Dacillos'. Both cancelled on him, as they were concerned about getting too involved and putting their families at risk. Emily did not want Sef to stay at her home either, and told him she too did not wish to get involved. She had a young son to protect. Sef said he understood, then said words to the effect of: 'At least I know who my true friends are.'

Chapter 15

The siblings

Teddy and Loiva had both wanted the very best for their children's future; however, their ideas on how to raise the children were different.

Teddy wanted them to have all the material possessions that he missed out on when he was growing up, says Emily. 'It was Ted's principle ... because when he was a young kid he never had that luxury,' she says.

Loiva, on the other hand, was a disciplinarian, and very protective. She did not believe in spoiling the children. Emily believed this stemmed from her being the eldest sibling in her own family. Loiva thought that if they were spoiled, her children would not grow up to be responsible adults.

Both Teddy and Loiva agreed, however, on the importance of giving the children a top-notch education. They enrolled Sef and Clodine in two of Sydney's best Catholic high schools. Sef went to Parramatta Marist High School, and Clodine to Loreto Kirribilli.

Emily recalls that until Year Ten, Sef was a straight-A student. Clodine did acceptably well at her studies, but her brother's grades outshone hers. She did not seem to harbour any resentment at this. She was more interested in her wide range of friendships, and in playing sport.

Emily says Clodine really looked up to Sef, and admired his intelligence. Like all siblings, of course, they fought, sometimes viciously, but these were verbal spats, not physical. Emily says Clodine was very strong-willed, independent and determined, and would not back down from an argument. But that said, Clodine respected her elder brother.

'She admired Sef ... even if they argued, it's just normal, but she admired him, she told me,' says Emily.

When he turned sixteen, Sef got his driver's licence, and soon afterwards Teddy bought him a car, the Ford Festiva. Loiva objected, worrying he would be out driving when he should be studying. But Teddy wanted Sef to have his own transport. In his little green Festiva, Sef would rack up speeding fines.

In 1998, Sef's final year at Marist Brothers, he made his parents proud by being nominated house captain of St Vincent House. It was a position of responsibility and leadership.

Pressure was always on the two children to perform well academically. Whichever child outperformed the other was always heaped with praise and was the subject of their parents' proud boasting to friends.

Sef told his family of his ambition to be a doctor. However, at the end of the year his Higher School Certificate (HSC) results were a big disappointment. Sef only gained a mark of 71.55, which ruled out entry into a university medicine course.

SEF HAD ALSO begun dating. He favoured women who were tall and leggy, and dreamed of having a model for a girlfriend. He took one girl to the late 1998 concert of boy band Boyz II Men at the Sydney Entertainment Centre. She was not impressed when Sef parked some distance from the venue because he did not wish to pay for parking, and made her walk. He told her he wanted to live in south central Los Angeles, the home of 'gangsta' rap, but she was unimpressed, and thought him pretentious. He wrote her eloquent love letters, but his feelings were not reciprocated.

This was a shame, as the girl was the daughter of one of Loiva's closest friends. Loiva would have liked to see them pair up, remembers the girl's mother, who does not wish to be named. She will be referred to as Jane. Jane says she got the impression from Loiva that when Sef went out on dates with different girls, Loiva was worried that things might become too serious, and that he might choose an inappropriate partner.

'I said, "Gosh Loiva, he's still young, don't worry,"' Jane recalls.

But Loiva need not have been concerned that Sef would become involved in a serious and meaningful relationship at this stage. It seemed as far as young women went, he lived in a fantasy world.

This is demonstrated by a website Sef set up perhaps as far back as 1998, which Tawas detectives would later discover. Supposedly the site was created by a young woman named Daisy Diaz. The home page of the site was called 'Daisy's Dedication page to Seffie'. There was a picture of an attractive young Asian girl with her hair in pigtails, and the caption 'here's an Old piccy of mE ...'.

A whole page, bedecked with pastel colours and pictures of teddy bears hugging, was full of gushing comments about just how wonderful and manly Sef Gonzales was. 'Sef or filoflava whatever it is that u call him, remember that he's a sweetie and a true friend (besides being caring, trustworthy, cute, adorable, kind, understanding, intelligent, and can sing in a way that makes any girl's heart melt!)' it read.

'Daisy' continued that she was sorry she had not had time to talk to Sef before she went on her 'trip' away and bemoaned the fact he never visits 'the cafe' any more, where 'we used to have heaps of fun together with the rest of the crew':

> *i know i'll be far away but i will never forget you, and before you know it i'll be there again! i owe you so much, actually i owe you my life! u were always there for me and when times get real tough, ur the only one I can genuinely count on. even though we've only know* [sic] *each other for 4months, u mean so much to me. remember that night I asked you to take me home? i was in such a mess. you didn't take advantage of me . . . you were such a gentleman and no matter what happens u'll always be that special man in my life (even if u just wanna be friends*smootch*) . . .*

It went on with 'Daisy' saying she wouldn't have minded if Sef *had* taken advantage of her — even though it wasn't his style, as he was 'a lot smoother than that' and 'such a gentleman . . . as ALL my friends say about u . . . "whatta man!!!!"'

The site included the graphic for Sef-G Productions — 'his company thingy', wrote 'Daisy' — and a raft of photographs of Sef, from Year Ten shots from his formal to pictures of him 'with his kick-ass r&b/rap group Definite Vibez'. It also featured pictures of Sef lying across a bunch of attractive girls' laps and smirking at the camera. And there was a photo of him naked from the waist up, his lean, chiselled muscles on display, in which he was supposedly posing for a Calvin Klein modelling competition; he was '3rd Runner-up' in the 'babyface division'.

The site also contained a poem for Sef — a 'Lil' dedication from me hun'. It began:

> *How could she ever fool around?*
> *Don't know what she was thinking 'bout*
> *While you were giving love,*
> *She let you down.*
> *Boy I know that you want to be alone*
> *Cause she broke you're* [sic] *heart*
> *And she sent you home*
> *And you're wondering why*
> *She was so cold.*
>
> *Well when they lie*
> *They have to lie again*
> *Cause the lying never ends . . .*

According to police, the whole site is one big lie. The text and photos on the website were discovered in the laptop that was seized from Sef's bedroom shortly after the murders. He had written the dedication to himself and posted it on the web for all to see.

Tawas detectives did manage to track down the girl in the photograph, who told them her parents were friends of the Gonzales family but that she had not seen Sef for years. It appears that Sef created the name 'Daisy Diaz' himself.

Sef seems to have perpetrated the story of Daisy, the girl he loved but who broke his heart, to later girlfriends. He also told a huge lie about 'Daisy' to Sheehy during the murder investigation, probably in an attempt to elicit pity. He informed Sheehy he was grieving for Daisy, who had been killed in the 11 September 2001 terrorist attack on New York's World Trade Center. He told Sheehy he had flown to

New York for her funeral and that he had been generous enough to pay for the girl's mother to fly over as well. The real girl in the photograph, however, was in fact alive and well, having lived in Chicago before returning to Sydney.

IN 1999, AFTER leaving school, Sef had enrolled in a medical science degree at the University of New South Wales. It was a course which, if completed successfully, would allow him admission into a full medicine course. However, whether through lack of interest or lack of ability, Sef did not perform well in the course.

Towards mid-2000, the time came to reassess Sef's goals due to his failure to get into medicine. Sef decided he wanted to become a lawyer, like his father. He enrolled in a course at Macquarie University. His parents were thrilled. What they did not know was that it wasn't a full law degree course, but a university bridging degree course with some law subjects. Sef told them it was a law course, and they had no reason to doubt him, says Emily.

Freddie says he does not believe his brother would have forced Sef to study something he didn't want to. 'Probably Teddy had dreams for Sef, but you do not know what Sef wants to do ... I'm sure Teddy would have been proud if Sef wanted to be a successful lawyer but ... Teddy's a very intelligent and reasonable man. I don't think he would force Sef to be something or someone he couldn't be.'

Chapter 16

Teddy's troubles

Immigration law is a very tricky thing. You are dealing with people's lives. If you are an immigration lawyer, people look to you as the person who can come up with a solution. If you don't succeed, they can become upset and angry. Hence Teddy's brush with the law in the late 1990s.

Around 1997, Teddy began attracting the attention of Department of Immigration authorities. The authorities believed Teddy was party to lies told by would-be immigrants on their applications for refugee status. Gaining refugee status from the Philippines is quite difficult. Despite the occasional activity of members of the New People's Army, a communist guerrilla group, in the southern provinces, the country as a whole is generally considered safe by Australian immigration authorities.

A number of Teddy's clients were refused visas on this basis, and appeared before government tribunals to appeal against the decisions.

One such case was that of Lilia Gaculais, which went before the Administrative Appeals Tribunal on 25 August 2001. Lilia Gaculais was the aunt of a would-be Australian citizen from the Philippines, Mr Blas, who had approached Teddy Gonzales while in Australia on a visitor's visa in

August 1996, seeking advice on how to get Australian residency.

Gaculais said that Teddy had been paid a fee of $1500 by her nephew to assist with the preparation of a protection visa application, and a further sum of $1500 upon a subsequent review of that application by the Refugee Review Tribunal.

She said Mr Blas had told Teddy he wanted to get permission to work in Australia legally, and that Teddy had said he could get him a work permit without any trouble and in a way that would be allowed by the Australian Government. Mr Blas's application read:

> I was a professional nurse by occupation while in the Philippines. While I had a full-time job, I had spare time after work and I wanted to have additional part-time work.
>
> It was at that time I again met Ben Claraval, a friend I had met a few years back. Ben said they were in need of a nurse to participate in their rural projects. Ben said they had a privately funded corporation that looked after the needy communities. Ben was willing to get me part-time work, so I accepted the job. Early in our visits to the town I was shocked to see how difficult life was in many of those areas. There were really small villages with just very few people in them. There was neither water nor electricity in these places. As time went by, Ben and I became even closer. We had several discussions about our work but it always puzzled me why he would request that I keep everything we did in confidence. I thought that we were doing something great which deserved to be talked about and probably duplicated by others. But it was his request and I respected this. At one time, though, I was approached by Catherine Gomez. She was part of Ben's

team. She said that we would not see Ben any more and that the project was to stop. I insisted on getting information from her as to Ben, because I felt that something was wrong. I would not let her go. After a while she said that she would disclose to me the situation because she did not want to endanger me. She said that the villages we visited were where families of New People's Army members lived and that Ben was a communist leader. She said Ben had been shot and killed. This disclosure left me in shock. I was in the midst of communists and I did not know about it. Even more shocking was the news about Ben's death. Two nights later Catherine came to see me. She was visibly upset. She said the communists had come to the conclusion that I had something to do with Ben's death. She said that an order had been sent to a liquidation team to have me killed. She said she did not believe I was involved and therefore wanted to forewarn me. It is for this reason that I had to leave the Philippines.

Mr Blas signed the document, knowing it was not factual. It was the decision of the Tribunal's Deputy President, Dr D Chappell, that Mr Blas's visa application be refused. However, Dr Chappell went further, stating that the allegations made against Teddy in this case were almost identical to those in a previous case brought before the Tribunal. He proceeded to make the comments about the conduct of certain migration agents:

It does not require the skills of a Sherlock Holmes or Dr Watson to discern the nature of the systematic pattern of immigration fraud and abuse emerging from these cases. It is very disturbing, however, to realise that it is a pattern which appears to have been allowed to continue over a substantial period of time without effective actions being taken to investigate and prosecute those responsible.

In fact, by that time Teddy had been investigated by the Department of Immigration. In July 1998, he had been charged with four counts of 'being knowingly concerned in the offence of providing false documents to an officer exercising powers under the *Migration Act*'.

Two of these charges were later dropped, but the other two went to trial in St James Local Court in central Sydney. Teddy maintained his innocence and fought the charges. Two of his female clients claimed Teddy had charged them $1500 each, and stated in court that Teddy had provided them with false typewritten statements to copy, in their own handwriting, into their applications for protection visas. Both the applications revolved around the women being unwittingly tangled up in communist activity and leaving the Philippines because they were fearful they would be killed by communists.

The women claimed Teddy left them high and dry after their applications were refused. One had complained to the immigration authorities. She told the court Teddy arrived on her doorstep when he found out she had lodged the complaint and coerced her into signing a statutory declaration that she had no complaint against him.

The problem for the women was that if their own versions were to be believed, they had cooperated in writing down the statements, knowing them to be untrue. They also had an axe to grind with Teddy Gonzales. They were therefore hardly reliable witnesses. The immigration charges against Teddy Gonzales were dismissed on 15 March 1999. Teddy was able to continue practising.

Undoubtedly, Teddy had made a number of clients unhappy. The question that would be asked after the murders was whether this provided sufficient motive for him to be killed. But too much time had passed between this period of Teddy's legal troubles and the murders, it seemed, and the police soon abandoned this line of investigation.

Chapter 17

One sweet day

The funeral for the Gonzales family was held on Friday, 20 July at North Ryde's Holy Spirit Catholic Church. There were close to 300 mourners present to say their last goodbyes. Three coffins lay side by side at the front of the church, each adorned with flowers and a photo of a smiling Gonzales family member.

The Claridades relatives sat in a front pew, with Sef. Emily was next to him, facing the photo of Loiva. The Gonzales family sat on the other side of the church, also in the front pew. The rest of the church was filled with friends of Teddy and Loiva as well as schoolfriends of Sef and Clodine. Detectives from Strike Force Tawas were present amongst the mourners. Also present as Sef's 'bodyguards' were two of his friends. Sef had convinced them he needed personal protection during the funeral.

Father Janusz Bieniek, from the Holy Spirit Church had been in Cairns when his parishioners were murdered, but had flown back to comfort Sef. 'I was so shocked I knew that I should be here and I would like to assist Sef as much as possible,' he says.

Father Janusz had helped Sef organise the funeral. He recalls that Sef was 'extremely emotional' in the lead-up to the funeral. Father Janusz prayed with him, but did not offer any speeches to try to comfort him. Nothing could console someone at such a time, he thought.

He asked Sef whom he would like to have speak at the funeral and Sef requested Father Rex Curry, now a parish priest at Manly on Sydney's northern beaches, who had met the family when they were at Chatswood. Father Janusz telephoned Father Curry and asked him if he would say the homily. Father Curry agreed.

Father Janusz remembers that he thought it would be too distressing for Sef to speak at the funeral and tried to talk him out of it. But Sef was insistent. 'Especially he wanted to have his speech, he wanted to have his talk,' he says.

So, on the day of the funeral, as the mourners came to pay their respects to Teddy, Loiva and Clodine, Father Janusz tried to give the boy strength to go through with it. 'Just before the Mass he was really shaking and crying. [I said] you have to do this, you have to be strong, not to cry, there's no time for that now.'

Father Rex Curry had not had the chance to speak to Sef before delivering the homily at the funeral. He'd just had the phone call out of the blue from Father Janusz, despite not seeing the family for years. Sef never spoke with him directly before the funeral, which he found to be unusual.

'I couldn't have access to him immediately after the slaying, he seemed to be shuttled from one place to another,' says Father Curry.

Father Curry's homily was more religious than personal in tone, revolving around the nature of Christianity, but he also made the comment that the evil forces responsible for the Gonzales murders would not triumph. 'I was trying to be as neutral at the time and as religious as possible,' he remembers.

Nevertheless, Father Curry observed what he describes as Sef's 'detached' behaviour at the funeral. 'He sang a song which was, again, highly unusual at the time of his father's and mother's death and sister's death ... there was very little empathy there,' he says.

The song Sef sang at the funeral was entitled 'One Sweet Day'. It had been a hit for pop diva Mariah Carey with the boy band Boyz II Men, the band that Sef had gone to see at the Sydney Entertainment Centre in 1998. The song spoke of being reunited with a loved one in Heaven.

Annie Paraan, in her eulogy for Loiva, told the mourners how she had last seen her sister that May, when she visited Loiva in Sydney. 'When it was time for us to leave Sydney, [Loiva] and I hugged each other so tight for a long while and tears kept running down our eyes,' Annie Paraan said. 'I was crying with the thought that we would be counting the years before we can see and hug each other again. I never thought it would be the last time I would see them alive.'

In her eulogy for Clodine, Liza commented on the tragedy of a young life wasted.

For most of the funeral, Sef, smartly dressed in a dark blue suit, sat with his head bowed. When it was his turn to come to the lectern, he retained his composure.

His eulogy for Teddy was eloquent, almost poetic. He paid tribute to his father, his hero and mentor, and referred to the time Teddy had risked his life to rescue Sef from the hotel in Baguio when he was a young child.

He recalled, as a child, lying against his father's chest and listening to his heart. 'The rhythm of his heartbeat planted life in me and at that early moment instilled all the strength that I needed to face the life ahead of me. A man like Papa does not die. His heart continues to beat in me and in all of you who have known him,' he said.

Sef told the congregation that his father had promised to reveal the meaning of his name when he turned 21 — which would be in September of that year — and now he would never know. 'I will never find out the meaning of my name because it was taken away along with my father. That part of me will always be incomplete, along with many other parts of my life that only Papa can fill.'

After his eulogy was completed, Sef took a breath, and, unheralded and with no back-up music, sang in a clear, sweet voice, about a lost loved one and how he would eventually rejoin the loved one in Heaven.

Journalists had been allowed inside the church for the funeral, which was quite unusual. In fact, there was an area at the side of the church set aside for media, recalls journalist Letitia Rowlands, of the *Daily Telegraph*, one of Sydney's major metropolitan newspapers.

'From a media point of view it was bizarre,' she says. 'There was a media section at the side and they gave us all photocopies of all the eulogies so we didn't have to take notes or anything. It was too easy in that way … Him singing was the most bizarre bit. Here's this kid who just lost his entire family, and he gave a eulogy to his dad, which was quite touching really, but he didn't cry and then he sings. The family were a wreck, [but] they were definitely supporting him. After he sang they were all hugging him.'

The burial of Teddy, Loiva and Clodine was a more private affair. Sef had insisted it should be attended by family members only.

The family made its way through Macquarie Park Cemetery to the three plots side by side in the Catholic burial section, to see the coffins lowered into the earth and to say their last goodbyes.

Emily would visit the graves once a week for the next three months and feel growing anger as the headstones for the family failed to be erected. Each grave simply had a temporary name tag on it. This was not good enough for her family, she felt.

Spurred by anger into action, she contacted the cemetery administration and asked why the plaques containing epitaphs had not been placed on the graves. She was told that a form had been sent to Sef some time ago, and that as he was the only immediate family member left, it was up to him to choose the inscriptions. The forms even offered him a choice of inscriptions. Emily spoke to her mother, Amelita, about this, but Amelita did not wish to bring up the subject with Sef.

A month or two afterwards, the plaques went up, and the family was happy with them. All three began 'Always living in our hearts'. Teddy's described him as a dearly beloved husband and father and a cherished son, brother and friend. 'An inspiration to us all', it read. Loiva's described her as a beloved wife and mother and a cherished daughter, sister and friend. 'Her sweet ways will always be part of us' was the last line. Clodine's described her as a dearly beloved daughter and sister and a cheerful friend to many. 'She will always be part of our smiles' was how Sef described his sister on the plaque.

Chapter 18

'Definite Vibez'

One of the distractions Sef experienced during his university studies was his wish to become big on the music scene. Emily believes Sef was lying to himself about really wanting to become a doctor or lawyer, such was his need to impress his parents. She believed his first love was music, and if he had been true to himself, he would have pursued that path in earnest. Instead, Sef tried to juggle music and study, with a devastating impact on his university results.

He joined an R'n'B hip-hop group, Definite Vibez, an all-singing boy band. He loved to sing, and like his father, was quite good at it. He developed an extensive CD collection of R'n'B music. He adopted the 'homeboy' look, with baggy pants and buzz-cut hair, a look that made his parents cringe.

While he was still in school, Sef had told Emily that his band had been offered a $40,000 contract by a major recording company, although it never seemed to come to pass.

Sef by this stage routinely lied to his parents when he was in trouble for something, such as not being conscientious enough in his studies. Loiva would become particularly aggravated by Sef when she knew he was lying but refused to admit it, says Emily. But Sef must have known before the end of his final school year that his HSC results were going to be very disappointing for his parents.

They did not approve of his involvement in the band, and when Sef had told them Definite Vibez had been offered a recording contract, they had been dead against his taking it up and dropping out of his schooling. Such was Sef's frustration over this issue that he had locked himself in the bathroom of their Blacktown home, threatening to kill himself. A concerned Teddy ended up breaking open the door and finding Sef, distraught but conscious, in the bathtub, with superficial cuts to his wrists.

Emily does not think Sef ever received counselling over this incident. It was something his parents liked to keep private; the details given to relatives were vague. Emily believes it was not a genuine attempt at suicide, but an effort to garner his parents' sympathy.

TOWARDS THE END of 1999, Sef proudly showed Emily a poster he had created for a dance party he was organising under the banner of 'Sef-G Productions'. Emily thought it looked quite impressive. The black poster showed a raft of pictures taken at the same time as some of the photos on 'Daisy's' website, of pretty girls in nightclubbing attire, lounging around with a few well-groomed young men, including Sef, who was decked out all in white. In bold yellow letters the poster announced: 'Impact Entertainment International and Sef-G Productions invites [sic] you to their Sydney Debut presentation ... JUICE ...'

'Juice' was the name of Sef Gonzales' first R'n'B hip-hop dance party, held at the inner-city Brooklyn Hotel. The poster announced DJs Moto and Pacheko, and the MCs were listed as Sef-G and Raff-D (an apparent reference to Raf De Leon). 'Exclusive pre-paid tickets' were $15, and tickets at the door cost $20. The poster also promoted 'Live Appearances by our Impact Entertainment Models'. Presumably they were the bevy of attractive young women featured on the poster.

AMANDA PEDRO WAS one of these young women. The seventeen-year-old had inherited her exotic looks from the mixture of her parents' heritage. Her mother was from Trinidad and Tobago, while her father was Sri Lankan. Amanda was vibrant, intelligent and caring towards others, traits also possessed by her outgoing and canny mother Belinda, a psychiatric nurse. Belinda doted on both Amanda and her brother Alan, who was two years older. Belinda instilled in her children a strong sense of self-belief. Together with Belinda's more private husband Vincent, they made a loving and close-knit family. Both parents were very protective of their children. (Their names have been changed in this book to protect their identities, at their request.)

Amanda was close friends with her cousin Sally Pedro (not her real name), who was a friend of Sef's, having met him a few years earlier when the students at her all-girls' school at Parramatta took Spanish classes with the boys of Sef's school, Marist Brothers Parramatta. Sally's brother, Dennis (not his real name), also knew Sef as an acquaintance, having been introduced by his sister, but they were not close.

In November 1999, Amanda agreed to go with Sally to a promotional shoot for a dance party at the Brooklyn Hotel. It was the first time she had met Sef, and she was immediately impressed. She had led a sheltered life, and this young man, dressed in a white suit and coordinating the photo shoot, struck her as being very together for someone of his age. 'He knew everyone at the shoot, and my first impression of him was that he was very successful,' she says.

Sef was more than impressed by Amanda. It became obvious by the end of the shoot that he was harbouring amorous thoughts about her, by the way he sought her out to chat. He said he would contact her when the poster was ready and send her a copy, and Amanda gave him her phone number. She was friendly to him, but that was as far as it went. 'I was never attracted to him [but] I thought he was a nice guy,' Amanda recalls.

From there, a friendship developed between Sef and Amanda. Sef would call her every few weeks but then drop out of contact, sometimes for a period of months, only to reappear just as suddenly. They would hang out at her house, go for a drive or to lunch, or spend hours on the phone. They talked easily about their thoughts and feelings on a vast range of subjects, including Sef's family, of whom he spoke with the utmost regard, particularly his father, whom he seemed to look up to. He talked with pride about how his parents still held hands as they walked down the street together. He showed her a picture of Clodine and mentioned how cute and sweet his little sister was. He seemed very loving and protective towards her.

When Sef and Amanda were together, he often told her she was beautiful and gave her a hug or held her hand. He said she was his best friend. When he was physically affectionate, Amanda tried to deflect attention from herself to another topic, trying not to hurt his feelings. After she met her future fiancé during the Sydney 2000 Olympics, Sef would often ask her how things were going with her boyfriend, maintaining it was just a friendly interest. But he would not become affectionate with Amanda when her boyfriend, a strapping champion swimmer, was around.

It did not really occur to Amanda to dwell on why, in the course of their friendship, she never got to visit Sef's house or meet his family. She did not even know he lived at home. She never had the opportunity to meet his close friends either, although she had heard him talk about his mate Sam Dacillo. But she never received the impression he did not have many friends; it seemed to her that Sef was always very busy.

In retrospect, it was no wonder that Sef did not invite Amanda into his world. It would have exposed the enormity of the lies he continually told her, in an attempt to build himself up in her eyes.

In a modest tone, he would tell her he lived with two friends in the city but that he also owned his own 'condo'. He had a black belt in tae kwon do, like his father. He told her he worked at a hospital as part of his medicine degree at the University of New South Wales. He would casually mention that he had to go work at 'the hospital' that day because 'they are paging me'. This was in addition to his organisation of dance parties and running his own bodyguard company as a sideline, he told her.

Sef would apologise for periods of absence, saying he had had to fly to New York for a few months to work on his business interests over there. He told her he jetsetted to the Big Apple of a weekend and was in the process of setting up his own modelling agency there. He falsely claimed to be negotiating for his agency to work with international cosmetic giant Revlon.

Such was Amanda's impression of Sef as a successful young man that she had no reason to disbelieve him. She certainly had no reason to doubt him when he told her he had cancer. Who would make up such a terrible lie?

He first told her he was suffering from cancer in early 2000, in an attempt to elicit more attention. Amanda and her mother were very worried about him. Then, many months later, out of the blue Sef arrived at their doorstep to announce his recovery. 'He rocked up at my door one day and said, "I'm in remission",' Amanda says.

Amanda was unaware that the only truth in the image Sef built of himself was that he had organised two dance parties: Juice, in December 1999, and then Juice 2 in February of 2000.

Amanda recalls the original Juice as being a great success. There were close to 200 people there, and Sef played the grand host, keeping himself busy by flitting from group to group. The DJs' music was great, and the only low point in the night was when Sef, along with a group of other young men, performed for the crowd. Amanda was truly horrified as she watched the boy band sing, with hackneyed coordinated moves and sickly-sweet lyrics. 'I thought he was shocking. I was so embarrassed for him when he got up [on stage],' she remembers.

However, the overall success of the dance party prompted Amanda to sell tickets for his next one, at another inner-city hotel. This one, despite also having a good DJ, was extremely poorly attended. Amanda organised for a group of her friends to buy tickets and attend. They were virtually the only ones there.

Amanda thought the poor attendance was purely due to where the venue was located. It was tucked out of the way and, unlike the Brooklyn Hotel, did not attract passing pedestrian traffic. Sef, though, had a far more dramatic reason for its failure — one that allowed him to come out looking good.

'He said to me that some drug dealers had approached him and offered him $70,000 to sell drugs in the club and they'd sabotaged him. That was his excuse, [because] through moral and ethical reasons he couldn't accept the money,' Amanda explains. 'I had $200 worth of money left over from the tickets I sold and told him to keep it, and he said, "I'll donate the money to charity." He always said he donated to charity. He made himself out to be a huge humanitarian.'

Following this debacle, it appears Sef decided there would be no Juice 3. But he did maintain an avid interest in nightclubs, DJs and hip-hop, and still moved in those circles.

Chapter 19

A dream turns sour

Teddy and Loiva sold their Blacktown home around the beginning of 2000, and purchased the lot at 6 Collins Street, North Ryde. It was about 30 metres from Amelita's house. There was an old fibro home on the block, which they demolished. They would build their dream home, although the process wasn't without problems. Teddy became involved in a bitter dispute over payment for the demolition of the old home by a Korean contractor.

As they had already sold their Blacktown home, the family rented a house in Numa Road, North Ryde, to live in while their new home was being built. Collins Street residents would often see Teddy in the street, supervising the building of his house, which was not progressing as quickly as he had hoped. At that time, builders were in short supply in property-mad Sydney.

Nevertheless, the house was finished just in time for Christmas.

THE BLESSING OF the home is a Catholic tradition. It is meant to provide peace, wellbeing and love to all who reside there.

Father Janusz Bieniek performed this blessing of the new Gonzales home in Collins Street in January 2001. He blessed room after room, the garage, and the garden as well, consecrating the dwelling with holy water. 'It's a spiritual blessing elaborated with scripture readings and prayers ... which involve the whole family,' explains Father Janusz.

The Gonzales family attended Mass at the Holy Spirit Church several times weekly. Teddy proudly told Father Janusz that Sef had became a devotee of Opus Dei, a movement that is part of the Catholic Church. It calls on the faithful to live their lives according to the Gospel, and to let their faith be known to others. Teddy also told Father Kevin Dadswell that Sef was involved with Opus Dei, while Sef was attending the university of New South Wales. Emily confirms Sef was indeed studying under an Opus Dei tutor while at the University of New South Wales, but once he changed to a different university, he dropped his studies of Opus Dei.

Sef's devotion impressed Father Janusz. 'I thought that he was a nice good man and the sort of external expression of his faith seemed to be quite impressive, quite uplifting, going to church and having meaningful discussions. We would shake hands and say hi,' he says.

Clodine had moved to Melbourne, attending Siena College, a Catholic school, from mid-2000, so it was just Teddy, Loiva and Sef living at 6 Collins Street.

Sef expressed to his mother a wish to move out, into accommodation at Macquarie University. Loiva had told him that was fine; however, if he did, he would have to support himself. She pointed out all the costs he would be up for. In the end, Sef opted to stay at home.

But increasingly, the relationship between Sef and his parents was becoming strained. Sef was going through a rebellious period, speaking back to his mother, which went against the grain of Loiva's upbringing. But he would not do this with Teddy. Teddy had a fiery temper and the fear of being yelled at by his father was enough to rein in Sef's rebellion when he was around his father. 'When his dad's angry, he's angry. You don't say anything,' says Emily.

Sef went through a stage where he seemed to be rejecting the Filipino culture. According to Annie Gonzales-Tesoro, Sef shocked his paternal grandfather, William, during one of William's visits to Sydney by saying, 'I hate Filipinos.'

'He saw himself as Australian,' Annie says.

Teddy and Loiva were both concerned about Sef's lack of attention to his studies, as Teddy once confided to Loiva's close friend Jane. 'I really studied hard when I was doing law and Sef is not even doing half of what I did,' Teddy told her.

Jane recalls discussing Sef's studies with Loiva. 'I said to Loiva, why don't you let him do what he wants to do ... are you sure you're not pushing him too much? And Loiva said no, that's what he likes,' Jane says.

Loiva complained to Emily that Sef was 'lazy'. Clodine was not around any more to help with the housework, and Loiva was left to do all of it.

By October or November of 2000, a close friend of Loiva Gonzales, Madeleine Azcona, a vibrant, say-it-like-it-is kind of woman, had became disturbed by a particular problem that seemed to be recurring whenever she visited the family's Numa Road rental house for dinner. She would place her wallet down on a bench and leave it unattended when she visited the Gonzales' house, and afterwards she could swear there was money missing from it.

After pondering the problem, she began to suspect it may have been Sef who was stealing the money. Teddy or Loiva would hardly be doing it, she thought. Not willing to put her friendship with Loiva at risk by making unfounded accusations, she devised a plan to see whether she was right.

One morning, she went to the bank to withdraw $100, in two $50 notes, and placed them inside her wallet. That day, she drove to the Gonzales home and picked up Sef for a prearranged appointment. He was coming to her house for a haircut.

Deliberately leaving Sef alone with her wallet lying on a table near the front door, Madeleine went upstairs and made a great show of calling out, 'I won't be long', so Sef knew she was still upstairs.

'I'm coming downstairs now,' Madeleine called out, after giving Sef sufficient opportunity to rifle through her wallet.

She was about to drop Sef home when she said she needed to use the toilet. Taking her wallet with her, Madeleine looked inside it and her heart sank. One $50 note was missing.

Madeline wasted no time in confronting Sef, explaining the trap she had set and stating that she believed Sef had stolen her money. Sef kept denying it, even holding out his arms and challenging her: 'Search me.'

Madeline told him that of course she was not going to do that, but that she and Sef were the only two people in the house when the money went missing. She told Sef if he looked her in the eye and told her he did not steal it, she would believe him.

Sef did as she asked. 'I didn't take it,' he said.

Madeleine decided to let it lie and not tell Loiva, but just be careful not to let her wallet out of her sight when she next visited Loiva's home.

She was extremely suprised to get a phone call from Loiva the next day. Sef had told his mother about Madeleine's accusation. Unfortunately for him, Loiva and Teddy had believed Madeleine's version. In fact, Loiva also suspected that Sef was stealing money from her own wallet, as much as $50 at a time, as well as stealing from Teddy and even from the tiler who was working on the house at Collins Street when they moved in.

Three days later, Sef called Madeleine and said he needed to see her. He drove around to her place that evening, offered her $500 cash and admitted to stealing the money.

Madeline declined the $500 from Sef, taking $200 to cover what she believed he had stolen in total. Most of all, she wanted to know why Sef had done it. Did he have a drug problem, or a gambling addiction? she asked him.

Sef said no.

'Then you have to have a reason — are you a klepto[maniac]?' Madeleine probed.

'No, I'm just an opportunist,' Sef replied. He added that previously he had swindled a friend out of profits from dance party productions, and that his parents had been forced to shell out the missing money to pay back his friend.

The whole experience left a sour taste in Madeleine's mouth, and seeing Sef's discomfort whenever she visited Loiva from then on made her feel ill at ease.

IT DID NOT help when, around March or April 2001, Sef wrote off his father's near-new Toyota Camry while he was driving out to Quakers Hill. Rather than borrow his son's car to get to work until he replaced his, Teddy had Sef drop him at the train station so he could make the trip to Blacktown each day. Sef hated public transport, recalls Emily, and Teddy did not want to force his son to catch the bus to nearby Macquarie University.

In addition to all this, Sef was suffering, at twenty years of age, an extremely humiliating and private problem. He was wetting his bed, and of course his mother, who did the laundry, knew it. It was one of those unfortunate physiological things, a habit from childhood he had never broken.

Through family friends, Loiva heard of a child psychologist who dealt with the problem by recommending an alarm system that was attached to the bed. Sef outright refused to accompany Loiva to the psychologist, so Loiva went alone. The psychologist told her there was not much he could do if Sef did not come to see him as well.

Frustrated, Loiva got the alarm system anyway, and persuaded Sef to give it a try. This behaviour couldn't go on, she told him; he couldn't be wetting the bed when he was married — his wife would divorce him!

The alarm system worked by detecting the first drop of moisture on the bed and setting off a loud, old-fashioned alarm-clock sound, forcing the bed-wetter to get up and go to the toilet, and thus training the body to do this automatically after a while. Sef used it for two nights, and Loiva heard the alarm go off as well. After that, Sef refused to use the device again. He couldn't get a decent night's sleep, he complained.

Shortly before the murders, Loiva and Teddy discovered Sef was falsifying his university results. Sef had offered to do the same for Clodine. She had refused and told her parents. Sef got in a world of trouble, and the problem escalated into a heated argument between Teddy and Loiva. It ended with Teddy threatening to go back to the Philippines and leave the family behind. But he loved Loiva and the kids too much, and there was nothing to indicate he would ever have gone through with his threat. However, the issue contributed to tension within the Gonzales home.

By this time Sef was failing university, and failing badly. Poor results had followed him from his pre-medicine course

CLOCKWISE FROM TOP
Teddy holds his young son
in the area of their Baguio
hotel that collapsed in the
earthquake, injuring Sef;
Loiva and Clodine in the
hotel, named Queen
Victoria after Sydney's
Queen Victoria Building;
the hotel wrecked by
earthquake damage; and
the hotel new and open
for business.

A happy, loving family — from Baguio (*top*) to the Snowy Mountains and a wildlife park where Sef and Clodine pat a wombat.

Scenes from young Sef's life.

Family fun: a digitally compiled image against an African setting which hung in the Gonzales home; they would joke to relatives that they had been to Africa.

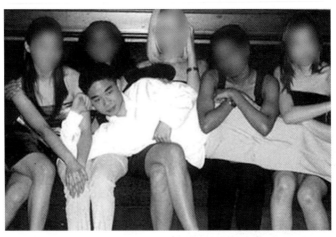

Sef at the photo shoot for his dance party, Juice, in late 1999.

Clodine, a blooming beauty, at her school formal in Melbourne in 2000.

Sef and his cousin Monica Gonzales during her visit to Sydney, May 2001.

One of the last photos taken of Teddy and Loiva (with her dog Ginger) on the couch in their home in May 2001.

News Limited

News Limited

ABOVE Grief overwhelms Sef's grandmother Amelita Claridades at the funeral, while Emily Luna looks on from behind.

LEFT Sef at the funeral, where he sang the song 'One Sweet Day'.

News Limited

News Limited

ABOVE Amelita and Emily outside court, with detective Geoff Leonard behind them.
LEFT Father Paul Cahill providing support to Sef at the funeral.
BELOW Annie Para'an, Sef's aunt in Baguio, whom Sef emailed asking for money.

Clodine's friend Michelle Dacillo, who gave evidence of 'rejected' calls to Clodine's mobile phone.

Sam Dacillo, used by Sef as an alibi for the murders when they went to Planet Hollywood for dinner.

Sef under arrest in June 2002. Behind him, on the far left, is Detective Paul Auglys, and on the far right is Detective Mick Sheehy.

at the University of New South Wales, to his pre-law course at Macquarie University. Whatever the case, he routinely missed classes, exams and assignments. He also appeared to be suffering from a string of illnesses during this period, and relied heavily on medical certificates to squeeze through into his next semester's studies. He would often use these to apply for 'special consideration', which universities can grant in circumstances where students suffer hardship that interferes with their studies.

From January 1999 right through to July 2001, Sef was routinely 'ill'. There were medical certificates for respiratory tract infections, mild asthma, chronic coughs, migraines, chest infections, viral illnesses, and so on. In one particular stroke of creativity, Sef told a doctor that he was training to compete in the Olympics and that this was interrupting his sleeping patterns.

As far as his first semester of 2001 subjects went, Sef had failed to complete essays in Communication and Citizenship Law Policy, and Anglo-American Constitutional History, and would get incomplete grades for both.

He had two subjects in which he had to sit mid-year exams — Law in Australian Society, and Politics. On 4 July 2001, he did not attend the Law in Australian Society exam that day. Earlier, Sef had sat for the Politics exams but failed, with a mark of 39 per cent. His parents would learn about it when the university results were posted on the Internet and mailed out on 20 July 2001.

Sef was staring failure in the face. It looked like he was going to bomb in all four subjects, unless the trusty medical certificates that he had lodged for special consideration would get him through. He was not facing expulsion — he would be allowed to continue through to the end of the year, at least — but his parents certainly would not be happy.

Loiva and Teddy had told Sef they would take away his beloved Ford Festiva if his grades did not improve. After all, Clodine was doing extremely well — why couldn't Sef try as hard? He used to be the academic one — what had happened? They had decided to see what his mid-year results were.

PART 2

Chapter 20

Wired

In late July 2001, Paul Auglys approached Emily, asking if she would take part in a police bugging operation on her nephew. The way the police put it to Emily was this: Sef by that stage was already contacting her, questioning her about things he had heard that she was saying about him. She was bound eventually to have a confrontation with him about the subject of his guilt or innocence, and what she saw that night at the house. So why not have that conversation under the protection of the police? They wanted Emily to direct the conversation, to tell Sef she knew without doubt that he had committed the murders, and that he had been in the house when she arrived at 6 Collins Street about 6 pm that night. She was to ask Sef how she could help him fix it so that the cops would not be onto him. The cops wanted to bug the conversation via a device inside Sef's car. Eventually, Emily agreed.

Emily spoke to Sef on the phone and set up the meeting with her nephew to take place on 25 July, just after lunchtime, in the carpark of her office block at Macquarie Park. At 2.01 pm, Emily hopped into Sef's vehicle, where they began to talk in Tagalog. There were at least four police cars containing officers from Tawas lurking in the carpark, as well as technical experts. A police helicopter floated within distance of a quick response, and heavily armed State Protection Group response officers were on standby.

Emily was terrified she would blow the ruse, but did her best. She wasn't doing this for the police or even for herself. She was doing this for her three dead family members. Although she feared her nephew, some part of her still loved him — but justice was foremost in her mind. She thought, her only chance of getting a taped confession from Sef was to extend love and understanding, not accusations.

The conversation, later translated from Tagalog to English, began with the banal. After hopping into the Ford Festiva, she asked her nephew: 'Why is this car too dirty?'

Sef replied that he hadn't had it cleaned yet and that the police had to change his personalised numberplate.

'Turn the engine off,' she directed Sef. Sef responded that the battery had run down and he had to keep the engine going to recharge it.

Then Emily began in earnest. 'I'm worried about you, because, Sef, I have to be perfectly honest with you, just like what ... [I] told you, I love you very much, you know that.'

'Yeah.'

'I'll do everything for you. Even until death, I'll do anything for you. I will defend you, I won't let anything bad happen to you. I'm scared, Sef.'

Emily asked Sef about the conversation at the Ferrers', on the Friday after the murders, about whether it had been raining when Sef said he parked in the carport and did not get out due to this.

> **EMILY:** You told me it was pouring that night. Sef, I
> know you've got something to do with what
> happened. But I understand, I understand, I was scared,
> Sef, because it wasn't pouring rain that evening ...

SEF: No, but when I drove in ... it was drizzling, that's
   why I did not get out of the car.

EMILY: Sef ...

SEF: But what are you trying to say, Aunty Emily?

The sharp sideways glance he gave her made her back-pedal
quickly. Holding his hands, she said to him: 'I know, I know, I
know, but I'm scared ... because — didn't you have a DNA
test last Sunday?'

'Yes,' he replied.

Emily pushed on.

EMILY: I'm scared, Sef. I feel that they're onto you.

SEF: No, because, that's, they're —

EMILY: It's just a matter of time.

SEF: [inaudible] everything ... I spoke to Michael
   [Sheehy] today ... And they, he said ...

EMILY: I don't believe everything that the police were
   saying. Because, you know, when they asked me
   questions, I would like to be sure that we have the
   same answers. That's the reason why I am talking to
   you now. I do not like the idea that I have to be the
   one pressuring you. Just like what I told you, I wish I
   did not [drop by] your place at six o'clock that night.
   I wish I didn't see your car there. I have a feeling that
   the reason why they're asking the times I left the
   office, the time I came to your house, even the way I
   rang the doorbell, how long I have been there, is
   because you said you [had] just been there not for a
   long time, because you were making a phone call.

SEF: No, I received a phone call in the car. But the
   reason ... the reason ... one of the reasons why I
   didn't step out of the car, because it was drizzling ...

but I didn't say that it was pouring down heavily, I
said it was drizzling, that's why I could not get out ...
I knew there was no-one in the house.

Emily pushed him further. 'I read your statement, you said it
was pouring, that's what you said to me.'

Sef began to ramble. 'That was on the night. Because ...
I said, I just said it was raining ... I don't remember my
words if it's pouring or ... all I remember was the dog was
there.'

Emily warned him he had to be careful about
inconsistency, but Sef said he had clarified everything in his
first statement satisfactorily.

'What about your whereabouts, it's all clarified?' she asked
him.

Sef answered, 'Everything has been clarified.'

Emily asked if Sef was really being honest with her, and he
assured her he was. She told him again she would do anything
for him, and returned to the subject of arriving at the house
on the evening of the murders.

> **EMILY:** You know why I didn't see you that night at
> once, because I was scared that you had anything to
> do with what happened. I was so scared. In fact, I was
> also thinking ... I just tell you honestly ... just
> between the two of us ... I was thinking that you're
> also a victim. I know it was my sister who died, but
> you are also a victim. In case you're the one
> responsible for what happened, I will understand it. I
> know how your parents treated you ever since you
> were a kid. I know they loved you, but —
>
> **SEF:** But Aunty Emily, you know I wouldn't do
> something like that.

Emily was getting nowhere with this tack, and Sef seized control of the conversation, getting Emily on the back foot over her accusation to him on that the first night, at Gladesville police station.

SEF: And see when, you know that week I just couldn't talk to you, because I was angry because [of] that night. I was crying, I was really upset. The first thing that you asked me was, 'What really happened?', like the way you asked it was as if I have something to do with it already.

EMILY: I know it was wrong.

Sef went on to tell his aunt that at first her accusation did not register, that nothing was registering with him straight after the murders, but the next day he began to get upset and ask himself why she had said that.

Emily asked why he had not spoken to her to clarify things.

SEF: Because at that point, I even told Uncle, I didn't have the energy to get angry at any[one] at the moment so I said . . . for Mama, especially. We were working towards her funeral, she wouldn't want any argument like that . . . for the sake of the funeral, I was gonna make peace with you, I was gonna forget about that.

EMILY: Yes.

SEF: But the reason why I was so upset that first week, because it just really hurt me that you thought I have something to do with it. But circumstantially I understand, because you told me you saw my car there . . . I started to realise if I was there I'll probably assume the same thing . . .

Emily apologised, then told Sef it was only because she was worried about him. 'I'm really afraid for you. But if you [have] any problem or anything, you know you can talk to me. Don't just talk to anybody, even with the police. If you're feeling anything, you tell me, and if you need my help, you know you can count on me. I'm telling you that now.'

Sef then laid on a guilt trip, and Emily immediately perceived it to be emotional blackmail. He told her he was contemplating suicide. 'The past two weeks, it's like, I'm dead anyway . . . I was, like, floating.'

He said he was trying to fight the feeling but it was constantly there. He said in the next couple of months he would iron things out at his father's work, liquidate the assets and donate the money to charity or relatives, then depart this world.

Emily tried to encourage him to stay strong, to go on.

They spoke a little about what she had seen at the house that night and Emily told him she had been there for about five minutes. Sef told her he was in the car and hadn't heard any noise when she arrived, and at first was so upset with her he thought she was making it up.

He said whoever had committed the murders had planned to leave a relative behind, either himself or his father. They had taken clothes from his closet and from Teddy's. 'They're planning to leave one of us so they can point a finger,' Sef told her.

The conversation ended 35 minutes after it began, with no confession. Emily had done the best she could. But she knew her nephew was smart. She had known from the outset that the chances of success had been slim.

SEF'S FIRST MENTION that clothing was missing from the house had been made to Mick Sheehy on 23 July, the day after Sheehy casually informed Sef that some bloodstained clothing had been recovered in the vicinity of Collins Street and would be sent for forensic analysis. (It was later found to be unrelated to the murders and connected to a construction site down the road.)

Three of his tracksuits were missing from his closet, Sef said. Sheehy asked Sef to prepare a complete record of the missing clothing. On 27 July, Sef came back with a curious list: a black leather jacket belonging to Teddy, and, from Sef's room, a grey tracksuit top, two black tracksuit tops, one pair of black track pants, one pair of grey track pants and a school blazer. Also on the list was a pair of green gardening gloves. Of all these items, the only one police had seized from the house was Sef's school blazer.

Meanwhile, the clothing used by the killer, as well as the murder weapon, had yet to be found. One night in late July, the surveillance team lost Sef for a few hours, as he was driving near Lane Cove National Park. Police began to fret that if Sef was indeed the killer, he'd had the chance to recover the items and dispose of them for good.

Sam Dacillo's sister Michelle and her father Sammy accompanied Tawas officers to Lane Cove National Park, where they had gone picnicking with the Gonzales family the year before. Police divers searched Lane Cove River for five days, recovering items such as a jammed bolt-action rifle, ammunition, house bricks, a cat collar and some cat bones. None of it was relevant to the Gonzales murders. The search was called off.

Chapter 21

Poison plot

One of the fascinating little snippets of information Sef had given Sheehy the night of the murders was that there was something on his laptop computer in his bedroom that might be interpreted in the wrong way by police. The family's home computer had already been seized, on 11 July, and Ritchie Sim had taken the hard drive to the accounting firm KPMG, which had the software to copy it for analysis.

The drive revealed highly unusual Internet search activity. Reams of searches had been done on poisonous plants and plant parts, even as late as 9 July 2001, the day before the murders. Someone using the family computer had taken an intense interest in how these poisons worked — specifically, whether they could kill.

Commands to find more about certain plant poisons had been typed into the computer under various search engines, bringing up a number of web pages. The headings of the web pages were quite frightening: 'Comparative lethality of selected toxins and chemical agents in laboratory mice'; 'Poisonous part of "x" seed'; 'Poisonous plants and plant parts'; 'Poisonous house plants'; 'Taste of "x" seed'; 'Sprinkling the end product with soup'. And, most disturbing of all: 'How to kill'.

The list of pages called up went on and on, and included information about how to use a particular seed to make poison, and how to mask the taste of this seed with peppermint or fruit. The searches dated back to 12 February 2001, and seemed to revolve around two particular seeds, both capable of being used to make lethal poisons. (The names of the two poisonous seeds researched extensively on the computer have been suppressed by the Supreme Court of New South Wales to prevent copycat cases.)

Police also located a flurry of e-mails that had been recently sent to and from the e-mail address sef-g@usa.net. On Wednesday, 20 June 2001, an e-mail had been sent from the 'sef-g' address to a seed supplier in the United States. It began: 'hi ... i would like to order the following, kindly let me know the total costs including shipment and handling, or let me know if my calculations are correct ...' The writer had ordered sixteen of a type of poisonous seed, calculating that the total cost would be US$8.50, and asked approximately how long they would take to arrive in Sydney, Australia.

The seed supplier had e-mailed back and airmailed the seeds to 6 Collins Street on 2 July, contrary to instructions from the person ordering them to hold the order for the moment. On 8 July 2001, after the person requesting the seeds rebuked her for not holding the order, and said he had just moved house, the supplier e-mailed to say she would send another packet of the seeds, free of charge, if the orderer sent her the new address.

There was also recent e-mail communication between the address sef-g@usa.net and a seed supplier on the far north New South Wales coast. On 26 June, an e-mail request had been made by a person signing off as 'sef' for a second type of poisonous seed. The writer stated that he had sent an Express Post envelope off the day before along with an order form and money for the delivery of the seed. The writer expressed the urgency of the delivery:

> *i have ordered some . . . seeds . . . as a gift for my mother's 60th birthday this weekend. she had been looking for those particular seeds ever since she saw them in florida last year.*
>
> *she lives up the coast and I will be heading there this weekend. Kindly make an exception for my order. I would like to receive it by the week's end so that I can bring them to her.*

On 28 June, the supplier promised to have the three packets of seeds in the mail the next day.

On 17 July, the police seized Sef's laptop from his bedroom. This computer was found to contain a raft of similar Internet searches to those conducted on the Gonzales' home computer. The laptop, along with the home computer, would be sent to police computer expert Jason Beckett for further analysis in September.

As with the family computer, numerous search engines had been used on the laptop to look up information on poisons. The words typed in to make the searches included: 'amino + acids'; 'murder + methods'; 'poisonous + plants'; 'cyanide'; 'poison'; 'underground + poison'; 'poisonous + substances'; and 'make poison'. Web pages accessed included some on biowar agents (biological agents cultivated for warfare). And there were also specific searches on the sale of the same two types of seeds that had been ordered by sef-g@usa.net on the family computer.

This information totally threw the police off-track, but began to make sense when relatives mentioned that Loiva had been hospitalised with acute food poisoning the week before the murders. Investigators got back in touch with Dr Cala, who had performed the postmortems, but had had no reason to look for signs of poisoning in Loiva's body. However, he had examined her upper gastrointestinal tract and stomach and seen no sign of the damage ingesting one or both of the poisonous seeds would be likely to cause. Loiva's body had since been buried, but Dr Cala had retained blood and tissue samples in case the need for further tests arose.

Tawas detectives looked at Loiva's medical records from Sydney Adventist Hospital, where she had been admitted on 3 July 2001. Loiva had been very ill, suffering fever, severe abdominal pains and bloody diarrhoea. The hospital doctors had had no reason to suspect deliberate poisoning, or to test for the presence of anything but the various bugs that often afflict human beings and cause similar symptoms. Loiva's illness had been put down to colitis, an inflammation of the bowel that could have been caused by a bad case of food poisoning.

During the search of Sef's bedroom on 17 July 2001, police located a curious item wrapped in tissues and concealed under a set of drawers. It was a film canister containing a clear liquid. The liquid could not be analysed for the presence of contents of either of the two poisonous seeds researched on the computers in any Australian laboratory, so was sent to the United States, along with samples of Loiva's liver, stomach and blood taken at the autopsy. Atlanta's Centers for Disease Control (CDC) tested the liquid and advised that it contained a minute quantity of a particular poison made from a seed, one of the two poisonous seeds researched, but nothing that would be fatal if ingested. But they could not test Loiva's tissue.

Those samples were later forwarded to Commonwealth Biotechnologies Incorporated (CBI) in Richmond, Virginia, which were able to test the tissue and the liquid. The testing detected no poison, but it was a different testing procedure, and Australian police were told the levels of poison detected by CDC would not have shown up using this different method. As for the tissue, CBI could find no sign of poisoning, but then Loiva had recovered from her illness prior to her death and the samples by that stage were very old.

Chapter 22

Kathy Wu

As far as chat-up lines went, it certainly lacked originality. But when Sef first laid eyes on the petite and beautiful Kathy Wu (real name suppressed by the New South Wales Local Courts), a 24-year-old of Asian background, he knew he had to say something to her. He fell for her, as the saying goes, hook, line and sinker.

It was on Monday, 14 May 2001, at the Macquarie Shopping Centre at North Ryde that Kathy first caught his attention. She was browsing in the stores and was just leaving a mobile telephone shop when she was approached by Sef.

'You look familiar. Do I know you?' Sef asked her.

'No,' Kathy replied.

Undeterred, Sef continued talking. They spoke for about five minutes, then Sef asked Kathy for her phone number. Kathy was apprehensive — she did not know this man from a bar of soap, as nice as he seemed — and refused his request. So Sef handed her his business card, from T Gonzales & Associates, complete with his phone numbers and e-mail address. He asked her to e-mail him, and she said goodbye.

The brief meeting played on her mind over the next few days, and her curiosity was roused. At the time she was in a long-term relationship with another man, but, like many women, Kathy could not resist flattery when it came her way.

Two days after their first meeting, on Wednesday, 16 May, Kathy dug out the business card at work and e-mailed Sef from her office computer. The e-mail was brief and casual, simply saying hello and asking Sef to tell her a bit more about himself.

The next day as she logged in to her work computer, she saw Sef had replied. Sef, eager to impress, had told her more than just a bit about himself — and not all of it was truthful.

He was, indeed, a mixture of Filipino, Spanish and Chinese. Yes, he did study at Macquarie University, but he said he was doing law. Then he descended into the realms of make-believe — in addition to working part-time at his father's law office at Blacktown, he also claimed he held down two other part-time jobs. He worked for a law firm in the Sydney CBD, he stated, as well as being a personal trainer at a gym. Kathy was duly impressed, having no reason to believe that what she was reading was fact embellished liberally with fiction.

The pair embarked on a modern-day flirtation, courtesy of the Internet. They continued e-mailing each other, their interest growing with every message that arrived in their in-boxes. Sef told her even more about himself: that he used to study medicine at the University of New South Wales, that his mum worked alongside his father at the Blacktown law practice, and that his family had moved recently into a newly built home at North Ryde. His sister, he told Kathy, was studying in Melbourne.

Kathy, in return, told him a little bit more about herself. She told Sef about her family and divulged the fact she had a boyfriend. Sef's response was that it was okay with him. He simply wanted to be friends. It is unclear if either of them really believed this as they embarked on a whirlwind romance.

Kathy decided Sef was essentially a nice person. She agreed to meet him for lunch the following week, on Tuesday, 22 May. They e-mailed each other to confirm the details.

That day, Sef arrived in his green Ford Festiva, picking Kathy up at work. They drove to a restaurant, Thai Smile, on Victoria Road, West Ryde. Over the spicy food, they talked about themselves, their interests. It was all very casual, but with each word Sef was becoming more smitten. After lunch, he asked again for Kathy's mobile telephone number, and by this stage she relented and gave it to him.

That night, Sef rang Kathy to thank her for lunch. That was it, thank you and goodnight.

The next night, he called her again, and once more the night after that. He rang her every night that week in May, though their conversations were brief, lasting about two minutes each. Kathy began to think about Sef a lot; she wanted to see him again.

At some point during this period, Sef took Kathy on a picnic to Lane Cove National Park, a short drive from his house. He took his camera, and used a whole roll of film capturing Kathy as she posed, smiling, amid the greenery.

Sef couldn't resist showing the photos around at home, lovestruck and gloating over Kathy's beauty to anyone who would listen. 'Look at her, Aunty Emily, she's very pretty, what do you think?' he asked Emily during one of her visits to the house in May.

'He was just excited and happy, I've never seen him so happy,' Emily recalls.

Emily agreed with Sef that indeed the girl was very attractive. Sef commented on her resemblance to his mother. 'Are you going to go to sleep with those photos in your hand?' Emily joked, not realising that Sef had framed one of the photographs and placed it next to his bed, so he could see Kathy's face before he went to sleep at night.

Emily knew that Loiva, who confided in her about almost everything, had a problem with the relationship. It became a source of argument between Sef and his mother, with Loiva pointing out the disadvantages of seeing an older woman, and Sef countering with reasons why Kathy's age was an advantage. Sef complained that his mother was still jealous of his girlfriends.

Emily knew Loiva did not have a problem with Kathy as such. It wasn't that she even knew her personally, or that she had a problem with her ethnic background, which was not Filipino. But she was concerned that the relationship was becoming too serious. The girl was older than Sef and held down a job, and lived in a place of her own. Loiva worried Kathy and Sef might move in together, and that this romance was a distraction he did not need when he was studying.

'She felt it was getting serious, because Sef was always out at night,' Emily says.

Sef decided that Kathy should meet his mother, a sure sign that things had progressed to a more serious level.

On Thursday, 24 May, Kathy and Sef went out for dinner. Sef asked her to drive to his house after she finished work, and leave her car there so that he could drive her to dinner. Kathy pulled up outside 6 Collins Street around 5.30 pm. She got on the mobile, calling Sef to say she was outside his house. He came out to greet her and escorted her into the tiled entry.

Loiva was waiting to meet her. She said a polite hello to Kathy, then retreated to the laundry, where she was in the midst of washing one of the family's dogs. Kathy followed Loiva to the laundry to see the drenched little animal, before returning to the front of the house and stepping out the door with Sef. She left with no feeling either way about Loiva's opinion of her; Sef's mother had simply been preoccupied with washing the dog.

The pair drove to a Japanese restaurant for dinner. They spoke more about themselves and their families. Kathy thought again what a nice guy Sef was, and wanted to see more of him. The conversation rolled around to the idea that Kathy should break up with her boyfriend so she could be with Sef. That night, Kathy promised Sef she would end her other relationship, but said she had to wait for the right moment. She wanted to spare her boyfriend's feelings as much as possible. Sef, impatient to have Kathy as his girlfriend, told her he wished they could be together straightaway, but that he understood she had to time the break-up properly.

After dinner, Kathy and Sef took a stroll in the grounds of the nearby University of New South Wales, sitting in a park and talking. When they arrived back at North Ryde, it was midnight, and Kathy did not go back inside the house. They kissed goodnight.

The following day, Sef rang Kathy at work and asked if she would come over to his place for lunch. He picked her up from work and they grabbed some McDonald's takeaway — quarter pounders with cheese were one of his favourites — on the way to his house. Sitting in the family room at the back of the house, they ate their food, then Sef showed Kathy his neat, orderly bedroom, with its single bed and rows of tiny aftershave bottles stacked neatly on the shelves, before Kathy had to return to work.

That weekend, Kathy broke up with her boyfriend, but did not tell him about Sef. On the Monday she told Sef what had occurred and that they were now free to see each other. She arranged to see Sef after work. Sef rushed to her office that afternoon and they drove separately to a street in West Ryde, where Sef said he liked to park and contemplate things. When Kathy got into Sef's car he gave her a necklace with a 'G' charm hanging from a chain. Sef told Kathy the 'G' stood for Gonzales, and the jewellery was a promise of an engagement. She was taken aback — it was so early in the relationship — but she smiled, not wanting to hurt Sef's feelings.

Kathy did not see Sef again that week because she did not like to go out often on work nights, but she spoke to him every night on the phone. Sef told her he loved her, but she didn't reciprocate. She was thinking how much she missed her old boyfriend.

At the end of that week, on the night of Friday, 1 June, Sef and Kathy went out for dinner at Oatlands House near Parramatta. At dinner, Kathy dealt Sef a crushing blow, telling him she wanted to get back together with her ex-boyfriend. Sef was devastated, but after a while said, 'Let's not think about this tonight and just enjoy the night.'

In Sef's car that night, Kathy and Sef had sex. She was sad she would never be close to him again, so she wanted to make love with him once. She then broke up with him and Sef, though upset, took it on the chin. 'You know what is best with yourself, I just want you to be happy,' he said.

So ended their brief relationship, but Sef could not let go. That weekend, as Kathy reunited with her ex-boyfriend, Sef sent her text messages, letting her know he missed her and wanted to talk to her. The text messages went unanswered. He sent her another message on Monday, saying he wanted to talk. He rang her at home and tearfully asked her how she could make him fall in love with her, then just leave him. Then he said he had to go and hung up. He rang back half an hour later, apologising, and asking if they could still be friends. Kathy told him she did not know if she could do that, as she felt guilty about what she had done, then ended the conversation.

Later that week, Kathy e-mailed Sef asking him if he wanted her to return his Year Twelve yearbook, which he had lent her. He had wanted to impress her with the comments written in it by fellow students, saying how smart he was. Sef replied immediately, saying he had things to do but could meet up for lunch the next week.

She drove to Sef's house the following Tuesday, 12 June 2001. Only Sef was home. Returning the book, Kathy chatted to Sef for a while, and he told her he was leaving for Brazil in a couple of weeks to be a back-up fighter in a tae kwon do tournament.

This was pure fantasy, but Kathy couldn't have known that. In fact she received an e-mail from Sef on 8 July, saying he was having a great time in Brazil going to parties on the beach. It was another of Sef's lies, perhaps his way of getting back at her, and indicating he didn't need her in his life to have a good time.

Chapter 23

Sef's first interview

Three weeks into the investigation, armed with the information that they had gathered, Tawas officers decided it was time to sit Sef down for his first electronically recorded interview. There were more than a few things detectives wanted to put to Sef for explanation.

Before they did this, though, Geoff Leonard approached New South Wales Police psychologist Rozalinda Garbutt, who had extensively researched the phenomenon of intrafamilial homicide — the murder of one family member by another — in the United Kingdom. She was asked to review the crime-scene photos, Sef's re-enactment video, the coroner's diagram of the location of the victims' bodies and the description of their injuries.

Garbutt noted that the killer had displayed 'high emotion', as evidenced by the excessive number of wounds and the location of the crimes, the family home. The closer the relationship between the victim and the killer, the more emotion usually shown during a crime, Garbutt wrote in her report for Tawas. And the 'overkill' apparent in the murders suggested the killer had lost control, although paradoxically there was also a degree of planning, in that the killer appeared to have waited for his next victim for a period of time. She concluded the murders were planned, yet the actual attacks were fuelled by emotion.

International research has concluded there are six factors that point to a killing that has been committed by someone within the victim's family. First, the killer uses a weapon from the scene. Then, there are multiple wounds, the victim suffers trauma to the head or face, the body is left at the place of death, the crime occurs in the victim's home, and a blunt weapon is used.

The murder of Clodine Gonzales, Garbutt noted, showed all six characteristics. Teddy's and Loiva's deaths showed five — they lacked an injury from a blunt object. On this basis, it was 'highly probable' the killer was a family member, Garbutt decided.

She noted that the killer had lain in wait for at least two of the victims, and the crime scene had been staged to suggest theft as a motive — Loiva's handbag and Teddy's briefcase were rifled through, and the wardrobe doors upstairs left ajar. The killer had spent a great deal of time at the scene, indicating a familiarity with the family and the house, as the killer had not been overly concerned about being discovered.

Planned acts against specific victims most commonly exist in cases of parricide (a child killing parents) or mariticide (the killing of a husband by his wife), the report said. Given that both parents were dead, and Loiva killed before Teddy, mariticide was not an option. And, of course, Clodine had been killed before either of her parents.

'The offender therefore is more than likely one of the children . . . who has killed their parents in a planned crime to achieve a specific goal,' Garbutt concluded. This buoyed the investigators, making them feel they were heading in the right direction.

MEANWHILE, THEY COULDN'T ignore other lines of enquiry. Even before Sam Dacillo was ruled out as a suspect, investigators had turned their attention to Clodine's ex-boyfriend, twenty-year-old Christopher Fernstat.

According to numerous relatives of the Gonzales family, Fernstat and the family had been on acrimonious terms because of his relationship with Clodine. Tawas detectives had wasted no time in tracking him down, and Fernstat was pulled into Sutherland police station to make a statement on 11 July, the day after the murders.

Fernstat had met Clodine at an under-eighteen dance party at Darling Harbour during Easter 2000. Clodine was with a couple of female friends and she approached Fernstat while he was dancing with a mate of his. They started dancing and chatting. Clodine gave Fernstat her mobile number that night.

Their relationship did not last long. They went out on six or seven dates, playing pool and computer games, over a period of about a month. Fernstat told police they had never had sex. Clodine had told him a bit about her family, that they were very strict Catholics and she was given no independence. Her mother controlled the whole family, she said.

Fernstat had met Sef a couple of times, and once met Loiva at the Chatswood shops. The last time he saw Clodine, she had sneaked out of her house to meet him at the end of the street between 11 pm and midnight. She thought her parents had gone to sleep early and would be none the wiser.

No sooner had Clodine arrived at the meeting place than Fernstat's mobile phone rang; it was Teddy Gonzales. Was Chris with his daughter? Chris assured Teddy he was not with Clodine, but after the call ended Clodine was shaken, upset and tearful. The young couple waited for three hours, kissing and cuddling, before she screwed up her courage to go home.

The next day, Fernstat received a phone call from Loiva, who told him the family had disowned Clodine and were going to send her back to the Philippines for her transgression.

A few days later, Teddy called Fernstat to inform him that someone had left an abusive message on Sef's phone. Was it him? Fernstat protested that it wasn't. Teddy, disbelieving, told him not to do it again. Fernstat asked after Clodine and Teddy informed him that her life was finished. Teddy threatened he would get Fernstat back for leading his daughter astray.

Clodine called Fernstat a week after the sneaking-out debacle, telling him she was in Melbourne staying with her aunt. They maintained phone contact, speaking every night for a month, during which period Loiva called Fernstat a few times, telling him not to contact Clodine.

Fernstat also was contacted by Sef via an Internet chat program. He told police Sef had threatened to kill him, and warned him he was a gang member. It sure scared the hell out of Fernstat, enough for him to call Clodine to break up. Clodine didn't take the threat seriously; she said her big brother had only been joking and just wanted to protect her.

Chris Fernstat had an ironclad alibi for the afternoon and evening of 10 July 2001. He'd worked until 5 pm, then walked around Hurstville shopping centre with his new girlfriend, bumping into a few mates on the way. There were several people who could verify his movements. He hadn't even known that Clodine was in Sydney.

Chris Fernstat quickly dropped off the suspect list.

FILIPINO LAWYER BERNADO DAVID, who worked in the same office complex as Teddy, alerted Tawas detectives to a conversation of Teddy's that he said he had overheard two months before the murders, in which the person on the other end of the line threatened Teddy.

Teddy had been arguing fiercely in Tagalog, then yelled, 'Fuck you!' into the receiver before slamming down the phone. David, who had stopped by during the conversation, told police Teddy was agitated, and David asked him what was wrong.

'I have a property transaction in the Philippines that fell through. My brother is over there acting as an agent for me. The other party has told my brother they are going to eliminate my family,' Teddy confided.

David said he had made a joke of it — asking how could they come to Australia and kill the Gonzales family when they didn't have a visa — but Teddy did not elaborate.

Tawas officers checked all the phone calls made and received from Teddy's office for the six months prior to the murders, but came up with nothing to verify a threatening call from the Philippines. The only possibility was a call routed through an AAPT switch in Indonesia. It could have come from the Philippines, and the timeframe fitted with a call Freddie made to Teddy asking him to get in touch with their parents.

Freddie Gonzales would deny knowledge of this supposed property deal gone wrong, and police could find no evidence of transactions to indicate a financial failure.

In a later statement, David would tell police about an incident that occurred around 1998, in which a disgruntled client of Teddy's had threatened to kill the Gonzales family. David said the client had come to him, complaining that he and two other family members had mortgaged their property in the Philippines to pay a AU$5000 fee to apply for residency in Australia. They were about to be sent home by immigration authorities, and felt duped by Teddy.

'I'm going to kill his family and I'm going to rape his wife,' David says the man told him in a fit of rage.

David says this was not the first time he'd had Teddy's clients coming to see him, hoping David could fix up the mess they were in. David says he liked Teddy — he and his family would occasionally go on holiday with the Gonzales — but was well aware that Teddy had attracted criticism from within the Filipino community for lodging unsuccessful refugee applications, allowing the applicants to stay in Australia for a year or so before being deported. David says he would not take on the jobs, instead telling the complainants to get Teddy to sort things out.

David says he also saw flashes of serious temper in Teddy. One particular incident occurred in the Blacktown building where they'd both worked since 1996. One day, an accountant in the building let a client park in Teddy's car space because it was past 6 pm, and he thought Teddy had gone home. But Teddy came back to the office, enraged, and visited every office in the building until he tracked down the culprit. Teddy advised the accountant in no uncertain terms never to do it again.

IN THE DAYS leading up to 1 August 2001, Mick Sheehy and Ritchie Sim stayed late at work, formulating their plan of how to conduct Sef's interview. Sim and Sheehy had worked together before, and Sheehy knew Sim's style was harder, more confrontational than his own. They decided Sheehy would put most of the early, clarifying questions to Sef before they took turns hitting him with the difficult stuff. It would be a sort of good cop (Sheehy), bad cop (Sim) style interview.

They knew this might be their only crack at it, that Sef might decide to shut up once the questions became more difficult. Sef was not obliged to tell the police anything. His cooperation was voluntary, although the way Sheehy saw it, he really had no choice but to cooperate with police if he wanted to convince his family members he was innocent.

Before the first recorded interview took place, a New South Wales Police profiler prepared a report that made suggestions about the way to approach Sef Gonzales, based on the information about him that police had gathered up to that date.

It noted that Sef 'appears to view himself with grandiosity' and 'appears to seek admiration from others'. It observed that Sef had a history of telling lies, in an apparent attempt to protect and enhance his self-esteem. 'Sef is likely to detail his own concerns in a lengthy manner. Sef likely feels superior to police at this time, yet wary of them', the report stated.

The suggestion for the first interview was to make Sef feel as comfortable as possible, and approach him in an informal manner. Sef should not be dominated in the interview, and police should not interrupt him. 'It is considered that Sef will be willing to talk to investigators. Investigators should capitalise on this willingness by allowing him to talk ... you are there to *listen* to Sef, and hear what *he* has to say. The use of silence should induce Sef to fill the gaps', the report said.

In phase two of the interview process, the profiler suggested, the inconsistencies in Sef's statement should be put to him, with Sef being asked to explain them. 'Each answer he gives will need to satisfy the interviewer, rather than satisfy Sef.'

A break should take place between that and the third phase, in which police should return to an informal tone and let Sef know about the crime-scene evidence they had to date, as well as the fact they knew about the pressures on him at home, and the humiliation he must have suffered for his failures, which would put Sef off-balance.

'Sef by now should be destabilised and probably at his weakest point in the interview. If there is a time when he will confess, this is likely to be it. So now you need to give him an "out" [a reason for him to make excuses for having committed the crimes]. Use a compassionate tone, and sympathetic approach.'

Upon these words of advice, the plan for the interview was completed. The detectives would follow the first two recommended phases, to begin with, and leave their options open to pursue the third.

THE INTERVIEW WAS held in a stark room at Chatswood police station and began at 6.06 pm. Sheehy warned Sef that he was not obliged to say anything, but that whatever he did say would be recorded and could be used in evidence. Sef was reserved but composed as the questioning began.

Sheehy ran Sef gently back over his version of what he had done on the day of 10 July, what he was studying at university, the route he took to Raf De Leon's house, and the phone calls he said he made and received. Then it was on to the night out with Sam Dacillo, and the pair's arrival back home. Sheehy confirmed with Sef that he had not seen the racist graffiti inside the house. They also went back over the road rage incident, just to clarify what had occurred. (Checks of video surveillance from the Shell service station in Wicks Road did not reveal any such incident on the night of 9 July.)

Then Sheehy broadsided Sef with a question.

SHEEHY: Do you carry a baseball bat in your car?
SEF: No.
SHEEHY: You don't have one at all?

Sef reconsidered, and his nervousness began to show as he stammered through his answer.

> **SEF:** I think I probably had some, well, I had a baseball bat
> at some stage but I don't know, I don't know where,
> where, where it is. I think I may have, 'cause I remember
> when we were in our old house we had it, I'm not sure
> if we, if we had it with us when we moved to Collins
> [Street] as well, 'cause I, I never saw it when we moved
> to Collins. If we did it may have been stored in the, in
> the shed, but I can check that for you tomorrow.

Sheehy asked if the bat was kept in any of the three cars, bearing in mind Sam Dacillo's statement that Sef claimed to carry a bat in the boot of his Festiva. Sef said no.

Asked if it was a wooden bat, Sef said it was, then he volunteered:

> **SEF:** There is a stage that I had it, I think in my car
> when we were in Blacktown. I had it, 'cause we,
> 'cause my dad, I think he bought a cricket bat as well
> as, just as, just to put in the boot of his car. Think it's, I
> don't know if it's still there.
> **SHEEHY:** Yeah.

Sef continued to ramble.

> **SEF:** And I had either a baseball bat or a cricket bat. I
> think there was a baseball bat in my car at some stage
> ... but I remember taking it out because it made
> rattling noises in the boot, and because I had my, I
> have a subwoofer there and there wasn't much space
> ... and I remember I took it out and I, yeah, I think,

the last time I remember having it I think it was when
we were at Numa [Road], at my, our previous address,
but I haven't had it in the car for a long time.

Sheehy worked his way around to asking Sef about the Sam
Dacillo calls on the evening of 10 July. The SMS Sef said Sam
had sent him around 5.20 pm did not show up on telephone
records, Sef was informed. The records showed that the only
SMS from Sam to Sef's phone that day was at 8.52 am. Could
Sef explain that?

> SEF: A lot of times the text messages are delayed. I think
> you can check that with Vodafone that it happens a lot
> of times. I could, sometimes I send a message today and
> sometimes the receiver does not receive it till the day
> after. I don't know, but that's, that's an explanation to it.

But Sam's SMS was received on Sef's phone hours earlier
than Sef said he received it, Sheehy pointed out. Despite this,
Sef continued with his own peculiar brand of logic.

> SEF: Sometimes when my SIM, another explanation is
> when my SIM is, reaches about fifteen messages and I,
> I delete a message so there's space for another
> message. Sometimes it delays again the receiving of
> the message, that's the only problem with the Nokia.
> That's, that's the only explanation I can think of.

Sheehy moved on to the phone call Sef said he received from
Sam at 6 pm, while he was parked in the carport at 6 Collins
Street. According to Sam's phone records, the only call Sam
made to Sef on that date was at 7.54 pm. Could Sef explain
that?

SEF: Yeah, I don't have any explanation why six minutes to eight. Yeah, I, my recollection of the conversation was at that time [6 pm].

On the same tack, Sheehy asked why Sef's records made no listing of a call to his mother's mobile phone around the time he was supposedly in the carport, trying to reach her.

SEF: The only, the only thing I can think of is that the call didn't get through. That's, I don't know, I don't, I don't have any possible explanation, that's all I can think of but I was sure I, I attempted to call her and that was the, that was the message that I got.

Asked about his recollection that it was raining around that time, which is why he did not get out of the car, Sheehy pointed out that Sef said he normally entered via the laundry door and that the path from the carport to this door was under cover. Sheehy showed Sef a photograph of the area he was referring to. Sef said this was not true, there was a gap in the covering of the walkway where the water poured through, and that water from the gutters also flooded onto the ground.

With that, the interview ended at 10.15 pm. Sef was visibly rattled, and he didn't look happy.

Chapter 24

A friendship ends

By the Thursday after the funeral of the Gonzales family, Sef had been living a fairly nomadic existence. Having worn out his welcome with family members, he telephoned his friend Amanda Pedro's mother, Belinda, and asked if he could stay at their home in Sydney's northwest for a few days, because the media were harassing him. Belinda agreed, but would quickly come to regret the decision.

When Sef arrived at their place that evening, Belinda observed that his hands were stiff and defensive at his sides and his head was bowed, but when she looked into his face she saw there was no emotion. In her opinion, as a trained psychiatric nurse, he wasn't just withholding emotion, it simply wasn't there. She had learned enough in her profession about psychopaths to know that they are incapable of feeling empathy for anyone except themselves. Instantly, her intuition told her Sef was guilty of committing the murders.

Belinda had always viewed Sef as a bit of a cold fish. On 21 June 2001 — less than a month before the murders — he had visited their house for her son Alan's 21st birthday party, which Belinda had videotaped. All the other kids were laughing and joking, but as Belinda trained the camera on Sef, she noticed he was silent and not joining in the merriment.

Belinda was always outgoing and affectionate towards the young people who visited her home, but she could not bring herself to be that way with Sef. It was as if there were some invisible emotional barrier he held out that she could not penetrate.

That first night of Sef's stay Belinda decided she wasn't going to be treated like a 'nincompoop' in her own home by this young man. After Amanda and Alan arrived home she made him aware of that. 'You know, Sef, the first person people will suspect is you,' she told him.

Sef immediately went on the defensive. 'Who said that? Give me their names,' he demanded. He said he would get straight onto his lawyers, if someone was slandering his name in such a way.

Before she went to bed that night, Belinda instructed her children to sleep in the same room and urged them to place a chair under the doorknob. Sef was to sleep on the couch.

Amanda, however, did not get to bed until about 4 am, as she and Sef sat up talking. Amanda, now a university student, had told Sef she understood if he didn't want to talk about the murders, but Sef seemed to *want* to talk about them. Amanda was taken aback by the way Sef could bring himself to go into graphic detail about what he had seen in his home on the night of the killings. 'He said, "My dad was covered in blood and stabbed, like, twenty times"', Amanda recalls. 'He was able to speak, he was able to give details about it.'

The next morning, it was still dark when Belinda sat down with Sef at the table and spoke to him for more than an hour. Sef talked extensively about his parents. He said his father had left him $5 million and that he wanted to use this money to help people. He said he wanted to be like his father. Belinda tried to scrutinise him, read his emotions, but Sef's back was facing a window and in the dawning light she couldn't see his face properly. 'I could not feel any empathy for him, and the sorrow I felt was for his family,' she says.

The following night, Amanda went out in the city, while Sef remained at the Pedros' home and watched a video with Alan and one of his friends. The movie they saw was *Meet the Parents*, the Robert De Niro–Ben Stiller comedy about a bumbling young suitor trying and failing miserably to impress his future parents-in-law. There is a particular scene in the movie in which Stiller's character pops a champagne cork and it flies into the urn containing the ashes of De Niro's character's beloved mother, smashing it to pieces. The boys worried about Sef's reaction to the movie, since his own family had just been buried. But according to Belinda, Sef showed no sign of being upset. He laughed at all the right parts of the movie.

During his three-day visit Sef told Amanda's parents he felt very close to them. 'You're my new family now,' he said.

Sef continued to drop into the Pedros' home unannounced over the next couple of weeks. At first Amanda had no problem with these visits; at this stage she was convinced of his innocence. However, she became disturbed at the way Sef would just walk into the house without knocking, one time wandering straight into her bedroom to find her; she could have been getting dressed or anything. She felt it was an invasion of her privacy.

During this period Sef asked her to come out with him to see a movie, and they went to see *Erin Brockovich*, starring Julia Roberts. Amanda couldn't believe it when Sef kept trying to put his arm around her and kiss her — how could he be behaving this way when his parents had recently been murdered? On the way out of the cinema, Sef told her he had been offered a recording deal due to the way he had sung at the funeral. In spite of her incredulity, Amanda kept trying to make excuses for his behaviour. 'I kept trying to convince myself, "He's really traumatised",' she says.

About two weeks after the funeral, two Tawas detectives came around to her house, looking for her cousin Dennis. At first, Amanda was indignant about the detectives' attempts to speak to Sef's friends. 'You don't know what he's been through! He's had cancer!' she fired at the police officer.

It was after this that the police informed her of all the lies Sef had told her. He had never been diagnosed with cancer, they said. He did not study medicine. Amanda's initial shock was soon replaced by genuine doubt about Sef's proclaimed innocence.

The lies provided enough reason for Amanda's father Vincent to decide to tell Sef not to come and visit any more. Bluntly, he told Sef he believed he had been less than honest with them about so many aspects of his life. He had betrayed their trust.

Amanda began to fear another visit from Sef. He would come around looking for her and she would drive up to her house, see his car parked outside, and keep driving around the streets until she saw that his car was gone, and that it was safe to come home.

When Sef telephoned her one morning she told him he shouldn't be calling her. 'He said, "Look, I just want you to know I forgive you abandoning me in my hour of need",' Amanda says. He also told her the police had lied to her family about him.

Despite her family's rejection of him, Amanda would always have a place in his heart, Sef said. 'Once this is all over, I hope we can be friends.'

THE FRIENDSHIPS SEF had before the murders — such as those with Sam Dacillo and Raf De Leon — seemed to wane around this time. Both Sam and Raf had been used by Sef as part of the alibi to divert suspicion from himself.

He took up with a new crowd, coming to rely heavily for emotional support on Dennis Pedro and Don McGregor, one of Dennis's mates, who would later become a Crown witness and have his name suppressed by the New South Wales Supreme Court. His name has been altered in this book. Don was a legal clerk and nightclub DJ whom Dennis introduced to Sef after the murders. Don and Dennis both enjoyed the nightclub scene in the city, and Sef soon joined their circle. He would frequent clubs in the city with them, particularly Connections nightclub. According to Amanda, he would go nightclubbing virtually every weekend.

On her twentieth birthday, which fell in May 2002, Amanda was at Connections, dancing with friends. She was afraid when she saw Sef approach her. He asked to talk to her in private. She refused, but Sef persisted.

He told her: 'In two weeks I'm going to be on television offering a six-figure reward for anyone who can offer information for a concrete conviction [of the killer]. You'll finally see that I'm innocent.'

That was the last time Amanda spoke to Sef, her former friend. She had come round to her mother's way of thinking: that he was a manipulative, remorseless killer. 'I feel like I don't hate him because I don't have the energy to hate him. I pity him, because he's fucked up, like, mentally,' she now says.

Chapter 25

The follow-up interview

Sef returned to Chatswood police station for a second interview two days after his first interview. He did not know that, compared with the interview he was about to undergo, 1 August had been like a walk in the park. The police had only been getting started on the inconsistencies in his statements.

Sef was accompanied the second time around by a grief counsellor, who sat quietly in the corner of the interview room, observing the action. Sitting in another room of the station, waiting to watch the interview via video-link, other investigators and psychologists were ready, if necessary, to recommend Sheehy and Sim hit Sef with all their ammunition if it appeared Sef was vulnerable to making a confession.

Sef told police he had been back to Collins Street to look for the missing baseball bat after the first interview, but could not find it. He thought it had probably been left in his father's Toyota Camry, which had been written off in an accident.

The police then dropped a bombshell. As well as Emily's statement about seeing Sef's car in the carport at 6 pm, they had information that a client of Teddy's had dropped some documents off in the Collins Street letterbox between 4.15 pm and 4.30 pm on 10 July. She had told police she observed a small blue-green car parked in the carport — could Sef explain this?

'No. I have no, I have no explanation for it,' Sef replied. Around that time, he would have been travelling from his father's Blacktown office to Collins Street. He left his father's office, to the best of his recollection, about 4.30 pm.

Sim next produced Sef's street directory, seized by police from his car. Sef had earlier told the police that he had looked in the street directory to find Raf De Leon's address, but it wasn't in his old directory, as the suburb was very new. He had also told police he did not have Raf's new phone number on him to call and ask for directions.

Sim informed Sef that Raf's street, Crestview Drive, was listed, and Sef agreed but said the suburb of Kings Ridge was not. Sim informed Sef police had found both Raf's current home and mobile numbers recorded in Sef's mobile telephone, but Sef replied he'd thought they were the old ones.

Sim's tone became harder as he pushed Sef on the issue of why he had not looked to see which suburbs had Crestview Drives listed, to see which was the closest to Raf's description of where he lived, near Blacktown.

SIM: So am I correct in saying you drove out there, got yourself lost. Is that right?

SEF: Yes.

SIM: And then you turned around and went home?

SEF: Yes.

SIM: When you say you got yourself lost ... did you use your street directory to get yourself unlost? *[Sim's voice drips with sarcasm.]*

SEF: No, I was lost in the sense that I wasn't sure how to get to this place, not lost in the sense that I didn't know

where I was. I knew where I was but I didn't know
how to get, I didn't know how to get to this place.

Sheehy took over from Sim, and brought up the subject of
the 000 call, his tone soothing. He produced the tape and
played it as Sef sat, looking shell-shocked, hearing his
screaming and crying voice played back for the first time.

The tape concluded and silence hung thick in the air. If
there was ever a point when Sef could excuse himself from
the interview, too distressed to continue, this was it.

> **SHEEHY:** Are you all right, Sef?
> **SEF:** Yeah.
> **SHEEHY:** Do you wish to continue at this time?
> **SEF:** Yeah.

Sef agreed with Sheehy that he made the call when he had
found his father, and that it was during this call that he found
his mother's body. Some time later he found his sister, he said.

Sheehy continued in his conciliatory tone.

> **SHEEHY:** In the opening of that 000 call you actually say
>   that someone's killed your family, then killed my
>   parents. I know this is difficult, but are you able to say
>   how you've determined that, when at that stage
>   you've only located your father?
> **SEF:** You don't, well, while I was on the phone, I guess I
>   was rambling, and I just, I wasn't picking the right
>   words to say on the, on the phone. I was just, you
>   know, to the effect I was just saying, you know, my
>   family had been hurt, and I think that I said they were
>   shot. And that's the first time I've heard that, and I
>   have, I mean, till now, I don't even. And I, I never

could recall what I said to the operator, I was just, just
remember rambling to the operator. In terms of what
I saw, I just, you know, that's what [I] say in my
statement and that's, that's just the best of my
recollection.

Asked why the family's cordless phone, usually kept in its
stand in the downstairs study, was found at the top of the
stairs when he had made the 000 call on his mobile phone,
Sef answered that he had probably clipped the phone to his
belt automatically, even though the phone line had been
dead.

Sef denied ever having seen the painted racist scrawl inside
the house, and said he did not know what colour the paint
was. Shown a photograph of it for the first time, he told
police he wrote with his left hand and that he did not see
many similarities between the scrawl and his handwriting. He
denied he had written it. He said he had not used blue spray
paint recently.

It was revealed to Sef that police had found what appeared
to be a small amount of blue paint on the sleeve of the
jumper he was wearing the night of the murders. Asked if he
had an explanation for this, Sef said there were decorative
blue-painted woodchips on the side path of the Collins Street
house. The dogs sometimes tracked blue chips onto the
garden pebbles nearby and family members were constantly
picking the chips up and depositing them back in their
rightful place. He would have handled the chips within the
last week, and could not remember the last time he had
washed his jumper.

Asked about the Human brand shoebox in his room, Sef
said it had been left behind by his cousin Monica, who had
visited Australia that year, in April or May. Sef said he had

never owned or used a pair of these shoes, and could not explain why they had left bloodied prints in the house. It was possible, Sef said, that his father had owned a pair of the shoes; he was trying to remember if he did.

'What you're saying, are you saying that you think your father may have had a pair of these shoes?' Sim asked him.

Sef agreed.

'Where do you think those shoes may be now?' Sim pressed.

'I don't know, they may have been taken. They may have been, I don't know, just, I'll have to check the house. I mean, if, if you're saying it doesn't match it, I'm just guessing, you know, what if whoever did this took the shoes as well, and 'cause just putting things together, they've taken some of my clothes from what it appears, that you're saying the police didn't take my clothes. And it just occurs to me, maybe if they took my clothes, they may have taken, you know, a pair of shoes as well, or more than a pair of shoes.'

Towards the end of the interview, Sim began to question Sef about the computer searches for poisons. At first Sef had nothing to say, but as Sim asked him about the various searches made, Sef began to imply that possibly it was another family member who had made the searches.

'Just with the plants, in case I might forget, the only possible explanation I guess is that my dad used the computer as well, and we just, we just put topsoil on the perimeter back yard . . . and we were planning to plant different plants there, and I remember accessing those, if my dad were researching plants . . . and if he was to, he was trying to make, to ensure that none of them was poisonous, that may be an explanation for why [he] would look up those particular sites. But that's, you know, that's the best thing, that's the best guess that I could . . .' His voice trailed off.

Sim let him know he thought this was an unbelievable explanation. He pointed out there were a number of searches on one specific poison, telling Sef what the poison was.

SIM: Could you give me a reason why your dad might plant a poisonous plant in your garden?

SEF: I wouldn't know, no. And I don't think he would.

SIM: Does that sound like a reasonable explanation to you?

SEF: Well it's the best guess that I could make of . . .

SIM: Sorry, it's the best what?

SEF: It's, it's the best guess that I can . . .

SIM: Guess? *[Disbelief rings in his voice.]*

SEF: . . . make of, what, what's here.

The interview concluded at 3.13 pm. At no stage had Sef shown a sign of being close to breaking into a confession. Just before the interview ended, Sheehy uttered the words Sef must have known were coming, considering everything he now knew the police were aware of.

'Sef, I have to ask you . . . did you have any involvement in the murder of your mother and father and sister?'

'No, I didn't.'

'Do you know of any person who may have had any involvement?'

Sef said he could only speculate. But he mentioned the name of a high-profile, extremely wealthy Filipino businessman. 'As I mentioned, yeah, that person . . . may have had something to do with it. After having heard, you know, different accounts from different people, that's all I can come up with right now.'

Sef left the station, never to participate in another recorded interview. However, his discussions with police were far from over, and he would continue to deal with Mick Sheehy, who he obviously felt was more sympathetic to him than Ritchie Sim, who did not seem to believe anything he said.

PERHAPS IT WAS sheer coincidence that on the day of his last nerve-racking interview with police — 3 August 2001 — Sef claimed to have received an anonymous e-mail nominating the same wealthy Filipino businessman he had mentioned in his interview as being behind the family's killings. The businessman cannot be identified due to a suppression order from the New South Wales Supreme Court, but suffice it to say that he is extremely wealthy and influential.

The e-mail, which Sef gave to Tawas investigators on 20 August, was written partly in Tagalog and partly in English. It nominated the businessman as having taken out a hit on the family. 'They were paid to kill three', it said, and went on to add that Clodine's being in Sydney had saved Sef's life. The e-mail said it was Teddy's good principles that had resulted in the deaths, and advised Sef to go through his father's papers for clues. It warned Sef to be careful.

On 6 August, Sef had contacted his cousin Monica Gonzales, Freddie's daughter, in the Philippines and asked her to make enquiries at her end about the businessman's activities. She did not even bother. She found the suggestion that the businessman was involved patently ridiculous.

Much later, an earlier, all-English version of the e-mail was found on a computer seized from Sef's Chatswood apartment.

Sef had moved into the high-rise, one-bedroom, $380-a-week apartment around the beginning of August 2001, telling his relatives the police had decided the high-security unit was necessary for his safety. (In reality, the police had said no such thing.) His family paid his rent and bills.

Chapter 26

The inheritance

Sef's 21st birthday fell on 16 September 2001. It was the day his father had promised to reveal to him the true meaning of his name.

One week beforehand, Sef rang around his relatives, inviting them to attend his birthday lunch at a Chinese restaurant in Coxs Road, North Ryde. One of the people he telephoned was his Aunt Emily. He told her he'd had a dream of his mother the night before, in which Loiva had spoken to him. Specifically, Loiva had told him in this dream that he must speak to Emily.

Emily agreed to come to lunch, as did Joseph, Amelita and the Ferrers. Sef arrived at the restaurant in his mother's white Toyota Celica, the car he had never been allowed to drive when his mother was alive.

It was a distinctly uncomfortable gathering. Emily, in particular, felt ill at ease, sitting directly opposite Sef. As the others talked amongst each other, Emily noticed that Sef hung his head in his hands. Emily waited for someone else to notice and comment on it. No-one did, and the conversation continued to swirl around them. 'I guess it will have to be me,' she thought, with an inner sigh.

'What's wrong, Sef?' she asked him from across the table.

'I've been getting headaches,' Sef revealed to her. He went on to say he'd had CT (Computerised Tomography) scans and that the doctors had detected brain tumours.

Emily was taken aback. She knew all about brain tumours; her husband had developed one, and Emily had been with him every inch of the way, as he consulted doctors and was treated in a public hospital under the Medicare system. Emily's husband had been lucky; he had survived his operation and recovered.

Emily questioned Sef closely, knowing the exact diagnostic process for brain tumours. Sef told her he had to have an MRI (Magnetic Resonance Imaging) scan to confirm the diagnosis.

Emily was extremely sceptical of anything he said by now, and felt another stab of disappointment in her nephew. She suspected Sef's talk of brain tumours was just another charade, another attempt to garner sympathy. It even occurred to her that Sef might have used the genuine trauma that her husband had gone through as inspiration for another of his schemes.

As they left the restaurant, Emily noted the new mag wheels and side skirting on her sister's car, and told Sef the vehicle looked good. Sef responded that his friends had bought the accessories for the car as a birthday present. Emily commented that he was lucky to have friends who were so generous.

NOT LONG AFTER his birthday lunch, Sef began to e-mail Annie Paraan, his godmother and Emily's older sister, in Baguio.

Annie, a senior banking officer, managed the account containing rental money from Teddy's apartments on Legarda Road, Baguio. The apartments were located on a prime lot of around 20,000 square metres. William and Belen Gonzales managed the property for their son and Annie would call on them to collect the rent and deposit it into Teddy's and Loiva's Filipino bank account.

Sef contacted Annie on 6 November 2001, seeking access to the account. In the e-mail, Sef stated that the funds were not subject to Australian probate. Sef was asking Annie to transfer a massive amount to him: AU$190,000. Annie Paraan e-mailed back, asking Sef how urgently he needed the money.

On 9 November, Annie received another e-mail from Sef reiterating his request, and saying there was no way the funds would become part of the probate matter. Sef explained to his aunt that he needed money because he suspected he had a brain tumour. He needed to pay, he wrote, for MRI scans and other medical procedures. 'Tell them we are not intending to transfer that money into my name', he wrote.

Annie sought the advice of detectives from Tawas, asking whether she should release the funds to her nephew. Their answer was no. Already Emily had advised Annie that if Sef indeed had a brain tumour, he could get free treatment in a public hospital. She got Annie to forward each e-mail to her and she would pass it on to Detective Paul Auglys.

To support his bid for the money, Sef had included a death certificate he had obtained from the Registrar of Births, Deaths and Marriages. Also, signed by a Justice of the Peace, a 'Reginald Matthews', was a document entitled 'Affidavit of Self-adjudication' regarding the funds. Legally, it meant nothing; such an affidavit did not exist in New South Wales. Tawas detectives located three Justices of the Peace in New South Wales named Reginald Matthews, none of whom had signed the document. Police believed Sef had forged it to give added legitimacy to his claim for the money.

Sef continued to send e-mails to his aunt requesting the transfer of the money, including one on 13 November, in which he asked: 'When do you estimate we might get the green light from the bank?'

Annie Paraan finally replied that she was not able to forward him the money, that she did not feel it was appropriate.

WHEN TEDDY AND Loiva Gonzales died they were both asset-rich and cashed up. Their assets in Australia alone were worth $1.5 million, while their real estate holdings in the Philippines were worth in the vicinity of AU$1.3 million.

The property at 6 Collins Street, North Ryde, was valued at $700,000, their furniture at $30,000. Loiva was very fond of jewellery, and together the couple owned approximately $10,000 worth. Teddy's white 2001 Mitsubishi Pajero, registration TED-11G, was valued at $54,325. Loiva's white Toyota Celica SX sedan, registration LOI–11V, was worth $18,650.

Teddy also owned Unit 31 at 15–17 Kildare Road, Blacktown, the commercial space from which his legal practice operated. Teddy's superannuation fund held $69,244.73, and there were also various accounts and trusts in the couple's names, totalling a few thousand dollars.

To ensure their children's future financial security, Teddy and Loiva Gonzales had created their last will and testament in February 1998, when they were still living at Blacktown. They appointed each other as the executor and trustee of the estate, in the event that one of them died before the other. However, if the surviving spouse were unable, for whatever reason, to fulfil this role, Amelita Claridades was to become trustee.

If one spouse died, each wanted the other to inherit their entire estate. However, the will also took into account the fate that would eventually become theirs: 'Should the surviving spouse die or should we die at the same time, the entire estate shall be divided equally between our two children, Sef Gonzales and Clodine Gonzales, in equal shares as joint tenants. We appoint Amelita Claridades to be the guardian of our minor children.'

The times of death would become important in the execution of the estate (if Sef were not to inherit), even though Teddy, Loiva and Clodine died on the same day, within hours of each other. Clodine died first, leaving Sef the sole heir of Loiva and Teddy. Loiva died after Clodine, but before Teddy, and in the eyes of the law left all her worldly possessions to her husband. And when Teddy died, his estate — including what he had inherited from his wife — would go to Sef.

That is, of course, what would have happened if Sef were not the chief suspect in the murders of his three family members. As it was, Sef legally would not be able to touch the funds of his inheritance for some time, if ever.

WHEN HIS FAMILY died, Sef was pretty much broke. He had exactly $551.33 in his Commonwealth Bank account. But after the murders, Sef's account balance took a rather dramatic turn for the better.

Three days after the murders he visited his father's accountant, John Stafford, who also managed Teddy's and Loiva's superannuation fund, but he was unable to get his hands on any money, as the estate had not yet been executed.

But he was getting money from somewhere.

On 23 July, three days after his family's funeral, there was a deposit of $9234.49 into Sef's account. The next day, 24 July, there was a further large deposit of funds, with $4152.35 being put into the account. On 26 July, a large portion of this money — $11,067.54 — was withdrawn. A number of other transactions were recorded between then and 24 October 2001, including the receipt of social security payments of $460.00 every fortnight.

Then, on 28 November, Sef came into a large amount of money. That day, a deposit of $45,000 was made into his Commonwealth Bank account. On 13 December, there was a withdrawal of $33,988.60. The next day, 14 December, a deposit of $7500 was made. The same day, $4000 was withdrawn. On 19 December, a further $5000 was deposited.

These were major financial transactions. Sef was not allowed to access his dead family's estate, so how could this sudden wealth be explained?

THE INTERNET IS an easy way to access a great many potential buyers. You can sell virtually anything. That was where an advertisement for a near-new white 2001 Mitsubishi Pajero was posted in the months after the Gonzales family deaths, with a sale price of $56,000. Accompanying the ad was a photo illustrating a Pajero four-wheel drive. The contact for interested buyers was listed at the bottom of the advertisement: Sef Gonzales, Chatswood. His mobile telephone number was beside his name.

Whether it was through this advertisement or by other means that Sef found a buyer for his dead father's Pajero is not clear. What police were able to confirm is that in the year after his family's murders, Sef sold his father's and mother's cars, in addition to his green Ford Festiva.

Teddy's white Mitsubishi Pajero, which he'd bought on 10 April 2001, was transferred into the name of Sef Gonzales on vehicle registration records on 27 November 2001. The next day, 28 November, the vehicle was transferred out of that name. Sef sold the Pajero in January 2002 for $52,590.

The green Ford Festiva Sef drove had been bought by Loiva in May 1995 and registered in her name. On 27 November 2001, the car was transferred into the name of Sef Gonzales. In March 2002, Sef sold that car for $12,000.

The 1996 white Toyota Celica — the car Loiva drove — had been bought by Teddy Gonzales in January 1997. On 22 November 2001 the car was transferred to the ownership of Sef Gonzales. On 1 May 2002, it was sold to another party for $23,500.

The three vehicles were not the only assets belonging to Teddy and Loiva that became part of Sef Gonzales' fire sale.

Teddy's sister, Annie Gonzales–Tesoro, recalls Loiva's love of jewellery and the fact Teddy owned an expensive Rolex watch. Many of Loiva's valuable pieces, as well as Teddy's watch, went missing around this time, she says.

In fact, Sef began pawning the family belongings on 1 August 2001, a little over two weeks after the murders. On that date, he pawned eleven items in exchange for $210 at Cash Magic at Top Ryde Shopping Centre. He told staff there he needed to get rid of the items because he had found a job in the United States. The items included a DVD player, video cassette recorder, microphone, Nintendo player and a few Nintendo games.

Tawas detectives were notified of the transaction after shop employees passed on Sef's driver's licence details to police, as required by law. Two members of Tawas were actually in Cash Magic, speaking to staff, on 9 August when Sef came in again and attempted to sell some jewellery, including a baguette diamond ring, diamond earrings and a pearl ring. He told the staff, 'I am a part-time lawyer and I need to sell them for my studies.' Sef did not strike a deal with Cash Magic that day but approached another store at the Top Ryde Shopping

Centre, Lindley's Jewellery & Giftware, where he was informed they did not buy second-hand jewellery.

On 18 August, Sef again went into Cash Magic and negotiated with staff to sell a ladies' Longines watch for $120. He came back two days later, but only got $80 for the watch. On 14 March 2002, Sef again went into Cash Magic and sold five items of jewellery, including two white-gold bracelets, one white-gold necklace, a white-gold pendant with diamond and a white-gold cross pendant with diamond.

Emily says Sef had asked his grandmother, Amelita, shortly after the murders if he could sell some of the family's smaller belongings to get cash. Amelita did not wish to object. Emily recalls visiting Sef soon after the murders and finding a number of his mother's perfume bottles which he had removed from the Collins Street house. Sef told Emily to take whatever she wanted, but she was appalled. She did not want anyone touching her dead sister's belongings. These minor items were never listed as part of probate, which meant they were not subject to the execution of the estate.

However, the vehicles and jewellery were part of the estate, and by selling them Sef was in breach of probate, which had been granted to Amelita, the executor of the estate. Through routine investigation, the police were the first to learn that the vehicles had been sold. However, their hands were tied. They could inform the family, and indeed did so, but after that their role ended. The estate was a civil matter. Their job was to arrest and attempt to gain a conviction against the family's killer.

Towards the end of 2001, Sef Gonzales went car shopping. It was at the Sydney Motor Show at Darling Harbour, on 10 October 2001, that he visited the Lexus stand and was referred to a dealership at Chatswood, where he ordered a $170,000 Lexus convertible sedan with an extra $5000 worth of accessories such as pin–striping and tinted windows. Sef told the Lexus salesman he was about to come into an inheritance from overseas. He laid down a deposit but soon had to cancel the order when he discovered he could not come up with the funds.

In December, Sef opted instead for a sporty silver 2001 Ford Cougar coupé from Brad Garlick Ford at Ryde. The car, imported from the United States, sold for around $45,000. Sef registered it with the personalised numberplate: 'TLCS'. These were the initials of each of his family members' first names, including his own.

In arranging a lease for the vehicle, Sef was required to provide proof of income. It was not until later that police discovered Sef had altered his bank records so that his social security payments came across as payments from Impact Music Productions.

Chapter 27

Countdown to murder

In June 2001, Emily visited her sister Liza and her niece Clodine in Melbourne. Clodine was extremely happy. She told Emily she had abandoned her dream of becoming a chef and instead had decided she wanted to be a teacher. She said she had told her father about her plans, and he had said that if that was what she wanted to do, she would have his blessing.

Teddy, the planner, was already mapping out the next few years of his life. He foresaw that Sef would eventually take over his law practice, and he and Loiva would sell the Collins Street home and retire to the Gold Coast. They would use some of the funds from the sale to buy Sef and Clodine their own units, so they had independence. Teddy was already teaching Sef the basics of conveyancing, which comprised some of the work performed at his law office at Blacktown. He was speaking to Sef about going partners in the purchase of a unit off the plan in a Mount Druitt development. He wanted Sef to have made something of himself, to have something to offer, when the time came for him to marry, like he did when he met Loiva.

Loiva, shortly before her death, was busy planning a ceremony for the following year, 2002, in which she and Teddy would renew their wedding vows on their 25th wedding anniversary. She wanted Amelita to make her dress, and to have her sisters Liza and Emily as witnesses. She was very much looking forward to it.

On Sunday, 1 July, Loiva was feeling very sick. She was passing blood, and had terrible stomach pains. She and Clodine, who was now in Sydney for the school holidays, visited Emily at her home. Emily had made them a Filipino dessert, which was one of Loiva's favourites. In fact, Loiva could never say no to sweets. Clodine ate some, but Loiva couldn't touch the dessert. Pale and listless, she sat clutching her stomach.

'I think I've got food poisoning,' she told Emily. The previous night, Loiva and the family had gone to dinner at a restaurant in Ryde. She and Sef had drunk tap water, and she thought that might be the cause of her illness, as Sef had also complained of feeling sick.

Emily told Loiva before she went home that food poisoning generally only lasted 24 hours, and that she should be feeling okay by the next evening.

Loiva made no contact with Emily for the next three days. On 5 July, a Thursday, she told Emily she had just got out of hospital the day before.

On the Tuesday night, Loiva had still been feeling extremely sick, and Teddy had said he would take her to hospital. Emily says this had prompted an argument between Teddy and Sef about whether she needed medical attention. Sef, for some reason, opposed the idea.

Teddy had driven Loiva to Sydney Adventist Hospital, where she was admitted overnight and underwent tests. She was to come back a month later for a colonoscopy.

Emily was surprised she had not been notified that Loiva was in hospital. When she went around to her sister's house on Thursday, she saw Sef, who also complained of being ill.

'He was holding his tummy. He said: "Oh, I'm also feeling very sick, like Mama."' Emily advised him to take some painkillers, but he said, 'I'll be okay.'

Then Sef noticed that Emily had driven over in her brand-new white Honda CRV four-wheel drive, and excitedly he went outside to inspect and admire the car. It seemed to improve his spirits. He showed no sign of sickness then.

Annie Gonzales-Tesoro recalls it was around this time, about a week to ten days before the murders, that Teddy made a cryptic comment to his father, William, over the telephone. He said words to the effect of: 'I have a big family problem I am dealing with. But I think I can solve it.' They would never know for sure what Teddy meant by these words.

After the food poisoning experience, Loiva relayed her fears to Annie Paraan and to her friend Jane.

'She was sad,' recalls Annie Paraan. 'Two things she talked to me about. She talked about her food poisoning; it was the first time that had happened to her. I got the feeling she almost died. She was talking about several tests she was scheduled to have.' Loiva also spoke to Annie Paraan about a problem concerning outstanding rent on one of their properties in the Philippines.

Loiva told her friend Jane she thought she had got food poisoning from eating Almond Roca, a sweet sold in tins in department and specialty stores. 'She said to me, "I nearly died,"' says Jane.

That Thursday morning before the murders, when Emily visited Loiva's house, only Sef and Loiva were home when she arrived, as Clodine had gone out and Teddy was working.

As Loiva prepared lunch for the three of them, Emily observed that Sef was morose. Sef told her unhappily that his mother wanted him to break up with his girlfriend, Kathy

Wu, so he could concentrate better on his studies. He told Emily he supposed his mother was right, but he looked very down. Emily listened as Loiva told him, 'Sef, believe me, the right girl will come when you finish your degree.' Emily commented to Loiva that she did not think any girl would be right for Sef, as far as Loiva was concerned.

After lunch, Sef commented to Emily that he believed people in the Opus Dei movement, which Sef no longer followed, were 'hypocrites' who pretended to be good people. Clodine was heavily involved in the movement. Sef told Emily that Clodine had chastised him severely for staring at a photo of a 'sexy lady' in a newspaper, wearing a bikini. Clodine had asked him, 'Why are you looking at that photo in the paper? It's indecent.'

Sef told Emily this as his mother was washing her chihuahua Ginger. Loiva, who was very concerned about her colonoscopy the next month, moaned to Emily, 'My poor Ginger, what's going to happen to her if I die?'

Emily assured Loiva a colonoscopy was not a life-threatening procedure. But, very seriously, Loiva set about showing Emily each step of her care for Ginger. Once she had shown Emily how to wash the chihuahua, she led her upstairs and showed her the stool where she placed her dog as she dried her with a blow-drier. She showed Emily the bed Ginger slept in, and explained how Ginger had her own toothbrush and had her teeth brushed every night before she went to bed. Loiva explained how each of Ginger's feet must be wiped off after the dog went outside to perform her ablutions, to ensure she wasn't dirty.

Emily still cannot relate these instructions without giggling. It was a comedy that preceded the tragedy. She knew Loiva babied her dog, but had no idea about the lengths she went to in her grooming. (After the murders,

Emily did take Ginger into her care, until she moved to a townhouse six months afterwards, and complaints from neighbours and the fact she also had a cat meant she had to give the dog away to a family friend.)

The following morning, a Friday, when Emily was paying another visit, Sef left the house early, dumping all his bedding into the washing machine for someone else to clean. It appeared he had wet his bed again. As Emily helped Clodine hang out Sef's bedding on the clothesline, Clodine complained of how inconsiderate Sef was in routinely leaving his dirty bedding in the washing machine. She said her parents had had to get the washing machine fixed due to damage caused by constantly washing the heavy bedlinen.

As Emily and Clodine chatted, Clodine told her she believed Sef was sexually active. Even when he was ten years old, she had discovered some 'adult' magazines in his bedroom, she said. Sef had claimed he was keeping them for a friend. Clodine had informed her parents, who were not impressed with Sef. Clodine also told Emily she believed Sef was accessing adult websites on the Internet late at night, as he often stayed up at night and slept in the next morning.

On Saturday, 7 July, three days before the murders, the Gonzales family went to a friend's house for dinner. Sef came along, as did Emily. Emily said everyone was laughing and chatting at dinner, except Sef, who was moody and silent.

The dinner took place at the home of one of Loiva's best female friends, also a Filipino. Her son, Brian, was three years older than Clodine and involved in the Internet technology industry. Brian was a bright, tall and handsome young man. Loiva thought he would be a wonderful match for Clodine. In the weeks leading up to the dinner, Loiva and her close friend had chatted excitedly on the phone like schoolgirls about Clodine's impending visit to Sydney and about setting up the pair, who had never met before. They arranged the dinner at the friend's house for the Saturday night.

Both women were delighted when Clodine and Brian hit it off immediately that night, talking to and gazing at each other like there was no-one else in the room. This only enhanced the merriment of the others at the table — all except for Sef. It must have been such a bitter blow to see his parents' obvious pleasure as Clodine talked to Brian, starry-eyed, while his mother had been dead against Sef's own relationship with Kathy Wu.

Clodine had, of late, been winning their parents' approval for her grades and her friendships in Melbourne, while Sef seemed to be earning nothing but their disapproval. They criticised his university results, his choice of women, even his haircut and the clothes he wore. He could never seem to win the praise he sought so desperately.

After dinner, from the other end of the family's pool room, Emily noted with concern that Sef was crouched in a corner, holding a pool cue. He was staring off into space. 'I noticed that — I thought what's wrong with this boy?' she says.

It was not the first time Sef had acted in a bizarre manner. The year before, at their Numa Road home, Sef had had an argument with his mother about his haircut. His mum thought it was too short. After the argument, Sef stood at a table with a butter knife and started banging the top of its blade in a stabbing motion, and staring off in a vacant manner. According to Emily Loiva had said to Sef words to the effect of 'Stop pretending you're crazy.'

Nevertheless, Emily took Sef's recent behaviour very seriously. She spoke to Loiva the following Monday, the day before the murders, and warned her that she feared for Sef's life.

'I told her that he might commit suicide, because he's very depressed. She said, "I don't think so. He's been like that for a week."'

That Monday evening, Emily visited the Gonzales home. She wanted to wish Clodine happy birthday. It was the day Clodine had turned eighteen, and the family were going out to dinner in the city to celebrate. The family were dressed up; Loiva had had her hair done and looked wonderful. Loiva gave Emily some chocolate cake to take home.

By about 9 pm that night, the Gonzales family had returned home. Emily spoke to Loiva on the telephone and she seemed very happy and bubbly. 'She was so pleased, she said, "Your brother-in-law [Teddy] took us to a very nice Japanese restaurant in Sydney,"' Emily recalls.

Emily also spoke to Clodine that night on the phone. She seemed to be as cheerful as her mother. That was the last time Emily ever heard the voices of her beloved sister and niece.

Chapter 28

Undercover

In September 2001, Tawas detectives decided to take another crack at getting a confession from Sef. Leo, an undercover operative (not his real undercover name), managed to bump into Sef at a Chatswood coffee shop while Mick Sheehy was having one of his regular informal meetings with Sef. Leo casually complimented Sef on his cool threads. In the undercover business, it is called a 'cold start'.

Leo portrayed himself as a gangster with connections in the police force. He was a man who could solve your problems for you. This was crucial, because police believed Sef would not confess to committing the murders to someone he saw as beneath him in the criminal pecking order. Tawas detectives wanted Sef to engage in a bragging contest with Leo — which he did to a certain degree. He told Leo he was a member of the White Dragons Asian crime gang — a gang police later ascertained did not exist, at least according to their databases.

In October, Leo was the man who got Sef into the exclusive Lexus stand at the Sydney Motor Show. Once a friendship of sorts had been established, Leo informed Sef that an inmate dying in jail would confess to his family's murders. Sef gave Leo floor plans he had sketched of the

Collins Street house, indicating where the bodies had been found and where the graffiti was on the wall. He even wrote 'Fuck Off Bloody Asians' on the plan.

None of this meant much to police, as Sef had discovered the bodies and had been shown photos of the racist scrawl, although the wording of the racist scrawl he wrote for Leo was slightly different. But they did compare Sef's handwriting on the paper to that on the wall.

What was most intriguing was that Sef wrote down his family's approximate times of death on the plan. He noted that Clodine's was 3 pm to 5 pm, Loiva's was 5 pm to 6 pm and Teddy's was 6 pm to 7 pm. Police had carefully guarded the times of death, knowing it was a detail only the killer would be able to pinpoint.

In the end though, Sef did not take Leo up on the offer of an inmate's confession. He did, however, make some interesting comments to Leo. On 15 October, he told Leo: 'People don't suspect me, it's just Sef with the little baby face. I have a split personality, I can hide what I do.' On 5 December, he said that his family had been murdered by contract killers due to politicking in the Philippines: 'I'm pretty sure it's all over, I've tied my loose ends really well.' Then, on 12 December: 'They've got nothing on me ... I'm pretty confident on what they've got on me, it's all circumstantial stuff.'

Yet on 20 December, Sef told Leo categorically that he was not involved in his family's murders. The decision was then taken to can the undercover operation.

Some investigators, Paul Auglys included, thought Leo should have been set up as a nightclub guru, someone who could exploit Sef's fascination with that whole scene and offer him the chance to become a big shot. Others, such as Sheehy, thought the outcome was to be expected. They wanted Sef to brag to Leo, to shoot his mouth off. Yet murdering your family wasn't exactly the kind of crime you went around boasting about.

IN DECEMBER 2001, Mick Sheehy and Detective Paul Sullivan visited Queensland's Gold Coast to interview the head of one of the seed suppliers whom 'sef' had e-mailed from the Gonzales' family computer. During their stay, they spoke to Sef's Uncle Edmund, who lived up that way, and Edmund convinced them to go to a psychic with him — one he had visited previously.

The psychic's name was Rhiannon, and Sheehy and Sullivan, the trained psychologist, were extremely sceptical. They decided in advance they would keep poker faces and not volunteer any information that could influence what she told them.

Edmund had been asked by the woman beforehand to bring along something belonging to Loiva. Edmund brought along a large Global brand knife. Loiva had given it to him when the Gonzales family had bought the Global brand block, and no longer needed the single knife. As a black cat with intense green eyes wandered around her home unit, giving the cops the evil eye, Rhiannon touched the knife. She said she could feel some connection between the knife and the murder weapon.

She told them she had communicated with Loiva's spirit and Loiva had told her that her son was the killer. Loiva had expressed her shock at having raised a son who was so evil. She mentioned that Clodine had been choked and also attacked with a silver cylindrical object. And the killer had worn running shoes that had no shoelaces, just like the Human brand shoes police believed the killer had worn. All these were details the police had witheld from the public.

She said that, after the murders, the killer had washed in open ground where there were buildings and a water supply. To Sheehy, it sounded like it could be Truscott Street Public School, which bordered nearby Ryrie Street. Rhiannon said that the killer had deposited a black bag containing a weapon and clothing in an open drain, within 2 kilometres of the Collins Street house. The bag would be found one day, she was sure, by a child playing with a ball. This event would have some connection to the name 'Lily'. It could be the child's name.

The two detectives walked away from the psychic if not converted, extremely impressed. So impressed that when they got back to Sydney they looked in the phone book to see if anyone living in the area had the last name of Lily (of various spellings). They found a female florist who lived right near Truscott Street Public School. The detectives visited her house and asked if they could have a look in the back yard. The woman was very good-natured about it. The detectives didn't find anything but a freaky connection. The florist said she had helped provide the beautiful floral arrangements for the Gonzales funeral.

STRIKE FORCE TAWAS was hearing murmurs from the Philippines, via Annie Paraan and Annie Gonzales-Tesoro, that Emily Luna knew more than she was saying. The relatives suggested via letters to investigators that they ask Emily again what she knew about the night of the murders. But they did not tell police what this extra information was.

On 7 December, Paul Auglys called Emily into Gladesville police station. He laid all his cards on the table, telling her he knew she had more to say. 'Let's just finish this,' he said to her.

Emily confessed she had not told him everything, that she had walked to the carport the night of the murders and had seen that Sef was not inside his car. Emily again mentioned seeing the coatstand through the glass panels.

Tawas Detective Michael O'Brien, who was sitting in on the discussion, realised the significance of this with the aid of his fresh perspective on the investigation. The pair showed her an electronic interactive display of the crime scene, at which point it dawned on Emily that the coatstand was not visible through the front glass panels of the house, but was located further back behind a pillar. If it wasn't a coatstand that Emily had noticed, what was it?

Emily had given police a number of statements already, spilling out more detail each time. Auglys decided that to clear things up once and for all. They would conduct a re-enactment at the crime scene of what Emily had seen. It began at 8.50 pm on 19 December, in about the same daylight conditions as would have existed at 6 pm on 10 July 2001, in the dead of winter.

Emily revealed several things on the night of the re-enactment. She told police that as she drove into Collins Street and parked her car on the street outside the home, she saw a swift movement from right to left behind the glass panel to the left of the front door. She said the back kitchen light had shone through to the front of the house. Repeatedly an officer attempted to replicate the movement until Emily said it was exactly how she remembered it as she pulled up on 10 July.

Paul Sullivan, 190 centimetres tall, was asked to stand behind the left-hand pane of glass to see if he resembled the coatstand-like object Emily had seen. No, he was too tall. Then a female constable, 159 centimetres tall, was asked to stand there. Her height was about right. The figure also looked like it had been wearing a cap, Emily said.

The female constable then sat inside Sef's car, which had been brought back to the house for the reconstruction, and

Emily admitted she could not see whether anyone was inside when the light was off. Maybe the car had been in a slightly different position. She could make out a headrest, however. But she thought it did not replicate what she had seen that night. By that stage it was dark. The reconstruction ended at 9.38 pm.

The police had tipped off the *Daily Telegraph* to come to the scene and take a photograph of Sef's car parked in the driveway. They told the *Telegraph*'s reporter that they had a fresh line of enquiry that revolved around a green hatchback. The story ran the next day. It would get tongues wagging. One of Sef's mates, legal clerk Don McGregor, would hear the news repeated on the radio that day and call Sef to let him know.

IN DECEMBER 2001, and then the following month, January 2001, Sef had two telephone conversations with his grandmother, Amelita. In these calls he would suggest that his Uncle Freddie was involved in the murders. Tawas detectives thought Sef told her this because he believed her to be a soft touch.

What Sef was probably unaware of was that his grandmother, like her daughter Emily, had by this stage become highly suspicious of Sef. The dignified, intensely private woman had been left with a deep sense of loss and sadness after the deaths of her daughter, son-in-law and granddaughter. The grief had etched itself on her face. But she was far from a soft touch. The 67-year-old woman's mind was sharp as a tack.

Amelita had suffered considerable hardship in life. She had raised and provided for six children in the Philippines. She had cared for her husband, Simeon, when he suffered multiple strokes late in life, gradually resulting in complete paralysis and later in a permanent vegetative state. This caring had worn her down, causing her to become ill, and there were times when she had to be hospitalised alongside her husband. Her concerned children convinced her to apply for a visa to the country she had visited and loved — Australia. While residency for herself and her children Edmund and Liza was approved, her husband's application was refused on medical grounds. Her children assured her that the move would be good for her, and Annie said she would care for Simeon in the Philippines. It was a tough, painful decision to make, but she separated in 1987 from her life partner, who died in 1992. Amelita Claridades had known adversity, but she was a survivor.

If she did not want to let on to Sef that she thought he was involved, it was because she was extremely fearful of her grandson. This, however, did not stop her from assisting police with some tantalising clues to possible motives for the murders. Aside from Emily, Amelita knew more than anyone about the dynamics within Loiva's family. Living only metres from their Collins Street home, she popped in all the time. Loiva would confide family problems to Amelita — sometimes in secret, if Teddy had asked her not to tell anyone outside the immediate family.

Amelita had made a statement to police on 16 July 2001 — the same day as Sef was doing his walk-through reconstruction at the murder scene — in which she told police that Clodine had been sent to Melbourne because she was caught out lying to her parents about her relationship with Chris Fernstat. However, she told police, she believed Teddy, Loiva and the children had all got along well since then and 'there were no problems within the family'. She had not wanted to believe her grandson could have had anything to do with the killings at that time.

Over the following two months, Paul Auglys had been heartened by the fact that Emily was coming around to trusting the police. So he gave Amelita a call, using his dealings with Amelita's daughter as a reference, and asked whether Amelita would mind attending Gladesville police station.

On 18 September, Amelita, who by this stage had moved to Melbourne due to her fear of Sef, was back in Sydney staying with Emily. She went into Gladesville police station to speak to Auglys. He could see, beyond the slight language difficulty, that the grandmother was no fool, and he found her quite cooperative.

Amelita told Auglys that day that she now believed her former statement that the family had not been experiencing any problems was untrue. She told Auglys that Loiva had often confided in her about 'issues' within the family, in particular problems she was experiencing with her children, and the methods she and Teddy adopted to deal with these problems. Amelita had told Loiva she disagreed with some of these methods, but her headstrong daughter had continued to do what she thought best in raising her children.

'One of the ways that Loiva and Teddy would show they were not happy with Sef and Clodine was by disowning them,' Amelita told Auglys in her second statement. She said she did not know of any occasion in which Sef was 'disowned' but she did know Loiva and Teddy were 'very disappointed' with Sef just before the murders due to his poor university grades.

'Sef had been caught by Loiva and Teddy changing his university grades after he offered to Clodine to do the same for her,' Amelita revealed. 'When Sef said this to Clodine she told her mother, who told Teddy, and they were very angry with Sef. Loiva told me that if Sef's grades didn't improve by next grade time then they were going to take the green Ford Festiva off Sef and make him catch the bus. Sef loves his car and would have been devastated if they took it off him. I know that he spent quite a bit of his money making modifications to the green Ford and he loved it.'

Amelita revealed she had spoken to Teddy about this issue and Teddy had expressed extreme disappointment in Sef, telling her he did not know why he worked so hard when Sef did not. 'He said that he was thinking of selling his business and moving to Queensland and leaving Sef and Clodine to live by themselves. I do not know if Teddy had said this to Sef and Clodine.'

Police got their first clue as to the timing of the murders when Amelita said that Sef's term grades were due to be given to his parents just after the time the killings occurred. At the end of June, Loiva had discussed the issue of Sef's results with Amelita and said she and Teddy were waiting to see them before deciding whether to discipline Sef. 'I do not believe that Sef had a very happy childhood in the Philippines or in Australia because of the pressure his parents put him under,' Amelita explained.

Then police learned of Sef's bed-wetting, and the fact that he had refused professional help for the problem. Amelita told police that Loiva had informed Sef he could never get married until he stopped this habit, as 'it was grounds for divorce'.

'Loiva told me that Sef thought that she was not supporting him and that she was putting him down.'

Amelita also gave police an insight into Sef and Clodine's sibling rivalry, particularly in relation to their scholastic results. 'I know that Loiva and Teddy put pressure on both Clodine and Sef equally and because of this Sef and Clodine turn everything into a competition. Clodine told me about a week before she was murdered that Sef was trying to interrupt her studies. She said that Sef would bang on her door while she was trying to study and come into her room and constantly interrupt her.'

The period Clodine was referring to was when Loiva had been taken to hospital for food poisoning. Sef would come into Clodine's room and 'pretend' to be sick.

'In my opinion Sef was interrupting Clodine because Teddy and Loiva were very pleased with the way that Clodine's studies were going and he did not want her to get a higher grade than he did in the HSC,' Amelita said.

She mentioned the incident that Emily also recalls, in which Sef took a knife from the kitchen and 'pretended to be crazy in an attempt to scare Loiva', stabbing the table with the knife. According to Amelita, Loiva told Sef to 'stop acting like he is crazy and that she is not scared'.

Amelita also suggested Sef's statement to police — that when he saw his chihuahua tied up outside the night of the murders he knew no-one was home — was a lie. She herself had often seen the dog tied up outside until late at night when the family was home.

She also poured cold water on the idea that the wealthy Filipino businessman whom Sef had implicated in the murders would have reason to know Teddy. '[This businessman] is very wealthy and I doubt if Teddy would have ever dealt with him due to our middle-class status in the Philippines,' she said.

The final paragraph of her statement was the most intriguing of all.

'The only other thing I can think of that I think the police should know is that I remember that Loiva told me that Clodine was able to get around Sef's passwords in his personal computer and see what he had been doing on it. Loiva told me that Clodine found something on the computer that Sef was doing and she told her about it. I cannot remember what she found but I don't think it was a very big matter.'

Clodine might simply have found out that Sef had been accessing pornography on the web. Had she discovered the web searches later found by police, she would have been in for a much bigger shock. Sef's research on poisonous seeds and how to kill someone had continued up until 9 July, the day before the murders. However, he was knowledgeable, to a certain degree, about how to protect various documents inside his computer from prying eyes.

It will probably never be known whether Clodine found these searches on poisons, or told her parents about them. It is important to note, though, that Clodine would have had every opportunity during the day of 10 July 2001, while she was at home and Sef was at his father's law office, to search his computer. As mentioned previously, police obtained telephone records that showed she would have had telephone contact with her parents that day after Sef left home for his father's office. A call to Cumberland Psychiatric Hospital from Teddy's workplace followed this contact with Clodine.

Police could only speculate on what Clodine had told her parents in this telephone contact. It could have been about perfectly pedestrian matters. But police knew she had a tendency to 'dob' on Sef in order to curry favour with her parents; she had already told them he faked his grades, and she let them know when he wet his bed.

Had Sef found out about his sister's snooping on his personal computer — whatever she had found — it most likely would have sent him into panic, and filled him with rage towards his sister. This rage may have festered inside him as he drove home from his father's office to 6 Collins Street on the afternoon of 10 July, while Clodine sat studying at her neatly arranged bedroom desk, with her back facing the door.

According to Detective Paul Auglys, the theory that Clodine's 'dobbing' had sparked Sef to go into a violent frenzy that day was kicked around between Tawas officers a number of times. They thought it was more likely Clodine had told her parents that day that Sef had been accessing pornography, or wetting his bed again, than about her having discovered the poisons material — and that Teddy had called Sef to account for this while Sef was at his office.

Unfortunately, all but one of the people who could explain to police what really happened were dead. And Sef certainly wasn't likely to tell them.

Chapter 29

A prostitute, a taxi driver and a second alibi

In early January 2002, Paul Auglys paid a visit to Don McGregor. McGregor had become close to Sef since his family's murder, and was something of a sounding board for him. McGregor would always try to cheer up Sef and just be there if his 'bro' needed a chat.

Auglys told McGregor that police did not believe Sef's alibi because of the two separate sightings of Sef's car at the scene, one about 4.30 pm by Teddy's client and the one about 6 pm by Emily. Auglys told McGregor Sef would be arrested imminently for the murders of his family. Auglys knew McGregor would pass this information on to Sef. Auglys sat back and waited for the next development. Of course, McGregor reported this startling news to Sef almost immediately.

Within the next few days, Auglys noticed with growing interest, as he monitored Sef's phone calls, that Sef, who paid occasional visits to brothels for sex, was all of a sudden very interested in the workings of the brothel industry. In particular, he was interested in the prices of various services and the rosters of brothels on Sydney's North Shore.

On 8 January 2002, at 11.07 pm, Sef, from his home phone, called La Petite Aroma brothel at Chatswood, where he was a client from before the murders, and asked for the names of girls who worked there.

At 11.11 pm, Sef called Willoughby's Interlude brothel. He asked the woman who took his call about the brothel's rates. The woman told Sef they charged $60 for a half hour and $100 for a full hour for body-to-body massage. For full service it would cost $100 for half an hour and $150 for one hour.

At 11.19 pm, Sef was on the phone to the Club 350 brothel at Chatswood, enquiring about rates. He was told it was $75 for half an hour, $110 for three-quarters of an hour and $135 for an hour. Sef asked if the girls there provided full service, to which he was told that for $75 he would not get sex, and that they did not do full service, only massage.

At 11.21 pm, Sef's fingers were still doing the walking, as he called Chandalay brothel at Roseville. Again he enquired about rates and services. Sef then asked if there were any women working that night, and was told there were four girls on shift.

Two days later, 10 January 2002, was a busy day for Sef. At 11.01 am, Sef sent an SMS text message to a prostitute at La Petite Aroma, with whom he had had sex before. He referred to her by her working name, Latisha (not her actual working name, nor her real name). It read:

> hi latisha ... happy new yr! I wish I knew ur real name:) would like to catch up with u sometime ... lunch or dinner ... when are u free?

The message had possibly been prompted when Sef sighted Latisha as she crossed the road at Chatswood at 10 am that morning. He had called out to her, but she had pretended not to notice him.

At lunchtime, Sef met McGregor at a chicken shop in the city, and mentioned having a matter of a sensitive nature to discuss. The pair went for a stroll in Hyde Park and Sef confided that he had a new alibi that could clear his name. McGregor was the first person to whom Sef confessed that his first alibi — about driving out to Raf De Leon's place — was a lie. He told McGregor he had actually parked his car at home after returning from his dad's office. Then he had walked to a service station on the main road near his home, caught a taxi to a Chatswood brothel and spent some time there, before catching a cab back home.

At 2.26 pm, La Petite Aroma's receptionist received a call later traced to a public phone booth at Chatswood. A male voice told her he was Detective Mike Rogers, from Gladesville police station. He was investigating a murder that had taken place in July, and the main suspect claimed to have been at La Petite Aroma during the murders. Did they have surveillance camera footage and the names of the women on duty that night? The canny receptionist said she could only take his number and get the owner to ring him back. He left a false mobile number. Police later confirmed there was no Mike Rogers attached to Gladesville police.

Twelve minutes later, Sef was at his Chatswood unit, calling Interlude brothel again. He again asked how long the brothel had been open and was told only a couple of weeks. He seemed to lose interest and got off the line.

At 3.41 pm, McGregor called Sef. Their conversation revolved around the subject of their lunchtime discussion in the city. Sef said he had organised to see his lawyer the following day. He stressed to McGregor that their conversations were to go no further than the two of them. He said if he decided to commit to the second alibi, he wanted it to 'go smoothly'.

'So anyway, go and investigate it, but then I think you need to volunteer it to them,' McGregor advised Sef.

Sef agreed. 'But, but then yeah, once again, you know, I haven't made my final decision on it, you know,' he told McGregor. He confessed concern that volunteering this new alibi to police could come back to bite him.

''Cause the only thing I'm afraid of is that thing we talked about today, if it doesn't tally. You know what I mean? Like it, it could blow up in my face again, you know. Like if it doesn't, if it's not solid enough as an alibi. Like you know, for one thing, if the person isn't found or doesn't remember. Like, there's so many problems, you know. But that's the only thing that worries me,' Sef said.

After they got off the phone McGregor got to considering what Sef had told him, and his mind began to work over the potential problems with Sef's story. He was trying to support his friend, but even McGregor could see there were too many unanswered questions in the alibi, too many holes, things Sef would need to clarify. He typed up a two-page document, full of cross-examination style questions he thought Sef should read through. It was quite comprehensive, with questions such as:

- *What time did he park there [at home]?*
- *How long did it take to walk to the service station?*
- *Was the taxi he flagged down on the street or in the service station?*
- *Who was the girl at the brothel?*
- *What did he 'have done' at the brothel?*
- *Where did he hail the taxi from to go home?*
- *How did he intend to explain to his parents why his car was there for hours and he wasn't?*

- *Why did he lie about his whereabouts that day?*
- *Why is he now telling the truth?*

McGregor also suggested that Sef would need a statement from the girl at the brothel, a statement from the brothel management, taxi records of pick-up and delivery each way and the times of these, video footage of him in Chatswood at that time, and to chase up whether the girl's hair and DNA were on the clothing he had given to police.

The document complete, McGregor called Sef at 5.28 pm. He said he had typed up a 'cross-examination thing'. He offered to fax it through to Sef and Sef agreed this was a good idea. 'You're an angel, brother,' Sef told his friend gratefully.

The next morning, 11 January, the fax had not come through and Sef spoke to McGregor again, saying he would try to pick it up in person.

Of course, all this activity was coming across the police telephone intercepts. Sheehy decided to pay Sef a visit at his unit, arriving there at 3.30 pm. Sheehy bluntly told Sef he believed he was not telling the truth about the murders, that he believed Sef was responsible for them, and that he would be arrested soon.

Sef, confronted with this statement from the officer he thought believed in him, replied that he did indeed have information he was holding back, because it was demeaning to him and his family. He wanted to consult his lawyers. Sheehy told Sef he should be interviewed by police about this new information.

Sef's mind must have been spinning at this revelation. It was one thing to hear it second-hand from McGregor, but from Sheehy it must have really hit home. What could he do to protect himself? Time was running out for him.

The next day, 12 January, Sef took a stroll down to Chatswood railway station, where he approached a taxi driver, Alan Altano (not his real name), and asked him to come around the corner so he could have a chat. He would pay him $50 for his time. He then asked Altano to write a statement for him verifying that Altano had driven him from North Ryde to Chatswood in July 2001.

Sef assured Altano the statement was not regarding anything serious to do with the law, and Altano, an elderly man who spoke halting English, assumed young Sef had simply got into some strife with his girlfriend and needed the statement to sweet-talk her around. Ripping a piece of paper from his diary, Altano scrawled the words:

I declare that I picked up Sef Gonzales from Shell Service station at Wicks Road, North Ryde in the second week of July last year and dropped him at Chatswood Station.

At Sef's request, Altano backdated the statement to 7 October 2001.

On 14 January, McGregor rang Sef. Sef seemed full of confidence, and said that he had good news about what had been happening. He said he would be able to substantiate what they had discussed. McGregor asked if he had got the necessary witnesses, and Sef said he had, at least partially. He stressed that he needed to package the whole alibi properly, so it would be 'foolproof'. The next day, he would meet McGregor to show him the statement he had obtained, telling McGregor he'd had it since October 2001.

In the following two days, Sef would speak to Altano a number of times on the phone, and tell Altano that he would send him a copy of the handwritten statement he had provided.

Detective Auglys listened keenly to the tapped phone calls, and it wasn't long before Tawas officers paid the cabbie a visit. Altano, worried about what he had got himself involved in, would spill the beans to police on what had really transpired. Police told him to maintain contact with Sef but to take careful notes on what they spoke about. The last thing they wanted was Sef finding out they knew he was in the process of working on a second alibi.

On 18 January, while Detective Brian O'Donaghue was paying Sef an early visit at his Chatswood unit, Sef told the detective about being with a prostitute on the evening of the murders.

By 9 am, Sef was on the phone to Mick Sheehy. Sef said his instinct told him to trust Sheehy, but he was concerned about police corruption and whether the other officers on Tawas were trustworthy. Sheehy assured Sef they were all professional cops.

Sef told Sheehy that on the night of his first statement, while his relatives were present, he couldn't tell them exactly what had happened, because they thought he was a virgin. And he originally had thought his family members had all died after 8 pm, so what did a lie about his movements before that time matter? Also, he was so terribly ashamed of having been with a prostitute the day his family was killed.

Sef said he already had a statement from one of the taxi drivers, and he had an idea who the prostitute was, but he was only about 70 per cent sure. He was confident he could recognise the other cab driver, but he had yet to find him. He was prepared to give police his full version after consulting with his lawyers.

Sef then brought up the subject of the plant poisons and admitted it was he who had researched them, but it was to kill himself, not his family. (Sef had told numerous friends he suffered cancer in the year leading up to his family's deaths, but in reality he had never been diagnosed with the disease.)

'When I had that episode with [Kathy], basically I was with her for two weeks. That night we slept together she basically told me that she had a boyfriend and that she was breaking up with me and that it was a one-night stand . . .

'Every moment after that I deteriorated. I went into self-destruct mode and I was planning to take my life. My grades had gone downhill and the only thing stopping me was I could not bear the thought of the pain I'd give my parents if I committed suicide. And that's why I did those months of research to get that plant. Because if I took that, it was a sure way of killing myself without being detected and wouldn't look like suicide, because it would have the same symptoms as cancer.'

Sheehy asked if Sef had actually obtained the plant.

'I had a sample and I managed to make a potion. I was just fermenting it . . . from my research I found out that [the poison] would slowly kill my organs and basically would look like cancer. So even with my friends I told them that I had cancer because I could not bear the thought of them going through the pain of me committing suicide.'

Sheehy told Sef the reason he was under so much suspicion was because he had told lies. It was important now that he told Tawas detectives the truth. He informed Sef he would be waiting to hear back from him, after he had spoken to his lawyers.

The following day, Sheehy would get an SMS from Sef. It read:

> *I am sorry I wasn't completely honest at the start . . . pls give me another chance and a little more understanding. Thank you for being open-minded.*

ON 28 MARCH 2002, Geoff Leonard was driving home along a freeway late one night when he received a call on his mobile phone from Sef's uncle and godfather, Edmund Claridades, ringing from Queensland's Gold Coast. Pulling over to the side of the road, Leonard listened to what Edmund had to say. It was very interesting indeed.

Edmund by this stage had heard via the family grapevine that Sef was formulating a second alibi, revolving around being with the Chatswood prostitute at the time of the murders. By now Edmund strongly suspected that Sef was involved in the murders, but was careful about confiding in family members because he did not want it to get back to Sef. But he could see how ridiculous it was for Sef to have maintained a false alibi for more than six months, preferring to remain a murder suspect rather than confess he had been with a prostitute. Edmund wanted to help the investigators get to the bottom of this.

On 27 March, Sef had made telephone contact with Edmund and said he was coming to the Gold Coast, and that he needed his uncle's help to decide something. Edmund offered to wear a wire for the police to record his conversations with Sef when he came to visit.

There were two advantages to using Edmund in this regard. First, as Sef's godfather, or *ninong* as a godfather is called in Tagalog, he held an important position in Sef's life. Sef might very well confide in his godfather, when he would not confide in other relatives.

There was also another distinct advantage. In Queensland, it was perfectly legal, without a warrant, to record a conversation with another person if one party consented to that recording. Any admissions Sef made during a visit to Queensland could still be used in a New South Wales court. Edmund was a willing party, and Leonard thought it was a promising idea.

Leonard made contact with the Queensland police, requesting they pay a visit to Edmund, discussing how the scenario might go down.

Unfortunately, Sef appeared to have struck car trouble in northern New South Wales and informed his uncle later the same day that he could no longer visit. Edmund had another idea, however. As an electrician, he was able to create his own telephone recording device. By disassembling a hands-free mobile phone kit, creating two microphones, and utilising a Handycam camera, he could record both his own voice and the voice of whomever he was speaking to on the telephone.

Between 3 and 9 April 2002, Edmund had a number of telephone conversations in Tagalog with his nephew, while his recording device rolled. During these conversations Sef continued his lies about his movements on the night of the murders. Most enlightening, though, was that Sef admitted to his godfather that his life had been spiralling out of control in the lead-up to the murders.

Sef admitted his parents had been restricting his use of his car, and said that on the night of the murders he had had special permission from his mother to use the car only because it was for Sam Dacillo's birthday celebrations. He had sneakily used his car despite his mother's ban at other times, he admitted.

EDMUND: I don't know, especially in that stage that you said the car is yours, that's why you can do as you please, that [is] still not true because I know … you're on the borderline that the car is to be taken from you.

SEF: At that stage I was on the borderline, *po [a Tagalog term of respect]*, I admit that, but at that day I was given permission to take the car and I know it was selfish and it was wrong …

In the course of the conversations Sef also admitted just how hard he had taken the break-up with Kathy Wu.

SEF: Mama doesn't approve of her.
EDMUND: Who, this [Kathy]?
SEF: Yes, she doesn't, Mama does not like her.
EDMUND: Hmm.
SEF: Because she is older than me, then she has a different religion.
EDMUND: Hmm.
SEF: But at that time, I thought, I really thought, that is, I really fell in love with her, I thought, I thought, that she really is the one.
EDMUND: Umm.
SEF: That even to Mama I defended her. Papa did not say anything about it. And that even to Mama I defended her.
EDMUND: Hmm.
SEF: Then even to Grandma, I told her I think, this is it.

Sef told his uncle he lost his virginity to Kathy and went on to say he really 'lost a lot' when Kathy broke up with him.

SEF: Anyway, at that stage it's hard to explain, but everything about me went downhill, all my grades failed, so basically my life went upside down. It's like I feel I'm trapped, that I don't know what to do, because I cannot study, then I feel like I'm getting deeper and deeper.

Sef told his uncle how he had felt suicidal and that he had researched a biological warfare drug that mimics the effects of cancer in the body. He was going to commit suicide — but not before going to a brothel. He elaborated on his brothel alibi to his uncle.

During this exercise, Edmund had probably come as close as anyone to tapping into the despair Sef had been feeling in the lead-up to the murders — although the way Sef told it, the despair caused him to feel suicidal rather than murderous. These words from Sef's own mouth added strongly to the evidence of motive — that Sef had killed his family due to the unravelling of his life.

Chapter 30

Linda Pham

Sef did not make any further moves to shore up his alibi until 27 March 2002. This could possibly be explained by his meeting a young woman by the name of Linda Pham (not her real name), a university student, and becoming distracted.

She first met Sef on 9 January 2002, while at Bondi Beach with some friends. The two got to chatting, and she became his girlfriend. The relationship progressed so quickly that they became engaged just two weeks afterwards, on 21 January.

Sef had told Linda about the misery he had gone through at the hands of Kathy Wu, and another fictitious girlfriend called Daisy, the 'mystery woman' on the website he had created several years earlier. He was heartbroken, he told Linda, deeply depressed and considering suicide, and Linda wanted to make it all better.

Sef confided in Linda that he'd been going to take a particular poison on the night of his family's murder, having concocted it using hot water and storing it in a bedroom. The poison would be untraceable in his system. He had gone to see a prostitute, he told her, because, filled with self-loathing, he had wanted to do the dirtiest thing possible before going home to drink the poison. He told Linda that even in the depths of his despair he had managed to perform well sexually with the prostitute; so spectacularly, in fact, that the prostitute had tried to give him a freebie, but he had pressed the money upon her, insisting that she be paid.

Sef told Linda he had been sitting around Chatswood near the taxi stand where, as luck would have it, after a few days he'd spotted the taxi driver who had taken him to the brothel. He asked her to post a photocopy of the statement to the taxi driver, which she dutifully did. She believed that Sef had been hardly done by, that the police were out to get him, and she wanted to do anything she could to help him.

On the night of 27 March, when Linda was about to take a shower, Sef told her to drop everything — they had to go and meet someone. 'This might be the girl I was with that night!' he told her.

That day, there had been a flurry of SMS messages between Sef and the prostitute Latisha — nineteen in all. Latisha had messaged Sef that she did not 'do privates' and could not talk, but Sef insisted on communicating with her.

> *Don't even know ur real name ... I don't want any of that ... I need ur help to prove my honesty ... can I pls meet with you, with my girlfriend. Pls. Can I call u pls?*

Late that night, Sef drove Linda to the New Orleans Café in Crows Nest, where he left her to order coffees while he and Latisha strolled to a nearby bus stop.

Latisha was not even sure she had been working on the evening of the murders, but Sef was insistent that he recognised her as the girl he had been with that night. He seemed nice, and Latisha wanted to help him. She told him that it would be his responsibility to check the brothel records to see if she was on that night, then they could take it from there.

Later, as Latisha hopped into the back of Sef's car, Linda observed a look of relief on Sef's face. He turned around and said to Latisha: 'You remember me, don't you?' and Latisha replied, 'Yes I do.'

In the days following, Sef persisted in sending Latisha SMS messages, putting pressure on her to check the records. Latisha began to get annoyed: if she approached her female boss, she would think Latisha was meeting clients privately and Latisha would get the sack. She had a young son to support. She urged Sef simply to visit the brothel himself.

Sef went to the brothel on the night of 2 April. He explained to the receptionist that he was Sef Gonzales, that his family had been murdered on 10 July 2001, and that he wanted to see the girls so he could recognise which one he had been with at the time. He said he thought the girl's name was Latisha.

He then went through a charade with Latisha as a minidisc he'd strapped to his leg recorded their conversation. Sef wanted proof that Latisha remembered him. (After his arrest, Linda found the recording under his couch and provided it to the police, through her lawyers.)

SEF: So you do remember me?

LATISHA: Yeah, yeah.

SEF: So as soon as they check the record and they are 100 per cent sure that you were working, then you will be 100 per cent sure you remember me?

LATISHA: Yeah. I am worried.

SEF: But right now you are about 80 per cent, not 100 per cent.

LATISHA: I do remember, I do remember, but I am just not sure if I was working or not.

Before going, Sef left his name and number with the receptionist so he could speak to the manager about the rosters. He was told to expect a call back either that night or the following day.

The next day, 3 April, the owner rang Sef, who explained what he needed. The police were onto him by this stage, and checked the rosters themselves. Latisha had been listed to work on 10 July 2001, but had cancelled all her shifts that week. Later, Latisha would remember that she had asked for the week off because it was school holidays and she needed to be home to look after her son.

Police enlisted an undercover female officer to contact Sef, posing as a book-keeper for La Petite Aroma. On 10 April, in her broad Aussie accent, she informed him there was no record Latisha had worked that night. Sef seemed taken aback, disbelieving, and incredibly disappointed. But he had committed himself, and it was too late to back out now. If his second alibi fell apart, he was in a world of trouble.

That day, as his desperation increased, he text-messaged Latisha. The previous day, 9 April, sick of his harassment, she had sent him the message:

Do not bother me any more, I've done what I can.

Upon hearing that the records did not check out, he adopted a more threatening tone:

[Latisha] I don't know wat ur boss has said but what u r doing is unfair. I taped our conversations to prove I didn't bribe. Will u help with a statement to end this?

Latisha, who was by now ruing the day she ever met Sef Gonzales, did not reply.

The next message from Sef came a little over a minute later:

Or do I just use the tape and do this the long hard way 4 both of us?

Sef's barrister, Peter Kintominas, provided police with a signed draft statement containing Sef's new alibi on 22 May. Although specified times were omitted, it allowed for the fact Teddy's client had seen Sefs car parked at Collins Street around 4.30 pm (as Sef had been informed of by police), but that Sef had not been at the house at the time.

He said that after driving home from his father's law practice he had parked in the carport, not going inside, as he did not believe anyone to be home. He left the car and walked down Collins Street into Wicks Road, and into the Shell service station. He got a taxi as it pulled into the service station. He went to Chatswood. He said he did not want to drive to Chatswood for two reasons: he did not want his car with its personalised numberplates recognised, and he would have trouble getting parking.

Entering the brothel, he was told he had to wait, and eventually requested a 40-minute session. After he left the brothel, he walked to the Chatswood taxi stand in Railway Street and hopped in a cab, travelling home. After being dropped off, he did not go inside the house, but drove straight to Sam Dacillo's house.

BY NOW, PAUL AUGLYS felt he probably knew Sef better than anyone else in the world had ever known him. Every weekday, and most weekends, he would come into work and slip on the headphones, catching up with the ongoing soap opera that was Sef Gonzales' life. From late July 2001, when intercepts were first granted on both Sef's mobile phone and landline, until Sef's arrest, Auglys would listen to some 8000 intercepted phone calls involving Sef Gonzales. It had become his entertainment, picking up the headphones of a morning and wondering what the little bugger was up to now.

He had never met Sef face to face and felt confident Sef would not pick him if he crossed his path in the street. But he felt he had got inside Sef's head during the course of the investigation, and in his dealings with key witnesses. He knew where Sef liked to go out, sticking to his usual comfort zones, such as a Japanese noodle bar in Chatswood and the ground-floor café at Chatswood Chase shopping centre. He knew that Sef had only a small group of friends, including Don McGregor and Dennis Pedro. He knew Sef frequented Connections nightclub in the city. He knew Sef had gone to the club's opening shortly after the murders, and felt comfortable there.

Once Auglys and Detective Gavin Wicks had gone to the club to check it out. The doorman had told him, 'Mate, it's $20 to get in.' Auglys had said 'No worries', handing over the cash and entering with Wicks. The tall officers stood out like sore thumbs. The place was crowded with diminutive people — Sef was one of them — and he and Wicks seemed to be the only ones who drank beer. No wonder the doorman had tried to warn them. The officers soon decided they should leave; they did not really fit the scene.

Auglys knew that Kathy Wu, who had appeared appalled when police had informed her about Sef's lies soon after the murders, had got on the phone to Sef straight afterwards and told him about the interview. She even continued seeing him for about a month before things fizzled out. He knew about the girls who followed, that Sef had a way of pulling the 'poor me' act to reel the ladies in. One of them, an immature schoolgirl, had not lasted very long. While Sef poured out his troubles, lamenting his family's murders, telling her how alone he felt, the schoolgirl would cut in with a totally irrelevant, trivial remark, and Sef would complain she wasn't listening to him. Better for her, Auglys supposed, that Sef soon grew tired of her. Not only for her own safety, but the phone bills — sometimes the calls lasted five hours — must have been through the roof.

He knew about Sef's imaginary friend Rico, with whom Sef said he worked at a factory. Linda Pham would hear a lot about this mysterious — and nonexistent — friend, whom Sef would refer to as a really dangerous character, a real tough guy.

He knew of Sef and Linda's arguments about her going out at night. One time when Linda went to a rave party at Homebush without Sef, he observed Sef trying to get his own back on her. Throughout the night, Sef would use his mobile continually to call Linda, pretending to be totally drugged out. 'Help me, Rico,' he would slur, before hanging up, then would do the same thing again and again. 'My battery's dying, Rico.' He'd hang up again. The whole time he was calling from the Chatswood area, probably home in bed, Auglys surmised.

It wasn't until 8 am the following day that Linda was concerned enough about Sef's safety to tell him she was going to contact the police. Sef called her straightaway, telling her in a normal voice that he was fine and at home now. He told her he had been out at a North Sydney bar with his mate Rico and some girls had begun chatting to him. Rico had wanted to go home but Sef decided to stay. The girls must have slipped something into his drink, because the next thing he knew he was waking up in a strange house, naked. Pure fiction. Pure Sef, Auglys reflected.

Auglys also knew what Sef thought of him. Auglys was the shadow, the cop who stirred up trouble by approaching all of Sef's friends and family, leaving his name and contact details, making them suspect Sef of murder. Whenever these friends would tell Sef about being approached by Auglys, Sef would explain that he was one of the new detectives assigned to the case, implying Auglys didn't really know that much about it.

Auglys did not visit Linda Pham until a few months into her relationship with Sef, but in the end decided the police had a duty of care to warn her that Sef was strongly suspected of committing the murders, for her own safety. He was well aware that Sef had sucked her in, but he couldn't quite believe that she did not suspect Sef's guilt.

On 7 March 2002, Auglys and Detective Mick O'Brien had paid a visit to Linda at her university, to try to get it through to her that Sef was a suspect in a triple-murder investigation. Linda was not very cooperative, telling police she knew about Sef's true movements on the evening of the murders, but would not tell them to the police until Sef himself was ready to give them the whole story.

Straightaway, Auglys had noticed Pham was wearing a pink diamond ring and earrings and he recognised them as having belonged to Loiva. As soon as he mentioned the jewellery, she put her hand protectively over the ring, obscuring it from the officers' view. Auglys told Linda the jewellery had belonged to Sef's mother and that he'd had no right to give it to her — it was part of the estate's probate and not his to give. Linda replied that Sef had bought the items for her and refused to take them off.

To Auglys it was apparent they would get nowhere with Linda. The unpleasant meeting ended when she uttered the startling words: 'Why are you harassing me? I don't care what he did, I know that he won't kill me.'

Not long after this meeting, Linda would lose her precious ring — an engagement present from Sef — when, during an argument with him, she began hyperventilating and, weakened by having the flu, passed out. When she woke up, Sef had taken the ring from her finger.

Nevertheless she would stay in the increasingly acrimonious relationship until at least a few months after his arrest. She would continue to visit Sef in jail. But they would fight bitterly over the subject of her freedom and Sef's displeasure about her going out without him. Sef would pretend he had spies on the outside, and would know whatever Linda was doing and if she was seeing other men. In the end, it all became too much for Linda.

Chapter 31

A newspaper interview

It was Sef Gonzales' homecoming — except the scene was all wrong.

The once well-cared-for house at 6 Collins Street stood dark and silent, its vertical blinds drawn. The lawn that Teddy had kept immaculate was now overgrown. Three carnations strewn by an anonymous mourner lay on the driveway.

Sef walked towards the mailbox, overflowing with envelopes addressed to people dead eleven months. He cleared the mail then walked towards the front door, retrieving a set of keys from the pocket of his black leather jacket. He found the right key and the door swung open. He led the media crew inside to the tiled foyer.

It was 31 May 2002, and Sef had reached a decision.

Several journalists from Sydney's major media outlets had been pursuing Sef for an interview for months. The circumstances of his family's murder and the question of Sef's guilt or innocence had been ongoing subjects of newsroom discussion.

Living life under a cloud of suspicion had now become too much for Sef. The pressure of being a suspect had steadily built. He declared he wanted a story run in the media so he could clear his name and also appeal for the 'real' killer or killers of his family to be caught. His reference to his family's 'real' killers — and the suggestion 'they' were waging a campaign of intimidation against him, lest he speak out — became a common theme in Sef's informal discussions with reporters.

Of course, financial benefit may also have been a motivation. The prolonged game of cat-and-mouse with the detectives of Strike Force Tawas had left Sef frustrated and impatient. The Gonzales family estate was still frozen. Legally, Sef could not touch a cent until his name was cleared. As far as ongoing income went, he had little. He earned a meagre amount performing manual labour at a small family-run Pymble factory that produced water-filtering equipment, as well as cleaning churches. Both jobs had been organised for him by a Catholic priest, Father Paul Cahill of Killara parish.

Sef argued vigorously that he should be paid for any interview he granted — and he wanted big money. A television current affairs program, he claimed, was willing to pay him tens of thousands of dollars for his story. He said he needed to be paid so he could afford to hire security to protect himself. Once he went public with his appeal to find the killers, 'they' were bound to become enraged, and would come after him. He feared for his safety, he said.

However, few — if any — media outlets in Sydney were willing to pay for Sef's story, no matter how great a story it might be, because he was a triple-murder suspect.

I first met Sef early in 2002, over an omelette at the Chatswood Chase café he frequented. I knew next to nothing about the case, not having covered the murders to that point, but my news editor, Andy Byrne, wanted to find out if there were any developments in the case. I called Tawas police, but they were closely guarding the release of information. If they weren't talking, I thought, I may as well try Sef himself. I had been overseas when the murders occurred; this would be my

232 • *Unmasked: The Gonzales Family Killer*

first crack at covering the story and I had no preconceptions about his guilt or innocence. To me, it was just another story.

I had obtained Sef's phone number from the Internet advertisement for his father's car, and gave him a call. Speaking as gently and sympathetically as I could, I tried to encourage him to tell me about his ordeal. I wasn't trying to ascertain his guilt or innocence then, I was just trying to get the story. We agreed to meet to talk things over.

I arrived at the Chatswood café first, and was uncertain if it was Sef who was walking towards me a couple of minutes later. I was struck by how tiny he was, casually attired in jeans and a black shirt. He barely reached my shoulder. He had a thin frame and stood no taller than 160 centimetres (five feet three inches). His skin was smooth without a hint of stubble, his cheeks chubby, giving him a baby-faced look.

Hesitantly we approached each other. His handshake was soft; his manner gentle and unfailingly polite. He led me to a table and graciously pulled out a chair for me.

This was no naive boy though. I could tell almost immediately. It was because of his eyes. They gazed evenly at me as we spoke — off the record at this stage — and I could almost see his mind ticking over as he paused to carefully choose his words.

At the end of our first meeting, he told me his father had taught him to be a good judge of character, and that he trusted me. In the following weeks, I would visit him once, on my own, at his Chatswood unit. I persuaded him it would not look good if he were to profit from speaking about the death of his family — particularly as he was a prime suspect in the killings. But an appeal for information could help.

So it was that on 31 May, I, police reporter for the *Daily Telegraph*, interviewed Sef — free of charge.

THE WIND GUSTED outside the sleek glass and concrete structure of 1 Katherine Street, Chatswood late that morning.

Sef's apartment on the eleventh floor of the Bentleigh building was a short walk from the ritzy Chatswood Chase shopping centre where he liked to browse through the clothing shops or grab a coffee. The apartment had one bedroom and a balcony with city views. The complex offered high security, with an intercom to screen potential visitors and a concierge desk in the lobby.

I buzzed on the intercom for unit 96, and Sef's soft voice responded immediately. Within moments, the elevator descended from his floor and Sef stepped out to greet me and *Telegraph* photographer Nathan Edwards. Sef was wearing his trademark hip denim jeans and black designer T-shirt. His black hair had been freshly buzz-cut, but today he was not wearing his thin gold round-rimmed eyeglasses, which gave him a studious look.

Again, it came as a shock to me that this 21-year-old was suspected of committing three savage murders.

We arrived at Sef's front door, marked by the black smears of police fingerprint powder. Sef claimed there had been a break-in at his unit earlier in the week, and that he had called the police, but he asked me not to mention it in my story. I agreed.

The police were sceptical about the break-in, I later discovered. Despite the tight security in the apartment block, there had been no-one caught on the video surveillance footage. Nor had the front-desk staff witnessed anyone acting suspiciously.

Sef suggested the intruders could have come and gone via the stairwell, thus avoiding detection by cameras. He implied these were the people who were responsible for taking away his family. Now, they wanted him.

Sef's apartment reflected his meticulous personality. Everything was in order. The beige carpet was spotless, and on his dining table documents were stacked neatly.

His bedroom, too, was neatly arranged. The bed was perfectly made, with not a crease in the comforter sitting atop it. Next to the bed was his desk, and a sleek grey laptop. It was probably the third or fourth he owned since his family's murder. Sef had had his computers seized for forensic analysis by police several times. Offhandedly, he remarked it was too difficult to reclaim the computers from investigators. He just kept replacing them.

In the lounge room, the surfaces and furnishings were cluttered with flowers and furry stuffed animals, apparently gifts.

However, what was most noticeable about the whole unit was what was missing. Not a single photograph of Sef's murdered family was on display. Three perfect studio portraits of his mother, father and sister, smiling and dressed up in their best outfits, that had been placed on his bedroom windowsill during my first visit, were gone.

Sef's large balcony, which looked southwest towards the city skyline, was devoid of furniture. The only sign of visitors was a large screw-top bottle almost full of cigarette butts. Sef apparently did not smoke, but his girlfriend Linda Pham did.

As we sat on his buttercup-coloured couch, Sef offered us both a glass of water before the interview began in earnest.

Sef began by describing his suffering since his family was murdered. He described the time since the murders as a 'struggle every day'.

'It's more of a daily battle, that I just try to get through the day and you know when I get past the day then I'm happy. And I just . . . I dread the next day.

'It's very difficult because there's a lot of — there's a lot of pain and anger inside of me. And on top of that I have to deal with the speculation that surrounds me and I have to deal with the kind of remarks that are said towards me or towards my family and a lot of the pain and the anger goes towards that. You know, the pain and the anger in a way amplifies the hurt of losing them and the biggest disadvantage in that is that I haven't had a chance to grieve yet. It's stopping me from grieving because I have to deal with so much first, and I think that's the biggest disadvantage of the whole thing.'

He spoke about how he had considered his future before the murders.

'The biggest struggle I face each day is trying to rebuild what I can and trying to see the future in a different way. In a way I've tried to do that by lying to myself, being in denial, putting up a façade for people to see, for myself.

'It's all I've got to go on, that façade keeps me strong even though it puts me in denial, it's my way of trying to move on, it's my way of trying to ignore the hurt, the pain, and ignoring the grieving, trying to live a normal life. But as time goes on I realise that I am just lying to myself, and I do need to face these things.'

He told of his dreams for his family, which were now lost.

'I guess the best way to describe it is imagine knowing your whole life for twenty years, for twenty years of your life, you've got a picture of how the world is, you've got a picture of what you want for the future and that future is strong in your mind.

'Now imagine just one day, all of that being taken away. The challenge isn't just rebuilding what you can with your present world. The challenge is trying to find out, even figure out, where to begin, and the greater challenge is to try and picture the future, because my picture of the future [I had] then is impossible now.

'There's so many dreams that I had with my family, my dad had a lot of . . . I mean, we were all very ambitious, there were a lot of things that we needed to do, and wanted to do together.

'At the moment, my sort of fairytale I've got is one day, I picture myself on a fishing boat with my son and my dad. Now it's difficult to picture that future, erasing your dad from that image, and that's my example of how difficult it is to even have a picture of the future to work towards.'

His sleep was troubled, he said.

'A lot of the times I wake up in the middle of the night with a lot of frustration and anger, a lot of the times I wake up and I'm close to tears, but yet I've run out of tears to cry.'

Sef expressed frustration about people's expectations of how he should behave after such a tragedy.

'That's one of the main things I deal with each day ever since, you know, the incident. People have, you know, their own ideas of how someone should act, and it's not my place to tell people what to think.

'They've got their right to make their own judgment, but I think what's unfair is that they expect you to act in a particular way, and if you don't act in that way they judge you differently. Say, for example, I don't cry — it can be interpreted in the wrong way, or if, for example, I go to a party to try and put some normality back in my life, that gets interpreted as he's recovered too quickly. And I think that's unfair because that, and whatever rumours that you spread and speculate, that's what makes it difficult to cope with the situation.'

Sef said he believed he was being judged unfairly purely because of the statistics of family killings.

'In many ways you feel that there's no presumption of innocence. You know, instead of the concept of innocent until proven otherwise, it's otherwise until proven innocent. And I think that's an unfair thing because ... I've been told that nine out of ten of these cases usually involves either a family member or someone who knew the family, and just on those statistics alone people like myself go through that speculation already, because of those statistics. And the unfair thing about that is that they forget about the one out of the ten who are innocent and they [are] just treated as the nine out of the ten as well.'

Asked about who was making these assumptions about him, Sef said he did not wish to 'point fingers'.

'I hear things through the grapevine. Usually it's people who want a convenient resolution for themselves. I don't blame them for making their own opinions, but it's unfair that they damage someone's name, which in some ways it's irreparable when you damage someone's name. It's worse than being put behind bars … in some ways already, you're being treated like a criminal.'

However, he said he was more concerned about his dead family's memory being besmirched than his own reputation.

'To me, I'm not really that concerned about that any more, because like I said my name has already been damaged to some degree [and] it'd be a tough time fixing that. My main concern is the damage that's done to my family's name in the way that a lot of speculations have been spread about my family members and I think that's very wrong because they're not here to defend themselves. I can do my best to do that but they're not here to defend themselves.'

Talking frankly about being a suspect in the murders, Sef said he would 'just have to stretch my patience'. He said he had been through 'the process' with police.

'I can't tell police how to do their jobs, it's not my position to do so. Having said that, I can't criticise them for [doing] their jobs.

'I know there are honest detectives on the case that simply want the truth as much as I do, I just leave it to them. It's not my place to tell them what to do.'

Sef said he suspected he knew who killed his family, although he would not say outright whether he had given any names to police.

'Well, I've given them all that I know and I'll leave that up to them. But you know the best that I can do is try and assist them in some way. One of my goals at the moment is in the near future, when I am in the position to do so, I'd like to offer a substantial reward to people who may have some information that will lead to a successful conviction, that will lead to some answers.

'I know that there are people out there who either know a friend or know a relative and know something about someone regarding what happened to my family and may be afraid to speak out and I can understand that. But if they are prepared to help, then I will do whatever I can to assist them and I'm sure that the police would do what they can to help them as well.'

Asked about the estate and his financial situation, Sef said he would prefer not to elaborate.

'I think I'd prefer not to comment on the estate. Just that, it's in its own process. I'm in many ways living independent of the estate. I'm doing my best to survive on my own. Some good friends have been able to help me with some employment and I'm still studying, continuing my studies.'

However, he had cut back on his studies following the murders.

'I'm doing it by correspondence. It gives me time to work and to try and survive on my own.'

Asked if he would ever be able to work at a law firm, Sef said he did not know.

'I'm not sure where my legal studies will lead me to. It's a hurtful process to even study it sometimes because I remember my dad too much, and before, every time I was stuck on something I'd always refer to him and now that he's not there sometimes it's hurtful to even study what I'm studying now. And one of the reasons I decided to do what I'm doing is because of him. And I was doing another course previously and I got inspired by him to follow in his footsteps. And now that, you know, there's no guidance in that direction and he's no longer there . . .'

Speaking about the support he had received, Sef referred to the ongoing support of a Catholic priest. Although Sef said he did not wish to name him, it is known that Father Paul Cahill had become a very strong supporter of Sef Gonzales since the murder of his family.

'He's more of a friend than a priest to me. He's known my family for over a decade and we lost contact a little bit but we have been in close contact lately and he has helped keep me strong,' Sef said.

Asked about the work he was doing — the church cleaning and factory work — Sef said he had received limited support from the family estate, and was basically supporting himself. Obviously manual labour was a new experience for Sef.

'A lot of the work that I do is more physical things, whereas it used to be a lot of desk jobs before, and it's my way of getting away from it all sometimes.'

He said he had sought compensation from the Victims of Crime Tribunal but that a ruling had not been made. It was still pending. (In fact Sef had earlier successfully claimed about $15,000 for costs such as his family's funeral before police advised the Tribunal that he was a suspect. Thus his further application for money was rejected.)

Asked whether he stood to inherit the family home, Sef said he did not know. 'Even though I may stand to inherit it in the future, at this stage it's not my place to decide what happens to the house — it's not my house,' he said.

The inheritance, which he agreed was probably worth around $1 million, was not a priority for him, he said. People had misunderstood the whole situation with the inheritance.

'I mean I've had people assume that I'm getting a large inheritance, you know, or that I've gone away, or that I'm just spoiling myself, they don't know what I am really going through.

'I haven't left, I've decided to stay because I wanted to face all these problems. I wanted to show in some way that I'm not running or hiding. I'm trying to face these problems the best way I can.

'If they want to allude to some sort of motive to inheritance, which is not in my control, the way I see it now is that it's more of a consequence than a benefit, that causes people to speculate about it. Every person who has a parent are bound to inherit from their parents but that's not a motive to anything.'

Sef said he had deliberately isolated himself from people to protect them from the problems he was experiencing. Asked whether his relatives' attitudes towards him had changed, he said he would prefer not to go into that subject in detail.

'I've maintained a relationship with my family, they um . . . I'd be selfish if I just assumed that I was going through all the hurt and the pain. They're going through their own grieving process and their own pain. I can't judge how they act or how they react on the speculations or anything like that because it's not my place to judge them. They've got their own healing to do and meantime I have to try to heal as well.'

He indicated he had learned who his real friends were through the ordeal.

'I've learned a lot about friendship through the months and I've learned a lot about trust, about who my real friends were, and I really thank them from the bottom of my heart for being there.'

He said he used to visit the family home to try to erase the images in his head of his family's bodies that night. But it did not work. He had not been back to the house for 'a while'.

'My images of that night are so very vivid to this day, and I don't think trying to forget them helps, because I have tried everything I can to do that but I can't deny myself that it's something that I need to accept.'

He said one of his main 'driving forces' was to set up a foundation in the memory of his family. He wanted to call it the TLCS Foundation, with the letters representing the initials of each family member. He wanted the foundation to raise funds for charities such as the House With No Steps, victims of crime, Kids Help Line, children's hospitals and cancer research. His father, Sef said, was devoted to charity work. He hoped this would spread some good from the 'evil' that had befallen his family.

'In some ways I've given up trying to make sense of the tragedy. I guess the best I can do is try and get some good out of it. Maybe that's a positive step if I try and do that.'

Sef said he would stay and fight to clear his name, and finalise this 'unfinished chapter' in his life. He hoped that after that, he could begin to heal from the trauma.

He finished the interview with a public appeal. He indicated that he was speaking to his lawyers about offering a six-figure sum for information about who murdered his family. Sef asked, and the *Daily Telegraph* agreed, to publish an e-mail address that anyone with information could contact.

'I know that somewhere out there, there is someone who knows something about someone, whether it be a friend or a relative who's afraid to speak out for whatever understandable reasons. Like I said, I'll do whatever I can and I'm sure the police would do whatever they can to assist whoever is brave enough to come forward with information.

'And I just want to leave them with one last phrase which my dad shared with me, and that's: "There's no softer pillow when you go to sleep at night than a clear conscience."

'And I think that if they take that to heart, it might give them a bit of courage,' he concluded.

THREE GRAVES IN a row, set amongst the plush green lawns and winding driveways of Macquarie Park Memorial Cemetery. The resting place for the Gonzales family was only a five-minute drive from Sef's new home at Chatswood.

Sef kneeled in front of his family's graves for the photographer, his black leather jacket and jeans contrasting starkly with the lavenders, light pinks and deep violets of the posies clustered around the headstones. His demeanour was calm. His elbow propped against one knee, he stared at the inscriptions as if lost in thought. He did not cry, nor did he speak.

Sef had agreed to the photograph, which would accompany the story based on his interview earlier that day. It was a macabre, uncomfortable task, but this was the most powerful image to illustrate the story.

Later that afternoon, Sef told us, Harry Potter from Channel Ten would also interview him at the grave site for the five o'clock news. It was a situation the *Daily Telegraph* was not entirely happy with. The story would no longer be an exclusive. Sef understood this, but said he had promised Potter he would be able to film there. He was steadfast, refusing to budge. We would not find out until many months later that Sef had been stringing us along: he had already done his interview with Harry Potter that morning before we arrived at Chatswood.

Sef then volunteered to take us to the house where his family had been murdered. Inside, the house was dark and musty. Belongings lay stacked in a haphazard fashion, as if someone had been interrupted in the process of moving.

The tiled foyer where Teddy had been found by police led to a nearly bare lounge–dining room on the left. This was where Loiva Gonzales had been found.

To the left of the foyer there was a small room — a study — where boxes and various personal effects were stashed. Here, Sef located a number of family photograph albums. We had requested some family shots. While we waited in the foyer, Sef flicked through the photographs, producing two dated ones.

The first showed the Gonzales family on a skiing holiday. Rugged up in their ski gear against the brisk weather, a happy couple were clearly enjoying watching their two young children at play.

The second photograph was taken at the family's house in Blacktown. A small Sef, dressed in a light blue jumper declaring 'I Love Soccer', was unsmiling, as his father, wearing shaded glasses, hugged him. Teddy wore a grin. Also smiling were Loiva to his right and a young Clodine.

One happy family.

Sef then led us to a central wooden staircase. It spiralled upstairs, onto a landing. This was the floor where Clodine had been found, in her bedroom, slumped against a wall near her bed. In a central area connecting the bedrooms were stacks of colourful women's clothing, which Loiva had taken so much pride in.

A table with religious ornaments was pushed up near a door. 'The police must have moved it,' Sef said distractedly, dragging it across the wooden floorboards and pushing it against the rail of the staircase. 'This is where my mother used to pray with her rosary. It's right in the centre of the house,' he said. He allowed us to take photographs as he stood beside the table, with its statue of the Virgin Mary and other religious symbols.

Clearly, the visit was taking its toll on Sef. Photographs taken, he sat down on the stairs and asked for a few minutes to himself. We walked back down the staircase and through the front door as Sef cradled his face in his hands.

A few minutes passed before Sef came outside into the afternoon sun, his eyes reddened, but with no tears visible. 'I'm okay now,' he said, offering a brave half-smile.

Chapter 32

An abduction

Mick Sheehy received the call late at night on Friday, 31 May 2002. Channel Ten had aired its interview with Sef, but the *Daily Telegraph* had yet to hit the streets.

Chatswood police had been notified of an assault at Beauchamp Park, on the corner of Havilah Road and Nicholson Street, Chatswood, around 8.30 pm. Ambulance officers had found Sef Gonzales lying in a gutter with a plastic shopping bag near his head. His car was parked nearby, and Sef later told police he had been on his way to a video shop when he was attacked.

Sef was transported to Royal North Shore Hospital. He complained of pain in his stomach, head, back, chest and groin. He appeared confused and disoriented, possibly suffering amnesia. Sef said he remembered working that morning with his father and having lunch with both his parents. Doctors examined Sef and found no apparent injuries. He underwent a CT scan for brain injury, but the scan results proved normal.

A short time later Sef appeared to recover his memory. He indicated that he had been assaulted, around 7.15 pm, because he had spoken to the media. He informed police that his attackers had dragged him into a car, put a plastic bag over his head and tied his hands together with plastic bands. They told him that he had been warned not to speak to the media and then he was knocked unconscious. He also told police that his attackers told him they knew where his grandmother, Amelita, lived.

Sef was cleared by doctors to leave the hospital shortly after 2 am. He told me two days later that he would prefer not to discuss the incident, as he was too distressed. 'I'm still recovering,' he said. He said the incident was being investigated by police, separate to his family's murder investigation. 'Other detectives are working on that part of it. I just have to wait.'

The abduction attempt on Sef Gonzales remains unsolved. Obviously, Tawas detectives were sceptical. Paul Auglys's suspicions were heightened when he went to notify Linda Pham. He was almost positive she was trying to suppress a grin when he informed her of the incident.

THE DAY BEFORE Sef granted interviews to the media and was allegedly abducted, he told police that he had received two threatening e-mails. The first e-mail had self-destructed when he tried to save it on his computer, he said. Sef showed the second dramatic e-mail to police. It read:

> *Make it easy on yourself. Confess to the police now. We know where you live in Sydney. I know you have a girlfriend. We will do what we have [sic] if you don't. If you care for your friends or relatives, confess!!! This is your last warning. If you offer a reward we will kill you. You cannot bring back your family. Your father deserved to die. Confess!! We have been watching you. Don't talk to reporters. You have a week to confess.*

Police traced the e-mail as having been sent from the Sydney City Internet Café eight days before, on 22 May 2002.

ABOVE Sef in May 2002, at his family members' graves.

LEFT The young Gonzales family shortly after their move to Sydney.

ABOVE The Gonzales house sealed off as a crime scene. Sef's green car is in the carport (*far left*), Loiva's and Teddy's cars are in the garage, and to the right is the front door.

LEFT Shane Hanley, Sef's neighbour, who entered the house with Sef and saw the bodies. Behind him is John Atamian's house.

The racist scrawl on the family-room wall, with a wall hanging removed and dumped on the floor.

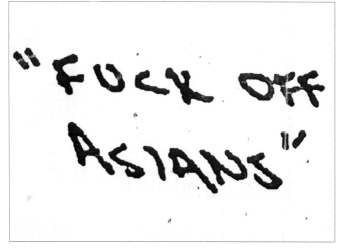

Sef's handwriting, obtained by police for comparison with the racist scrawl.

Teddy's briefcase contents scattered as part of the crime scene 'staging'.

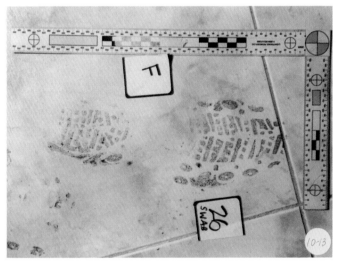

A bloody shoeprint in the hallway, left by a Human brand shoe sole and enhanced by police with chemicals.

Loiva's handbag near the dining-room table, a short distance from where her body was found.

More staging — blood was found on the floor underneath the handbag and contents.

Clodine's bedroom as it was found. Blood enhanced with chemicals is in the foreground and to the right is the desk where she had been studying.

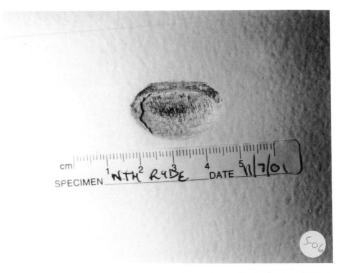

One of the impressions, probably left by a bat, in the gyprock wall in Clodine's room, above where her body was found.

Sef's meticulously neat room, showing the Human brand shoebox in the bottom right-hand corner, underneath the K–Swiss box.

Sef on the upstairs level of 6 Collins Street in May 2002. He stands next to his mother's Catholic shrine and behind his right shoulder is the door to Clodine's room.

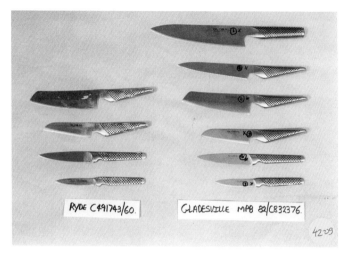

RYDE C491743/60.   GLADESVILLE MPB 82/C832376.

4209

The four knives found in the Global brand knife holder in the kitchen (*left*), compared with another set of the knives bought by police (*right*). The largest knife, and possibly the second largest, are the same as those used in the murders.

ABOVE The jumper that Sef was wearing when police arrived on the night of the murders.

RIGHT A magnification of the jumper's left sleeve, showing the blue paint on the fibres.

Unfortunately, rotating video footage picked up no likely suspects.

On the same day as he told police about the e-mails, Sef reported the attempted break-in at his unit. He told police that he had woken between 2 am and 3 am to the sound of shuffling noises at his front door. Police inspected the front door and found three fairly superficial gouge marks near the lock. They did not believe Sef. They formed the view that either he had made the gouge marks himself, or that they had already been on the door.

THE DAY THE *Daily Telegraph* hit the streets carrying Sef Gonzales' story, a well-meaning member of the public called the Crime Stoppers hotline to give the officers from Tawas some information.

The caller said she knew her tip was a long shot, but she felt compelled to pass it on. She reminded the police about the murder of a twenty-year-old western Sydney woman in 1996. Edwina Powell had been stabbed to death by a pizza delivery man in her Kingsgrove unit. The caller said that the killer, Rouben Diaz, was Filipino and that he had written in blood on the walls. (Some early media reports on the Gonzales murders incorrectly reported that the racist scrawl on the wall at Collins Street was written in blood.) Diaz may well have been on day release from psychiatric care when the Gonzales murders occurred.

In June 2002, Rouben Diaz, then aged 25, was still under psychiatric care. He had been found not guilty of Edwina Powell's murder by reason of insanity. But once the tip was passed to officers at Tawas, they were obliged to follow it up. So Auglys and Detective Senior Constable Darren Murphy visited Cumberland Psychiatric Hospital to find out what Diaz's movements had been for the period of the Gonzales murders. (Coincidentally, it was the same hospital that Teddy's office received a call from the day of the murders.)

The staff at Cumberland Hospital were not keen to let the officers inspect Diaz's medical file, lists of visitors and telephone calls made and received, or reveal details of his movements on 10 July 2001. However, Auglys managed to speak to Diaz himself. He told Auglys he had been on release the day of the Gonzales murders to attend a religious conference at Homebush SuperDome. He said he had gone there with his brother and brother's girlfriend, who had picked him up from the hospital at 5 pm, taking him straight to the conference then back to the hospital, dropping him off at 10 pm. He could not remember going anywhere else except the conference that night. Diaz's brother confirmed that he and his girlfriend had taken Rouben to the religious conference and that Rouben had not left his sight the whole time.

Later, police got a warrant to seize Rouben Diaz's medical documents, which showed he had in fact left Cumberland at 11 am that day, gone to the city with his brother, then to his father's house and on to Homebush, returning to his hospital ward at 11 pm. Any further attempts, however, to interview Rouben Diaz or his brother's girlfriend were stymied by the Diaz family's lawyer.

Tawas had checked out the lead, but could not go any further. In view of the mass of evidence gathered against Sef Gonzales, however, Tawas detectives did not lose any sleep over the former pizza delivery boy.

PART 3

Chapter 33

Under arrest

By now, Strike Force Tawas officers were growing quite concerned at Sef's increasingly erratic behaviour. They viewed his mention of his grandmother and where she lived in his account of the alleged abduction as a direct threat against Amelita's safety. The police believed the more Sef felt he had to 'prove' his innocence, the more he would step up his charades, such as receiving threatening e-mails and experiencing an attempted break-in to his apartment. Who knew what he would do next, and who would be hurt in the process? As well, Sef had already come through with his second alibi, which police believed they could disprove, adding weight to the evidence already collected against him.

Crunch time had come. So, after eleven months of playing the waiting game, they decided to move in on their target.

At 6 am on 13 June 2002, Tawas detectives held a briefing at Gladesville police station. Then Geoff Leonard, head of Tawas, Mick Sheehy, Paul Auglys, Brian O'Donoghue, Darren Murphy and Mick O'Brien jumped in their vehicles and drove to the Bentleigh apartment building at Chatswood. They met up outside and were greeted by an independent officer from Chatswood police who would, according to protocol, observe proceedings.

At 7.35 am, Sheehy went to the unit block's intercom and buzzed apartment 96. He and Sef had a brief conversation. Sef buzzed the police into the foyer, and went down to meet them. Sef and the police then took the elevator to the eleventh floor. When they reached the front door of Sef's apartment, O'Donoghue told Sef that the police had a warrant to seize a computer and various items of his clothing. He handed a copy of the warrant to Sef. Sef read the warrant, then opened the front door for the detectives.

Sef was instructed to stay with Auglys during the search. It was the first time they had met face to face. Sef asked Auglys if he could fetch his wallet. He wanted to make a phone call to his solicitor, Craig Saunders. Sef tried repeatedly to telephone Saunders, but, possibly because of the early hour, was unable to contact him.

The search began in Sef's bedroom. It lasted almost an hour, before Saunders rang Sef back. The search was halted so that Sef could confer with his solicitor. Then Sef handed Sheehy the phone and Sheehy spoke to Saunders.

At 8.31 am on 13 June 2002, more than eleven months after the murders, came the big moment. Ironically, it was Sheehy, the officer Sef trusted, the one Sef believed would save him, who delivered the blow, neutrally couched in official police-speak.

'Sef, as you are well aware, you have been a suspect in relation to the murders of your mother, father and sister for some time now,' Sheehy began.

'Yes,' Sef replied.

'I want to inform you now that you are formally under arrest for the murder of your family, and what I propose to do, following the execution of this search warrant, is to convey you to the Chatswood police station and give you the opportunity to participate in a further interview, if you wish to do so.'

'Okay,' Sef said.

'I want you to understand you are not obliged to say anything unless you wish to do so. Anything you do say will be recorded and may later be used in evidence. Do you understand that?'

'Yes, I understand,' Sef said.

After being informed of his rights by Sheehy, Sef turned to Geoff Leonard, who was coordinating the search of the unit.

'Mr Leonard,' Sef began politely, telling the senior cop this might be the last opportunity he had to speak to him: 'When this chapter in my life is completed, I would like you to put the same effort into the investigation to catch the real killer.'

Leonard gave a noncommittal reply.

Sef got on the phone to his solicitor again, then Sheehy took the phone and spoke with Saunders once more. The search of Sef's unit resumed, and took a further hour. Sef, at the request of police, took them down to the unit block's garage. The detectives searched Sef's car and storage area.

Shortly afterwards, police escorted Sef into a police car and took him to Chatswood police station. It was shortly after 10.15 am.

It took a while for detectives to get in touch with Sef's barrister, Peter Kintominas.

Kintominas said he would travel to Chatswood police station, but could not be there before 1 pm. So they all awaited his arrival.

FOR SUCH A short statement, the New South Wales Police Media Unit press release caused much excitement in newsrooms across Sydney and hit the airwaves almost immediately. Apparently no journalists had been the wiser as to what was going down except for Harry Potter, who got the hot tip and managed to get footage of detectives at Sef's apartment building.

The media release said that police had arrested a 21-year-old man in connection with the deaths of three people at North Ryde on 10 July 2001.

The throng gathering at the steel-mesh fence at the rear of Chatswood police station grew steadily once news of the arrest was released. Radio journalists filed frequent updates, with not much more to add each time. Everyone played the waiting game. Print journalists took turns doing cigarette and coffee runs. But photographers and TV cameramen stood rooted to the spot. The image of Sef being led from the station was not to be missed.

Eventually Sef emerged at 1.40 pm, having refused a police interview on legal advice. He was flanked by Mick Sheehy and Paul Auglys, both of whom towered over him. Sef wore his glasses and blue jeans, beige suede shoes and a khaki sweatshirt jacket. Unlike most suspects who are 'walked' in front of the media, Sef eschewed the towel or jumper over his head. He walked straight-backed with his head held high as police led him to an unmarked car.

For TV crews, the race was on. They jumped in their vans, cameras at the windows, and followed the police sedan up the road to Hornsby Local Court. It was not a long journey, and the Channel Nine crew chased the car all the way, the camera trained on the small figure in the rear of the vehicle.

Mick Sheehy and Paul Auglys were also in that particular car. Auglys turned to Sef and told him that he knew all about him, that he'd listened to all his phone calls, some 8000 of them, and although Sef did not know him, he knew Sef.

Almost an hour and a half later, Sef Gonzales walked into the Hornsby courtroom. Linda Pham sat quietly at the back of the room. The Gonzales family was represented by Loiva's brother Joseph. Most of the onlookers were media representatives.

Sef's barrister, Peter Kintominas, attacked the police case against Sef as 'tenuous' and said his client would strenuously fight the charges. 'It is certainly in his interests to fight and clear his name, because once he is acquitted of these charges he will be able to inherit,' he told the court.

Bail was not applied for that day, so Sef left the court to spend his first night in custody.

BECAUSE HE HAD been formally charged, Sef Gonzales' fingerprints could be entered straightaway into the Commonwealth fingerprint comparison database, to be checked against those found during the investigation of still-unsolved crimes. Beforehand, Sef's fingerprints could only be compared to evidence gathered as part of the Gonzales murder investigations.

The computer silently did its busy work during the night, and the result it came up with for Tawas officers the next day left them gobsmacked.

In the early days of July 2001, a major food and beverage company had received a letter alleging contamination of its products.

> *Three of your products have been poisoned. By now they are on supermarket shelves. This is what you get for treating employees like garbage. Good luck in finding the infected cans before somebody dies. Go to hell!!!*

The company (whose name has been suppressed by the New South Wales Supreme Court) had reported the threat to the New South Wales Police, but the crime had never been solved. However, the letter-writer had been a little too clever, also sending letters to the Australian Federal Police (AFP) and the Australian Quarantine and Inspection Service (AQIS), alerting both agencies to the threat and saying the company was unwilling to act on it due to profit considerations.

From the back of the envelope containing the letter sent to the Federal Police, fingerprints had been detected. Those fingerprints were a dead match with Sef Gonzales'.

The poisoning saga now took on a new significance. Computer expert Jason Beckett was asked to go back through data from the two computers seized from the Gonzales' Collins Street home. Sure enough, on the laptop seized from Sef's bedroom in July 2001, Beckett found numerous searches for the food and beverage company's website, the AFP website and the AQIS website conducted in the latter part of June 2001. Even better, Beckett recovered from the laptop copies of the letters sent to the food and beverage company as well as the AFP and AQIS. The letter to the company had been deleted, but was able to be restored.

Sef Gonzales was in even more strife now. In August 2002, in addition to three murder charges he was already facing, he was slapped with a charge of threatening product contamination.

EVEN THOUGH SEF was behind bars, Tawas detectives were not yet done with Linda Pham. They felt she was withholding information relevant to the triple murder. The officers were extremely interested in what Sef had said to Pham about his second alibi — that he had been with the prostitute Latisha during the murders.

Tawas brokered a deal with Pham's family, who had been forced to fork out for a lawyer to represent their daughter. On 25 June 2002, Pham, her father and her lawyer sat down with Paul Auglys and Darren Murphy at an inner-city police station for an interview. Pham arrived wearing the pink diamond earrings Sef had given her, though Sef had already taken back the ring.

Auglys put it on record that Tawas investigations had led police to believe Linda had 'actively assisted' Sef in his attempts to manufacture evidence and coerce witnesses, to divert suspicion from himself. The police had offered an inducement for Pham to be interviewed. The deal was this: anything Pham told police that day would not be used against her in criminal proceedings. There would only be two exceptions: if she made false statements during the interview, or if she later lied in court as a witness, and her statements during the interview contradicted her testimony in court, then the interview material could be used to prove she had lied under oath.

Pham stated that she understood these conditions.

Pham outlined what Sef had told her about his previous relationships, and said that long ago Sef's first serious relationship — before Kathy Wu — had been with a girl called Daisy. Daisy was allegedly a virgin and Sef had preserved his virginity for the girl that he probably thought he would marry, Pham said. Sef had found out after sleeping with Daisy that she hadn't been a virgin and he was heartbroken, even though Daisy had blurted out during intercourse that Sef was the best guy she'd ever been with.

'So he broke up with her and then he went out with this other girl, I think called [Kathy] . . .' Linda explained.

Pham went on to describe how Kathy had broken Sef's heart, having sex with him then rejecting him, when he had thought she would be his long-term girlfriend. Sef had gone into a deep depression, she said.

In all seriousness, she repeated the incredible story Sef had told her about how he planned to commit suicide but did not want anyone to know, how he had researched a poison that was not in any medical book and thus was untraceable. She said Sef explained he had ordered the poisonous plant part and extracted the poison using hot water at home. She confirmed the name of the poison Sef said he had created — the same poison Sef had told Sheehy he'd made. She thought Sef had told her he kept it in his bedroom. She described how the poison would collapse his lungs and heart and kill him in three days.

'But then he had to tell his friends, like he was preparing his friends, saying, telling everyone ... "I've got cancer" and, um, 'cause he was just preparing them for that time and he was ready to do it ...'

Pham described how Sef had planned to see a prostitute to do something self-destructive and 'totally against his morals' before killing himself. Sef had told her he had never been to a brothel before.

'And he made that, his confession to me ... he asked me am I okay with that [having seen a prostitute] and I thought, well in his state, I thought, yeah.'

She said Sef had told her how he had sat for days near the Chatswood taxi stand watching taxi drivers, hoping to pick the face of the driver who had driven him to the brothel on the day of the murders, until finally he managed to recognise him. She told how Sef had asked her to hold on to a copy of the statement the cabbie had written and that she had made a photocopy and posted it to the cabbie's address on Sef's instructions.

Next, Pham described how she and Sef had gone out to dinner one night and he had ignored her, as he was completely preoccupied with texting someone. Sef did not show her what he was messaging, but later that night he had suddenly dragged her out to see Latisha at the café in Crows Nest. She said she remembered Latisha saying in front of her after the meeting that she recognised Sef as a person she had been with on the night of the murders.

Asked how it was that Sef got Latisha's phone number in the first place, she said Sef had gone back to the brothel and recognised her by the perfume she was wearing, as well as by her face. He then pretended to be a drug dealer and got her number that way, Linda said.

Pham had gone along with Sef's version of events unquestioningly. For example, during the meeting at the café with Latisha, she had patiently hung out and killed some time by going to buy a packet of cigarettes, despite the fact it was getting very close to her midnight curfew. She hadn't wanted to break the curfew, she said. Her parents had the power to enforce it by taking away the brand-new car that had been delivered to her that very day.

Chapter 34

Incarceration

Sef was sent to Silverwater's Metropolitan Remand and Reception Centre (MRRC). A relatively new jail, it held about 900 maximum-security prisoners on remand. This meant they were waiting for their day in court, when their guilt or innocence would be decided.

At first Sef was placed in protective custody. This was largely because of his size, which would make him an easy target for more hardened inmates. However, as time wore on, he was relieved of this status. He shared a cell with another inmate, and seemingly settled in well.

Life in jail has its own routine. Inmates must provide their own television sets in their cells. And contrary to what the public usually sees in movies about prisoners, they do not eat meals communally at the MRRC. Instead breakfast, lunch and dinner — in the form of an airline-style heated meal — are served to them in the cells.

That is, unless a prisoner works in the MRRC's workshop, as Sef did. He would awaken about 6.30 am every morning, eat breakfast in his cell, then at 7.30 am start work in the workshop. He assembled headsets, the ones passengers use on planes for movie screenings, and packaged them. The working inmates broke at noon for lunch at the workshop.

Work finished at 3 pm, and the prisoners were served a very early dinner in their cells at 3.30 pm. Then they were free to watch television, read or write letters. However, Sef was not allowed to use the Internet, which he seemed so fond of. Its use was strictly prohibited inside the MRRC, for obvious security reasons.

Sef began working out, beefing up his muscles. At first he got along all right with his fellow inmates, and would not have been the first at the MRRC to protest his innocence. Many were convinced by the earnest young man; after all, a lot of the MRRC's residents had an abiding mistrust, even hatred, of police.

Sef Gonzales had been imprisoned in the MRRC for 216 days when his obvious frustration with incarceration led him to put pen to paper. A three-page letter was received by the *Daily Telegraph* in mid-January 2003. Dated 14 January 2003, the letter was addressed to 'The Editor' and signed by Sef Gonzales, inmate number 336593, with a return address of MRRC, Private Bag 144, Silverwater 1811.

The pretext for the letter was, ostensibly, a debate that was raging in the Sydney media at the time about offenders who were granted bail and then reoffended. The *Telegraph* had led the campaign to keep those charged with offences behind bars.

This is what Sef wrote:

> *Over the past weeks countless articles have been written criticising and debating over bail decisions and the current state of our legal system.*
>
> *Sadly, the most basic and most fundamental artery in this complex debacle has been constantly overlooked: innocent until proven guilty. It lives in the heart of a democratic society. Too many people are ignorant of the*

distinction between a police arrest and a conviction. Instantly, a person is branded a criminal the moment he or she is arrested and placed behind bars.

If you decide this is acceptable, then we should farewell democracy. What will protect the average citizen? — your parent, brother, sister, friend, you, if a detective decides that you are a suspect for a case that needs to be closed.

You have to wait an eternity (this is what it feels like when you are caged like an animal in a maximum-security prison) before you have your day in court when they will finally decide whether you should have been locked up in the first place.

I concede it is extremely important to protect every person's liberty from criminals. But again let us not forget the above distinction between a convicted criminal and a suspect.

Anyone can be accused of anything. It's too easy. A fair society should not scapegoat. A just society should not settle for 'guilty until proven innocent'. We must be careful not to fix a negative with a negative. It sounds like a basic, old cliché. But when things get complicated and frustrating, often the answer lies in the basics.

Perhaps the solution lies in improving the processing in the court system, NOT in politicians telling magistrates how to do their jobs just to score some election points.

Maybe we should look at a more efficient court system with a maximum set amount of days by which a defendant should immediately have his or her day in court (like in other democratic countries). This way a person won't need to wait years for a trial date only to be found 'not guilty' and have irreplaceable years stolen.

Won't this further protect society if an innocent person in custody is vindicated sooner so that the police can realise sooner that they have made a mistake and go after the perpetrators who are NOT in custody.

The bottom line is, unless a person has been fairly convicted (not just arrested), you never really know if the person you pass in the street is the actual rapist or killer that you saw reported on the news, not the suspect who was arrested yesterday. We need to be careful in jumping to conclusions and judging people rapidly and wrongly just because we need a resolution. We need an efficient system that will determine a person's guilt sooner rather than later, but we also need to make sure we convict the right people. The system should allow judges to do their jobs swiftly.

We should focus on that and leave the judging to the people trained and paid to do it. The anticipated problem in this suggestion is that there are too many cases to process. The jails are full and congested especially during election time. Well maybe it wouldn't reach this stage if the job was done properly in the first place — make sure that a fair system is in place before packing our jails.

I am not only living and breathing this injustice, but I have seen first-hand what it does to those who still have families. I live with fathers, sons who are still waiting after years of stolen birthdays and Christmases for their day in court. They may be guilty. But how can you credit back those lost years if they are innocent? How do you explain to a victim of years of torment that the actual perpetrator may still be out there?

I have met people who after months of waiting, each moment trying to survive in a violent environment, have their charges dropped because the police finally decide they changed their minds about going to trial. (They are not sure after all.) There is no compensation for that!

> *Every problem has a solution. But a 'quick fix' popularity contest to score election points is not the solution, neither is judging when it is not our place to. If we are not careful about which step we take, this problem will become worse and in the process lose the democracy we cherish.*

After signing the letter, Sef included a curious after-note: a poem about the injustice he felt had been dealt him.

> *18 months since I lost my family*
> *216 days in incarceration*
> *my alleged guilt continues to be unproven*
> *so in the eyes of the law, I continue to be as innocent as the truth in my heart.*
> *Surely the injustice cannot be that difficult to identify.*

Whatever Sef thought could be achieved by writing this letter, it seemed to be a cry for help from someone who felt wrongly done by and powerless in their situation.

The *Telegraph* management decided not to publish the letter. As Sef had been charged but not yet convicted, publishing the letter could result in contempt of court if it could be shown to have the power to sway a jury's view, whether in favour of a defendant's innocence or guilt.

However, my boss thought that something should be done in response. I agreed, and wrote a letter to Sef, floating the possibility of another interview with him, although, after the interview-and-abduction debacle, and the story I broke on the supposed abduction afterwards, I was doubtful Sef would respond.

It was not he who contacted me as a result of my letter, but an extremely concerned solicitor from the law firm Benjamin and Khoury, which acted for Sef. Sef's lawyer, John Clarke, seemed to be under the impression it was the *Telegraph* who had approached his client. Sef apparently had not informed him of the letter he had written to the editor.

Clarke's consternation increased at hearing this piece of news. Obviously the *Telegraph* could publish Sef's letter if it wished to run the gauntlet of the law, and as a result cause legal complications for his client. Clarke requested the letter not be published. I told him the *Telegraph* did not plan to publish the letter, but wished to have the first exclusive interview with Sef down the track — whenever his lawyers felt the time was right.

Clarke promised to do what he reasonably could, and the letter never appeared in the newspaper. Clarke had no way of knowing then that he would not be seeing the case through to the end of Sef's trial.

The *Telegraph* never heard another word from Sef Gonzales.

Chapter 35

A quest for freedom

On Friday, 21 March 2003, when Sef had spent almost a year in custody, his bail application was heard in the New South Wales Supreme Court in Sydney. The courtroom was packed with about 40 people, including Emily Luna, who watched from the rear of the court as her nephew's face filled a large video screen. With the technology now available, which enables an interactive video-link between courts and prisons, there is often no need for Department of Corrective Services staff to physically transport prisoners to court.

Sef Gonzales sat behind a desk in his dark green prison-issue tracksuit, watching as proceedings began. As well as the decision regarding his freedom, this would be the first time that the public would hear the Crown case outlining the motives for the crime, and details of the investigative tactics of Tawas detectives.

Representing the Crown was Mark Tedeschi, QC, Senior Crown Prosecutor, acting for the Office of the Director of Public Prosecutions. His deadly legal oratory had helped claim the scalps of some of New South Wales's most notorious criminals, among them the backpacker serial killer Ivan Milat, and Kathleen Folbigg, the woman convicted of the murder of three of her children and the manslaughter of a fourth. Tedeschi would be trying to keep Sef locked up until his trial.

On the other side of the bar table was Sef's barrister Peter Kintominas.

Tedeschi began by talking about how Sef's life had been unravelling — his faking of his grades and the break-up with Kathy Wu — and how Sef's parents had threatened to cut him off. He painted the situation of a young man so desperate to regain control he was willing to kill his entire family. He spoke of Sef's desire to get his hands on his family's money.

Peter Kintominas argued vigorously and at length for his client, saying Sef had no reason to flee to the Philippines when he could be due to inherit a large amount of money. However, given the seriousness of the allegations against Sef, he was fighting an uphill battle.

In addition to these verbal arguments, Justice Whealey had been handed a number of statements to aid him in reaching a decision. There were statements from Emily Luna and Amelita Claridades arguing that Sef should remain in jail and, on the other hand, some statements of support for Sef from his friends and associates. More than anything, the statements by his family demonstrated that Sef had been cut off by his mother's relatives.

Amelita stated that from the time of the murders she'd had her suspicions about who was responsible. 'I suspected my grandson Sef Gonzales, who is the son of my daughter Mary,' she'd told police.

'Since the time I made my second statement to police on 18 September 2001, where I outlined my suspicions and feelings about Sef, I would say that my relationship with him has slowly deteriorated,' her statement continued.

Amelita then went on to describe her fear of Sef.

'Not long after the murders I started having concerns about Sef and fears for my safety. This was compounded by Sef continually telling me lies about his movements on the night of the murders. In conjunction with this I became the executor of the deceased estate. I knew at that time that Sef was interested in being given the property of the estate and this raised concerns for me. Upon being executor I became even more concerned for my safety as I knew how much Sef wanted to receive property from the estate.'

These fears were such that in late July 2001, a few weeks after the murders, Amelita fled her Collins Street home and moved to Melbourne. She later sold the North Ryde house, which has been knocked down and replaced by a massive brick construction much like the Gonzales home. But even though she lived in a unit in a different State, she told police, she still did not feel safe. (In fact, Amelita did not move back to Sydney until mid-2002, after Sef's arrest.)

'After moving to Melbourne in late July I felt a little safer although as I was living in the same street as one of my other daughters, I did not feel 100 per cent safe.

'Sef is well aware of the address of my daughter living in Melbourne as his sister Clodine was residing with her up until the time she was murdered and Sef would often correspond with her through the mail.'

As a result of these fears, Amelita moved to another Melbourne suburb, to make sure she could not be traced by her clever grandson.

'Due to these fears concerning Sef, and my knowledge of him being resourceful, I have not changed my address details from my old address for my bank accounts and Centrelink pension. I am reluctant to change my address details as I fear that Sef may attempt to identify my address and cause me harm.'

Amelita then referred to Sef's abduction and the alarming veiled threat Sef had said he received about his grandmother — that his abductors had said they knew where his grandmother lived. Amelita said she was doubtful about the authenticity of Sef's abduction report, and that her concern for her own safety increased because Sef had thrown in the reference to her when he reported the incident to police.

'I take this statement to be an indirect message to me that Sef may do something to harm me, as I am the executor of the estate. During the previous eleven months or so since the murders, I am aware that Sef has inappropriately sold items from the estate and received large amounts of money. As such this demonstrates to me his desire to receive property from the estate.

'Furthermore, I feel that Sef has mentioned this threat relating to my address during the abduction in order to cover for anything that may happen to me at a later time that he may be responsible for.'

Since Sef's arrest, Amelita told police, her concerns for her safety had been somewhat relieved. However, she feared for herself and her relatives if he were released.

'I am extremely concerned now Sef has been charged with the murders that, if released, he may attempt to cause harm to both myself and my daughter Emily, who is also involved in this investigation ... I have concerns that if released Sef may cause harm to myself or other family members or even attempt to leave the country.'

She told police she believed prior to his arrest Sef may have been planning to leave the country with the money he gained from selling estate property.

'I have previously had several conversations with Sef since the murders where he mentioned an intention to leave the country and travel to America. In different conversations Sef has mentioned that he wanted to visit family relatives and also to continue his father's businesses in America. Sef does have a number of relatives in the United States and the Philippines. To the best of my knowledge, I think that the rest of Sef's extended family is of the suspicion that he is responsible for the murder of his family.'

Amelita then said she feared that Sef would be further motivated to harm her by his wish for the estate property.

'In relation to the estate and me being executor, a few months ago I appointed my son Joseph as the contact person for Sef's legal representatives as I was feeling more and more pressured by them. The legal representatives have since been dealing with Joseph and I learned this week, on Thursday, 27 June 2002, from Joseph that Sef's legal representatives are raising the question of who is going to pay for their fees.

'I am not prepared for these costs to be absorbed by the estate and I am preparing an appropriate response for Joseph to tell Sef's legal representatives. I feel that if Sef finds out that I am not allowing the estate to pay for his legal representation that he may have more motivation to cause me some harm.'

A statement made by Emily Luna was also tendered to the bail hearing. In Emily's statement, she told of visiting her sister's home at 6 pm on 10 July 2001, and how she had thought that Sef was home on the evening of the murders. She stated that she had informed police about her fears for her safety while Sef was still free in the community.

'I am still in fear of him because if he murdered his family, then it would be nothing for him to harm my family or me.'

She stated that after the murders, she was too scared to sleep in her own home and stayed with her family in hotels. She and her husband then sold their house at North Ryde and moved to another, undisclosed location.

'Since the murder my relationship with my husband has broken down and we are now separated. I believe that the murder of my sister, her husband and my niece in some way contributed to this breakdown. After my separation I moved to Melbourne to be with my mother who also moved away from Sydney. The reason I moved to Melbourne was so that I felt safe being in another State away from Sef.' (Emily had moved away in March 2002 and came back in May 2002. During this period she stayed working for the same company, which allowed her to work from home while in Melbourne.)

Emily stated that she had moved back to Sydney for personal reasons, but had not wished to make this move due to her fears of Sef. However, since his arrest and detention her fears had subsided and she enjoyed being back in Sydney.

She also expressed concern that Sef might try to use estate money to leave Australia and change his identity.

'Sef speaks Tagalog fluently and would have no problems surviving in the Philippines if he were able to get there.

'After the murders Sef told me that he was planning on going to Hawaii to stay with a friend he has there. He told me that this friend would look after him and let him stay with him or her as long as he wanted. I have no idea who this friend is or where in Hawaii this friend lives.

'I know through conversations with Sef that he uses the Internet a lot. Through this use he may have made friends with people living anywhere in the world and may have places to go and stay if he was able to leave Australia.'

Emily stated that Sef was aware of the location of her workplace, as he had been there to see her.

'Prior to Sef being incarcerated, when leaving work I would ensure that I was not being followed by taking different routes home each afternoon and by leaving at different times. When driving I would also check to see if the same car was following me. Since the arrest of Sef I have been able to drive home without worrying that someone was following me.'

She said that after the murders, because she feared Sef, she had talked to her son about changing schools. (While in Melbourne she enrolled Gerard in a Victorian school, but once she returned to Sydney, he went back to his old school.)

'I discussed this with him and he told me that he did not want to change schools. Due to the emotional trauma that Gerard had already gone through with the murders and later my marriage break-up with his father, I decided that it would be best to leave Gerard in the school he was in. To ensure his safety, I spoke with the school principal and advised her of my fears regarding Sef.

'When I heard that Sef was abducted in May 2002 I instantly thought that Sef was becoming desperate and was now making up stories to prove his innocence. This abduction made my fears worse that my family or I may be harmed because of Sef's desperation to prove that someone else was responsible for the murders of his family.'

Emily stated that since Sef's arrest she had been able to resume her normal life and start to socialise again with friends. However, if he were released on bail, she would be in fear again that he might harm her or her family, so he would not have to go back to jail.

These statements, of course, were at odds with the picture painted of Sef by his supporters. Indeed, two of them were willing to bet their homes on the fact that Sef would not flee. Obviously, they were convinced of his innocence.

Vivian Raz and her husband Benjamin owned their home in West Pennant Hills outright. It was valued at $650,000. Vivian, who had known Sef since 1999 and had been Loiva's friend, was willing to post bail for Sef for any amount up to $200,000, and use her home as security. She made a statement that she was willing to have Sef released into her custody, as she was aware there were concerns Sef would be a flight risk.

'While the police made it clear from a very early stage that Sef was a suspect, he made no attempt to leave Sydney. Instead, he sought employment with the assistance of Father Paul Cahill of the Immaculate Heart of Mary Parish, Killara.

'I believe that Sef is aware of his obligations to attend court as required. I was impressed by Sef's commitment and his respect for the judicial system and his commitment to studying law and [to] follow in his late father['s] footsteps.

'I believe that Sef is prepared to attend court when required to prove his innocence and intends to strenuously defend the current charges against him. I therefore believe that Sef will attend court when required to, as he has shown his maturity and respect for the judicial system.'

Also willing to put up his house as security for Sef's bail was Luis Chito Perez, a bank officer of Cherrybrook, and a friend of Vivian Raz. He owned the house outright with his wife, Teofila Perez. The house was valued at $530,000. Perez was willing to put up $50,000 for Sef's bail against the net value of his property. He also attested to the fact he believed Sef would attend court when required.

Bernado David, Teddy's lawyer friend, had also offered to let Sef stay in his home if granted bail. His wife, however, suspected deep down that Sef had something to do with the murders. Yet David did not want to offend his parish priest, Father Nards Mercene, who was influential in the Sydney Filipino community and had asked David to help. David was of the opinion that Sef probably would not get bail, so, unbeknown to his wife, he submitted a statement to the bail hearing.

'As a legal practitioner, I fully understand the nature of the charges and my legal responsibilities in acting as a surety in relation to the bail undertaking. In the event of Sef Gonzales being granted bail in respect of the charges, I am prepared to provide him with accommodation at my home with my family and ... on any terms as required by the court.'

David said he believed Sef would not flee Sydney if granted bail.

'I believe that at all times since the deaths of his family, Sef Gonzales has maintained his innocence and sought the opportunity to be present to clear his name.'

David's statement indicated belief in Sef.

'Sef Gonzales' father and I became very good friends and we frequently had lunch together and discussed our work and our families. Subsequently, we met socially as families. From my observations, I found the Gonzales family to be close, loving and strongly religious.

'I first met Sef Gonzales in or around 1996 at his father's legal practice. I understand that he was studying law and from time to time he would provide assistance in his father's practice. I was particularly impressed by Sef's commitment and his respect for the legal system.'

David said he had prepared a room at his house for Sef to use, in anticipation of a 'favourable outcome' to the bail hearing.

Catholic priest Father Paul Cahill, who since Sef's arrest had visited him weekly in jail to offer support and comfort, gave a statement that he had known the Gonzales family from 1991 to 1995, when he was a parish priest at Chatswood and Sef Gonzales was one of his altar servers.

'As parish priest, I got to know the family quite well, including Sef Gonzales who was a very bright and cheerful youngster. In or around 1995 the Gonzales family moved from Chatswood to Blacktown at which time I lost contact with them, although young Sef did call in once or twice when he was in Chatswood to tell us how he was doing in his new school.'

Around 1995, Father Cahill moved from Chatswood to Killara and lost contact with Sef and his family. He saw Sef on the television news in July 2001, in connection with the murder of his family.

'I attended the funeral and went to the graveside with Sef and did my best to console and comfort him in his hour of sorrow. Afterwards I gave him my phone number and promised I would do what I could ... to help him.'

Some weeks after the funeral, stated Father Cahill, Sef called him and asked a question to the effect of 'Can I do some work in the church so that I can spend some quiet time working and praying?' Father Cahill said that he gave Sef the job of cleaning part of the church so he could earn a little money to assist in paying his rent.

'I also asked one of my friends if he could provide Sef with a couple of days a week work so that Sef would not have to go on social services which Sef wished to avoid.'

Father Cahill said Sef had always been a happy and enthusiastic boy, full of life. He retained this air after the murders, although he was more subdued now.

'He is calm and accepting of the heavy cross he has to bear and he also realises that the police would naturally have to consider him as one of the suspects. He seems to have accepted this with some stoicism.

'In all our discussions about the deaths of his family, Sef has maintained his innocence and has expressed to me his concern that the crime is fully investigated and that justice should prevail.'

Justice Anthony Whealey rejected the bail application, however. He found that there was too high a risk that Sef would flee if released into the community. Sef hung his head in despair at the decision. The prospect of remaining in jail appeared to have brought him to tears.

ON FRIDAY, 16 MAY 2003, another bombshell was dropped in the Gonzales case. Reporters knew that in addition to the three murder counts Sef had been charged in August 2002 with threatening product contamination. However, due to a suppression order, the media had been unable to publish the fact that Sef had been charged in relation to the matter, let alone refer to the alleged circumstances.

After a legal campaign led by the *Daily Telegraph*, Justice Michael Grove of the New South Wales Supreme Court lifted the suppression order and the media was free to publish. The charge related to the threatening letter received by the food and beverage company and copied to the Federal Police and Quarantine and Inspection Service. Police alleged that in the three weeks before the murders Sef Gonzales made anonymous threats against the company, saying he would contaminate the firm's products.

Justice Michael Grove told the court this offence was allegedly committed so that Gonzales could deflect attention from himself and inhibit the successful investigation of an earlier attempt to kill the victims by poison. Reference was made to Loiva's hospitalisation with food poisoning symptoms a short time before the murders.

The charge that the media could now report was that between 25 June and 7 July 2001, at North Ryde, Sef Gonzales 'did make a statement believing the statement to be false with intent to induce a food and beverage company to believe goods had been contaminated'. It was alleged the statement was made with the 'intention of causing public alarm and anxiety'.

Peter Kintominas had argued vehemently that the lifting of the order would prejudice his client's ability to have a fair trial, due to the publicity it would attract. Kintominas said there was concern about his client's case becoming a '*cause célèbre*', in the Azaria Chamberlain and Ivan Milat class of matter. 'People read about it, they talk about it, and they go on and on about it,' he told the court.

Chapter 36

The estate

By May 2003, Sef Gonzales was virtually broke and had been in custody for eleven months, with nothing but brief and sporadic appearances in court via video-link from Silverwater jail.

He had no money to put up for his defence against the three murder charges. So, through his legal team, he applied for a court ruling to allow him to access the money from his dead parents' estate for his legal defence. It was a situation without reported precedent, anywhere in the world.

On 8 May, the legal battle for the money began in the New South Wales Supreme Court. Sef, through his solicitors, brought the action against his grandmother, Amelita Claridades, who was executor of the estate.

The key issue was whether Amelita would be breaching the trust of the estate by releasing funds for Sef's defence, argued Sef's legal representative Brian Rayment, QC, during the brief preliminary hearing. If Sef turned out to be innocent, Amelita was in breach of the trust by refusing to release funds to Sef. On the other hand, if he were guilty, then she would be in breach of the trust by making the payment to him.

It was a legal catch-22. The complicated civil case was set down for full hearing on 30 May. Brian Rayment, QC, again represented Sef at that hearing, while barrister John Wilson represented Amelita. Sef, in custody, was not present.

Wilson argued that it was premature to rule on whether Sef should have access to the funds, when the criminal proceedings had not been finalised and there was no verdict on his guilt or innocence. After all, if Sef were found guilty, then he could not legally benefit from the estate of his victims.

Rayment, however, argued that by the time a verdict was handed down it would be too late for his client. The need for the money was urgent; it would make a vast difference to the nature of Sef's defence at his forthcoming committal hearing, which it was estimated would last at least two weeks. Sef's defence team would be able to test the evidence against their client for the first time. At the committal, a local court magistrate would decide whether Sef should stand trial on the murder counts and the threat of contamination charge. The consequences, were Sef not granted the money to put up a powerful defence, could be grave for his client.

In support of this argument, Justice Campbell was handed a document from Douglas John Humphries, Director of the Criminal Law Division of the New South Wales Legal Aid Commission, a government-funded agency that tries to ensure that people without the money to pay a legal firm will gain adequate legal representation.

Humphries wrote that Sef would be entitled to a Legal Aid defence for the committal. However, he would be granted a solicitor only. The allocation of a solicitor to the committal hearing would have a five-day cap, at a rate of $600 per day. That would allow three days of preparation and two days for the actual hearing. The cap would only be exceeded in 'exceptional circumstances' with the approval of senior Legal Aid executives.

This meant that, with Legal Aid, funding, Sef would have a solicitor representing him in court for only two days of a committal hearing anticipated to last much longer. And this solicitor would be up against Senior Crown Prosecutor Mark Tedeschi, QC.

A statement from Sef's solicitor, Dieb Khoury, indicated the amount of work needed to prepare the defence case.

'The Crown brief [of evidence] which has been served in this matter includes thirteen volumes of written and other materials, a volume of photographic material together with a CD containing the negatives from 29 rolls of film, 24 audio CDs of telephone intercept material, and in excess of 2000 pages of material relating to exhibits and exhibits listings. A study of all the material in the Crown brief will take at least ten days. In addition, there would be considerable time required and substantial work necessary to coordinate, order and tabulate the brief and to prepare a detailed chronology, index, case outline and observations for Counsel', he wrote.

In a written submission, Rayment reiterated the need for the funds.

'If the application were refused then the plaintiff would be deprived of the benefit of private representation on the committal, and would be provided with the assistance as detailed in the affidavit of Mr Humphries.

'If the plaintiff is committed for trial without the benefit of cross-examination of Crown witnesses, he may be disadvantaged at the trial ... effectively the plaintiff would not have the benefit of a properly prepared committal proceeding and would be meeting the Crown evidence for the first time at trial.'

Rayment also pointed out in his submission that it was not suggested the people who would inherit the estate if Sef did not were in necessitous circumstances — they did not need the money.

However, it appeared the last thing those people — Teddy's parents, William and Belen Gonzales — were concerned about was getting their hands on their dead son's money.

The letter they sent to Roland Barros, the solicitor representing Amelita and the estate, in October 2002, in reply to his enquiries about their position on the matter, made it clear that the reason they did not want Sef to access the funds was a moral one. They did not say outright they believed Sef was responsible for the murders. But the tone of the letter said it all:

> *While we are aware of being possible beneficiaries of the estate of our beloved son, Teddy, this does not bear on the great moral responsibility we feel and carry as parents of Teddy Gonzales. Words cannot describe and convey our grief, loss and outrage over what befell him, our daughter-in-law and our granddaughter.*
>
> *Please do not think that your letter first brought or raised this specific matter before us. We have seriously and thoroughly thought out and weighed the issue for more than a year, and after considering all the information we could obtain and gather from those in charge of the case in Australia.*
>
> *We have to refuse any part of the estate of our son, Teddy, to be used in any manner, directly or indirectly, for the defence of Sef. Such is the only position we can morally live by, in deference to the memory of our son, Teddy, and be able to live by our conscience.*
>
> *We will greatly appreciate that you communicate this to Mrs Amelita Claridades, the executrix.*

Justice Joseph Campbell had a lot to weigh up, and he adjourned the case pending its decision.

ON THURSDAY, 12 JUNE, the decision was handed down. Sef was denied access to his parents' estate.

In his judgment, Justice Campbell referred to the principle of public policy whereby a person who unlawfully kills another person cannot acquire any benefit that arises from the death of that person. He then looked at whether the policy applied in Sef's case.

'The *Forfeiture Act* 1995 confers on the court a discretionary power to relieve against that rule of public policy. However ... the court cannot grant any such relief when the unlawful killing is murder.

'If it is ultimately not established that Sef Gonzales killed any of his parents and sister, this rule of public policy will have no scope for operation.

'If it is ultimately established that Sef Gonzales murdered his parents and sister, the effect of the rule of public policy will be that he is unable to take the benefits which would otherwise flow to him under the will of his father.

'If it is eventually established that he killed his father unlawfully, but in circumstances which do not amount to murder, and he is able to persuade the court to exercise the discretion under the *Forfeiture Act* 1995, he will be entitled to all or part of his father's estate.'

Essentially, Justice Campbell found that Sef's guilt or innocence had not been established, and therefore, he was not entitled to the funds from the estate.

Unfortunately, this left Sef's lawyers, Dieb Khoury and John Clarke, with an outstanding bill for $480,000, according to Bernado David, who says he was shown the total bill of costs.

While an appeal was launched against the decision rejecting access to the estate, David was asked to help with fundraising for Sef's private legal representation at the committal hearing, just in case.

David visited Sef a number of times in jail during this period and Sef prepared a 'To whom it may concern' letter outlining his angst at the unfairness of being accused of his family's murder, to be used for the fundraising. Along with this letter, Sef sent David a touching letter thanking him, Vivian Raz and Father Paul Cahill for their support.

'I know that even though my family is no longer here, they continue to watch over me. I also believe that they guide angels here to help me. Like Tita [Aunty] Vivian Raz for example,' Sef wrote. 'I feel that you are one of those angels too. I only hope that some day I be given the opportunity to be someone you can all be proud of. And some day to be able to thank you.'

David put out a few lines of enquiry in the Filipino community about Sef's appeal, and was promised money that never came through.

SEF GONZALES' COMMITTAL hearing was long awaited. It had been delayed time and again as his lawyers lobbied to access money from his dead family's estate.

The purpose of the hearing was to test aspects of the prosecution case against him. If Sef's lawyers could cast sufficient doubt on the validity of prosecution evidence during the committal, the charges against him could be dropped and he would be a free man. If, on the other hand, the magistrate found that Sef had a case to answer, he would be committed to stand trial for murder in the Supreme Court.

Despite the devastating blow of having been denied access to the estate, Sef's solicitor Dieb Khoury did not give up fighting for the funds on behalf of his client. Ironically, in going to the New South Wales Court of Appeal to challenge the decision of Justice Campbell, Sef was racking up an ever-increasing legal bill.

On Monday, 18 August, at Sydney's Central Local Court, the committal was finally about to start before Magistrate Deborah Sweeney. The media were there in force, and the Tawas detectives sat to one side of the bar table, waiting for proceedings to begin.

However, the legal gymnastics that had typified the case so far were to continue. Dieb Khoury requested another adjournment, as the Court of Appeal decision regarding the estate funds was still pending. Mark Tedeschi, QC, vigorously opposed an adjournment, arguing that the case had dragged on for far too long already.

Magistrate Sweeney refused the request for the adjournment. Then Khoury, who had worked on the Gonzales case since the beginning, said that if that was the case he was no longer able to represent his client. He and his colleague, John Clarke, gathered their belongings and walked out of the court, leaving behind shocked faces in the public gallery and Sef sitting on his own in the screened-off dock.

Now Sef was unrepresented. It was arranged for a Legal Aid lawyer to come into the court, and the proposition of Sef's applying for Legal Aid representation was discussed. However, the application would take time to be processed, and Sef did not have that time. Sweeney had just refused to adjourn the case. So the bulk of the massive brief of evidence against Sef — folder upon folder of material — was served on him as he sat in the dock.

Sweeney asked Sef what he wished to do.

He replied in a quiet voice: 'Your Worship, there is nothing further I wish to say at this time. All I ask is that I have time to go through the material in the brief.'

Sef was given a three-day adjournment to peruse the massive brief, and told to be back in court on Thursday.

Meanwhile, the Court of Appeal came back with its

decision on the estate late that Monday afternoon. The appeal was rejected. Sef could not gain access to his family's money.

THE FOLLOWING NIGHT, Sydney barristers Winston Terracini, SC, and Philip Massey were sitting in a city pub frequented by the legal fraternity. They were enjoying a catch-up over a few ales. Terracini, the son of a motor mechanic and a clergyman's daughter, had a tough, down-to-earth personality and 25 years' experience in the law. His long list of clients included notorious jailed underworld figure Neddy Smith, a cohort of disgraced detective Roger Rogerson, as well as the man with the golden tonsils, radio broadcaster John Laws, whom he had represented in a contempt of court matter.

Terracini ran the city chambers where Massey, who also specialised in criminal work, was based. Like Terracini, Massey had a forceful personality, as well as a droll sense of humour and a genuine passion for the law.

Both accepted Legal Aid clients as well as the privately funded ones. It meant reduced fees, but Terracini believed it was essential to do that kind of work. The financially disadvantaged deserved decent representation just as the wealthy did, he felt.

Terracini's and Massey's conversation turned to the news in the papers that morning: Sef Gonzales' lawyers walking out of court, and the rejection of the appeal for the estate funds.

They were not to know that back at Silverwater jail, Sef was complaining about his lawyers' walkout. One of the jail guards took pity on him and gave him a few names of barristers to contact. On that list was Terracini. On Wednesday, Terracini was contacted by Sef.

Terracini would oversee the case. Massey, as his junior, would do most of the research and legwork and the actual representation at the committal.

Father Paul Cahill dug up at least $10,000 of his own savings to pay for Sef's private legal representation at the committal. Later, Legal Aid would fund Sef's actual trial.

That Thursday, Terracini was in court along with Massey. Terracini did not pull any punches when he told Magistrate Sweeney that he believed whatever work had been done on the case by Sef's previous lawyers had been in the pursuit of 'other areas' — an oblique reference to the bid to access the estate — and not necessarily in preparation of a rebuttal of the Crown's case against Sef.

'I'm absolutely staggered at how on earth it has taken this length of time,' Terracini said. He told Sweeney he would be ready for the committal to proceed on Monday. It only allowed for three days' preparation time, but he believed it could be done. His client had already been in custody too long, he said.

Chapter 37

The committal

It had been a busy weekend for Massey, poring over the massive brief. But by Monday morning, 25 August, he felt he had his head around it. That morning, the commital hearing began in earnest. The venue had shifted to Downing Centre Local Court, just up the road from Central Local Court.

Legal argument took up most of the day. The first witness did not take the stand until the following morning. Emily Luna was about to have her first day in court.

First, a 40-minute video reconstruction at the Gonzales home was played to the court, with Emily describing to Detective Paul Auglys the movement behind the left glass panel that she had seen when she arrived with her then eight-year-old son Gerard at her sister's house around 6 pm on the night of the murders.

Massey decided to test Emily on this.

MASSEY: Had you stopped your car when you saw that movement or was your car still in motion?

EMILY: It was still a little bit in motion so I was just about to park my car then off the street.

MASSEY: So were your lights pointing towards the door, the lights of the car pointing towards the door, or —

EMILY: No, because I was just parking then and my eyes
just got attracted to the movement there.

MASSEY: That movement you say you saw. You say you
were attracted by the movement. How long did you
observe? Did you keep watching the door after the
movement stopped?

EMILY: No, no, it was just like one or two seconds, just,
because I was parking my car so I couldn't really just look
at the door. It was really — my eyes just got attracted
from looking at Sef's car when I first drove into the
street, and then my eyes got attracted to the movement
that I saw and then I was parking my car then.

Emily said she got out of her car to go to the front door,
pressed the doorbell a number of times, and didn't hear any
dogs barking. Ginger, one of Loiva's dogs, would come across
the hallway and she would start barking at the door.

Massey then broached the subject of the figure Emily said
she had seen through the frosted window panel at the left side
of the front door. She said she at first thought it was a person,
then her son said it was just a coatstand. Emily said the figure
appeared to be wearing a cap, with the peak facing downwards.
A jacket was just below it and it looked like the back of the
jacket was facing her, probably because of the curved shape.

MASSEY: So what you observed though was a shadow
rather than the coat itself, would you agree with that?

EMILY: I cannot really — it's not — would it be
shadow? I don't know if you'd call it a shadow but
definitely there was a figure there.

MASSEY: So there was a person there, are you saying?
You use the word 'figure' a number of times, what do
you mean by 'figure'?

EMILY: If you ask me now I can tell you now that it's a person. But if you were to ask me then, I thought it was really a coatstand because I actually thought that the coatstand was standing there.

MASSEY: So you'd agree with me then, that now your mind and memory is that it was in fact a person. Are you saying that now — that your memory now — is that it was in fact a person?

EMILY: I don't know, I don't know, I can't answer that question.

Massey further questioned Emily on what the figure was.

MASSEY: It is very important that you try to remember because you've used 'figure' as being what you saw. You've given descriptions of this coat. Is it your recollection that it looked like a person?

EMILY: That evening I did say to my son that I thought there was a man and then my son said, 'Mum, it's only a coatstand.'

MASSEY: Now, this man that you saw at the window, and this hat and coat you say you saw through the window, you'd understand that they'd be quite important, wouldn't they, for the police to know that sort of information?

EMILY: Sorry, can you repeat that question again?

MASSEY: You seeing a movement at the window?

EMILY: Yes.

MASSEY: And you seeing what you thought now, you say was like a person. You first thought it was a person at the time through the window at six o'clock on 10 July 2001, that'd be something very important wouldn't you think that the police needed to know, wouldn't you think?

EMILY: Yes, that would be helpful information.

MASSEY: It would be very helpful information, wouldn't it?

EMILY: Because it's the truth, yes.

MASSEY: Was there any reason why you didn't tell the police about it and include it in your statement of 10 July and 13 July?

EMILY: On 10 July that was my very first statement. We were still in panic. I was in shock about the incident. The questions asked of me were basically one question, one answer. All I know is, all I said was, I saw Sef's car and I didn't want to go into any further details.

Massey continued.

MASSEY: So you'd agree with me that your statement so far is very detailed, would you agree with that?

EMILY: It becomes more in detail every time, yes.

MASSEY: But as you agreed before, one of the most important pieces of information was that you say you saw [some]one in the house and you didn't tell the police that. Can you give an explanation for that?

EMILY: I don't know, I'm sorry, I don't know. I can't answer that question.

A relieved Emily was dismissed from the witness stand shortly afterwards. It had been a testing time in the box for her. She knew the defence lawyer was just doing his job. But how was she to explain, on a question-and-answer basis, just how long it took her to trust the police — and give all the relevant information?

The next witness to take the stand that Tuesday was the taxi driver whom police alleged Sef paid to write the statement that he had taken Sef from Wicks Road, North Ryde, to Chatswood on the night of the murders.

The man, whose real name was suppressed by Magistrate Sweeney, drove an ABC taxi, and had been a taxi driver for four years. In the following text, as earlier, I call the driver Alan Altano. Prosecutor Sarah Huggett questioned him about a three-page log of jobs for his taxi dated 10 July 2001. Altano did his best to answer, in his halting English.

HUGGETT: Did you in fact pick up Sef Gonzales from a petrol station at North Ryde and take him to the Chatswood area on the afternoon of 10 July 2001?

ALTANO: No.

HUGGETT: Do the records show that during the afternoon of 10 July 2001 your taxi was not in the North Ryde area?

ALTANO: That's right.

Magistrate Sweeney allowed the logs held by the cab company to be tendered, despite Massey's objection.

Altano said he drove only one cab that day.

HUGGETT: When Mr Gonzales asked you if you would write the statement that you've seen this morning, why did you agree to do that?

ALTANO: He looked very honest to me and I thought . . . I mentioned that this is not — don't take this, it's not for a legal matter, it's just, it's for anything like that, but is it for your girlfriend or something, and he said yes it's nothing important.

Massey cross-examined the cabbie. He asked Altano about the log of records, which showed various codes relating to the jobs allocated to his taxi that day. Massey noted Altano had made trips around Sydney, with destinations including the city and Vaucluse. He showed Altano the records. Asked about the machine to the front right-hand side of a driver in a cab, Altano explained it dispatched jobs to drivers, who logged on to a particular system when they wanted to pick up passengers in a certain area. Massey probed the meaning of the records with Altano.

MASSEY: That's about 16.07, [the suburb] Gordon, on that first page that we were just looking at before?

ALTANO: Yep.

MASSEY: And it's got log in approach. Does that suggest that you, as you said … indicated on that machine beside you?

ALTANO: Mm-mm.

MASSEY: Where you want to go to, is that right, you want to go to Gordon and that's what that records?

ALTANO: No, I had a passenger wanted to go to Gordon and I log on, just in case to get if there is a job from Gordon to take it, so.

MASSEY: When you say you had a passenger are you saying that from your personal recollection or from what you're looking at, these records?

ALTANO: That's what usually happens when you log on approach, that means we have a passenger and dropping to certain area. Do you want to pick up from that area providing if you can pick it up in ten minutes.

MASSEY: No, but what I'm asking is it's not your personal recollection that you're going to Gordon at that time. That is just what is indicated on these records. Would you agree with that?

ALTANO: I don't know what to answer of this question.

MASSEY: What I'm asking is —

ALTANO: Yeah.

MASSEY: You yourself don't remember as of today's date taking someone to Gordon at 16.07 on 10 July. You don't remember it personally, you're just recalling it from these records. Do you agree with that?

ALTANO: Well, I would say I wouldn't remember the passenger, yeah.

MASSEY: You wouldn't remember —

ALTANO: The passenger I had to drop to Gordon. But it was a long time ago.

The records showed that the cabbie, after reaching Gordon or while still on the way there, rejected passenger pick-ups offered to him. At 17.07 he logged out of the computer system until 18.15. In that period he was not working the cab. The next entry, when the cabbie recommenced work, was at the suburb of Pennant Hills.

MASSEY: And . . . the next entry for where you recommence is at Pennant Hills at 18.15?

ALTANO: Mm–mm.

MASSEY: Where you put in log-in vacant?

ALTANO: Where I got logged out there, um, most probably because my wife works at Macquarie Shopping Centre and I usually go around that time 5.30 [pm], I go and pick her up and we go home together.

MASSEY: Where do you —

ALTANO: Pennant Hills. So that's the time I got logged out and then I maybe — And we went home and had a coffee and I log on again and start working again.

MASSEY: Now, I don't want to know your actual address —

ALTANO: Yes.

MASSEY: But you say you're going home, what suburb you're going home to, just the suburb.

ALTANO: Pennant Hills.

MASSEY: Pennant Hills?

ALTANO: Yes.

MASSEY: When you say Macquarie Shopping Centre, where's that? I know I'm showing my ignorance but —

ALTANO: It's North Ryde, yes.

MASSEY: It's in North Ryde?

ALTANO: Yes.

This was an unexpected gift for Massey, who truly had not known where the shopping centre was located.

MASSEY: So you think that between — that you're probably in North Ryde some time between 17.07 and 8.15 *[sic]* on 10 July 2002 —

MAGISTRATE SWEENEY: 18.15, 6 —

MASSEY: 18.15, sorry, 6.15.

ALTANO: Yeah, that's a period usually I don't really mind not working because I'm worried about 5.30, pick up my wife.

MASSEY: My question was really — I ask questions and you just answer them —

ALTANO: Yeah, sure.

MASSEY: The question was —

ALTANO: Mm–hm.

MASSEY: You were in North Ryde some time between that period?

ALTANO: It's possible, yes.

Massey told Altano he did not wish to get him into trouble with ABC Taxis, but asked if he ever accepted 'cashies' while he operated his cab. Altano answered that he did not work on commission, he was an owner–operator. In other words, he had no reason or inducement to take cash jobs and hide them from the taxi company. The records Massey was looking at were not for the meter itself, but just to show what he was doing at a particular time. There were records in relation to the charge meter, he told Massey, and Massey asked to look at them. Altano said they were with his accountant, and undertook to try to retrieve them.

MASSEY: I imagine that when you were giving your statement on 18 January with the police you were a bit concerned, were you?

ALTANO: Yes, because I didn't take it seriously when I met him. And then when I found out because I told him [the] statement I gave you, it's just, shouldn't go to [the] police because it's got nothing, because he told me twice can he use me as nothing serious. I thought maybe is for his girlfriend or whatever. I said okay I'll just write down something for you but then I realised it's a big case and after that I just didn't want to have anything to do with it.

MASSEY: I'll put a scenario to you. Some people might, where they find in fact [they are] an alibi witness, change their story to police so they can get out of being involved in it. Is this what happened to you?

ALTANO: No.

MASSEY: The date 7 October 2001 which is the date which you say Mr Gonzales said to write, why did you write the incorrect date? Why did you do that?

ALTANO: I was just having a very quiet day and he just pulled me off the rank. I didn't want to lose my position because he just wanted to go around the corner and talk. So he just gave me $50 and I accepted it and I said you know I gave you something to just forget about it and go back to rank again so I was working after that.

MASSEY: But he didn't give you $50 to write a statement did he?

ALTANO: No he just — I give you this for your time.

MASSEY: For your time, so? And that was before you even spoke about the statement.

ALTANO: When he started he just said I'll pay you for your time, can we just go around the corner and talk.

Massey asked Altano about his original conversation with Sef.

MASSEY: Now, when you had this initial conversation with him you did recognise him, didn't you?

ALTANO: There was a time I did and maybe asked his name once I think.

MASSEY: But you did recognise him, you'd seen him before?

ALTANO: Yes. I'm sorry, could you repeat the question please?

MAGISTRATE SWEENEY: In which time, when he approached?

MASSEY: Yes, asked and answered.

It was a victory for Massey. Altano had admitted he recognised Sef when he approached him at the cab rank, leaving open the possibility he may well have given Sef a lift before. And it seemed he may well have been in the North Ryde area at the crucial time on the night of the murders.

Huggett, in re-examination of the taxi driver, did her best to stem the damage. She was not about to let Massey get away with this 'asked and answered'.

HUGGETT: Did you recognise the man when he came to your taxi at Chatswood and provided the $50 for your time? Did you recognise the man?

ALTANO: The face was familiar but I can't recall that —

HUGGETT: Do you know why the face was familiar? Do you know in what way the face was familiar?

ALTANO: Because I work the Chatswood area so he's probably been in my taxi before. I don't know.

This, undoubtedly, was not the response she had hoped for. It would have been quite likely that Altano recognised Sef from media coverage of the Gonzales murders. Huggett finished her re-examination then sat down.

Bernado David was up next. He spoke about the incident two months before the murders, when he went into Teddy's office to speak to him. David said he observed Teddy was on the telephone and was 'quite agitated'.

MASSEY: When you use the word 'agitated' can you describe what he looked like and what he was doing?

DAVID: He was on the phone and he was shouting, he was angry at that time.

MASSEY: Did you hear what he said?

DAVID: I don't remember right now but I heard something —

MASSEY: Was it in English or in Tagalog?

DAVID: In Tagalog. It's more or less ...

MASSEY: Beg your pardon?

DAVID: It's a curse word.

MASSEY: It's a curse word?

DAVID: Yes.

MASSEY: What would this roughly translate into in English, this curse word?

DAVID: F— you.

MASSEY: 'F— you'? You can actually say the word for me, Mr David.

DAVID: I've already said it.

MASSEY: 'F— you' means fuck you?

DAVID: Yeah.

MASSEY: Did you hear anything else in the conversation?

DAVID: No.

David said he told Teddy to put the phone down, and suggested that they go outside and he calm himself down. They went to the toilets then went outside and had a conversation. David asked, 'What's wrong, Ted?' Teddy was angry and frowning.

MASSEY: He then said [referring to the statement David made to police], 'I have a property transaction in the Philippines that fell through. My brother is over there acting as an agent for me. The other party has told my brother they are going to eliminate my family.' He — did he say that to you?

DAVID: He said it in Tagalog.

MASSEY: So it was in Tagalog?

DAVID: Yes.

MASSEY: How did he say it, from the intonation of his voice? How did he say it, angrily or —

DAVID: When I ask him what's wrong, what's wrong? And he said, well, I've got this telephone conversation that somebody overseas — and he said something about a property construction crashing and that's it.

MASSEY: But he didn't also speak about someone going to eliminate his family?

DAVID: Well, he said yeah, somebody had threatened him and his family.

MASSEY: How did he say it, though, was my question. Not what language, but how did he say it? What was the intonation of his voice and his emotions as you observed them?

DAVID: He was angry, he was agitated, he was worried at the time.

MASSEY: He was worried?

DAVID: Yes.

MASSEY: In your statement you then said that you, after a while, you'd gone to the toilet and then you said to him: 'How can they come here and eliminate you? They don't have a visa.' You were trying to put some humour in it, were you?

DAVID: That's so.

MASSEY: Did that seem to assist him at all? Did he find it humorous?

DAVID: Well, he laughed at that because he knew he was an immigration agent.

David said he and Teddy never discussed this matter again.

Chapter 38

Committed

The next day, Kathy Wu took the witness stand. Before she was asked anything, she asked if an order suppressing her real name had been granted. The magistrate assured her it had. She was then questioned briefly by the prosecution about her twelve-page statement to police made on 26 July 2001, which outlined her relationship with Sef.

When Philip Massey, in cross-examination, began to ask a question, Kathy Wu cut in, saying she had signed the statement but couldn't really recall its contents. Massey asked if it was basically correct, and she said some of it was.

MASSEY: Right, which parts aren't correct?

WU: Which are or aren't?

MASSEY: Which aren't. I'm assuming that the number that aren't correct is less than the number that are correct, or is it the other way around?

WU: Most of it's correct.

MASSEY: Most of it, so, which ones aren't correct?

WU: I think the date in paragraph 11 [referring to the paragraph in her statement that says 24 June, when she in fact meant it was 24 May when she met Sef at his house and he took her out for dinner].

MASSEY: What else is in there that's not correct?

WU: In paragraph 14, I don't recall kissing him [when they visited the grounds of the University of New South Wales].

MASSEY: When you say you don't recall, you say in your statement: 'And I may have — and we . . . may have kissed each other.'

WU: Yes, I may have, so I don't recall —

MASSEY: So you may have?

WU: In fact I don't recall most of the things in this statement, it was so long ago.

MASSEY: But if you made the statement at the time, which was within a month of most of these events or two months —

WU: Yes.

MASSEY: Of most of these events, would you agree that your memory probably would have been better [back then]?

WU: Probably would have been, but as I said I was there [in the police station, making her statement] for the whole day. I was really tired and I was hungry and all I wanted to do was go home. So when I signed the statement I just basically signed it and I trusted the inspector had, you know, written what I had told him, and —

Under further questioning, she continued not to recall aspects of her statement.

MASSEY: What else in there, do you think, is not correct?

WU: I can't really say because, as I said, I really don't recall most of this.

MASSEY: Now, if I suggested to you that the difficulties in your memory may arise probably [because of] the publicity that's involved in this, what would you say about that?

WU: What do you mean?

MASSEY: The publicity involved in this matter. That you don't want to be involved in this matter. What would you say about that?

WU: No, I don't remember, because it was more than two years ago.

Wu went on to say that although she couldn't recall most of her statement, there were only those previously mentioned two things that stood out as being incorrect. They first met on 14 May. After that they exchanged e-mails before going out several times to dinner or for lunch. The first time she actually went out with Sef was 22 May — eight days after they first met. They broke up on 1 June.

MASSEY: So the relationship extended really in the sense of personal contact, other than e-mails and telephones, only from 22 May till about 1 June, only about ten days?

WU: I suppose.

MASSEY: During that time, when you were speaking with him or e-mailing him or even having dinner with him, or lunch, did he speak about his parents?

WU: Only that his parents had a law firm and his sister studies interstate.

MASSEY: Was there anything more extensive than that, in your conversation with him in regard to his parents?

WU: I don't recall.

MASSEY: Did you have a conversation with him regarding his parents and his relationship with you?

WU: No, never.

MASSEY: Now when you met his mother, how was she with you?

WU: She was washing her dog, so she didn't really pay much attention to me.

MASSEY: Did she speak to you at all?

WU: She said hello.

MASSEY: And how did she say that, can you remember?

WU: No, I don't recall.

MASSEY: But it was basically, would you agree with this proposition, that Sef took you in to meet his mum, she said hello, and he took you out to dinner?

WU: Yeah.

MASSEY: That was basically it?

WU: Yeah.

MASSEY: She certainly didn't — she wasn't angry with —

WU: No, she was washing her dog.

MASSEY: She was washing her dog and she didn't seem concerned about you, from what you could perceive?

WU: I don't recall.

MASSEY: When you say you don't recall, is that because she didn't seem concerned?

WU: I don't think so. She was busy with her dog, as I said.

MASSEY: Did you have any physical contact with his mother?

WU: Physical?

MASSEY: Yeah. Did she give you a kiss on the cheek or something like that?

WU: I don't recall.

Kathy Wu was dismissed from the stand and fled the court building, hiding her face as she was pursued by media crews.

The next witness that day was Patricia Tonel, Teddy Gonzales' secretary, who was in the office on the day of the murders. In her original statement to police on 11 July 2001 she said that Sef arrived at the office at 10.50 am and left about midday. But her statement of 1 February 2002 said he would have left about 3 pm. Tonel admitted in court to being incorrect about the times in the first statement and said Sef arrived at the office at about 1.30 pm. There were only Teddy, Loiva and herself in the office that morning, and no clients visited.

> **MASSEY:** And you say in your statement of 1 February
> that he left around three o'clock, but you're not sure?
> **TONEL:** Yes.
> **MASSEY:** Could it have been as late as 4.30 [pm]?
> **TONEL:** I'm not sure but I think he left earlier than that.
> **MASSEY:** Right, but you're not sure about three o'clock
> either?
> **TONEL:** No.

Sef arrived at the office after Tonel got back from lunch. She said she usually went to lunch about 12.30 pm, and was out of the office for around 45 minutes. Teddy and Loiva were the only people in the office when Tonel left. After Sef arrived, he had a number of conversations with his father. Sef called a bank, something to do with a client, and Tonel heard him on the phone doing this.

> **MASSEY:** Right, but none of this was — would you say
> that any of the reactions between Mr [Sef] Gonzales
> and his father [were] in an angry way that day?
> **TONEL:** No.

MASSEY: So there were no raised voices?

TONEL: No.

MASSEY: What about his mother, was there any —

TONEL: No.

MASSEY: So what, were they just like normal?

TONEL: Yes, I think, yeah.

MASSEY: You said in your statement that you don't recall him kissing his mother goodbye that day?

TONEL: No. I remember him kissing his mother when he got there but not when he left.

Tonel conceded that maybe Sef had done so, and she might not have seen it. She said at some stage after Sef arrived at the office he was fixing a computer for about ten minutes. He took out the central processing unit and was going to take it somewhere to be repaired. Sef probably did this about fifteen minutes after his arrival.

He took the computer outside, possibly to his car, and came back and rang a bank. A man from a computer shop rang and spoke to Loiva. Sef was gone for about fifteen to twenty minutes. He returned and then went into his father's office and Teddy gave him a file to take to the bank.

Next Huggett commenced her re-examination.

HUGGETT: Ms Tonel, you were asked the following question. The answer, if you just listen for one moment, the question was could he, could Sef have left around 4.30 [pm] and you answered: 'Not sure, I think earlier than that.' How much earlier do you think it could have been that Sef left?

TONEL: Probably an hour earlier.

HUGGETT: Than 4.30?

TONEL: Yeah.

ON THE THURSDAY morning, without preamble, Magistrate Sweeney gave her ruling. She found there was a 'reasonable prospect' that a jury would convict Sef Gonzales. 'The evidence ... is sufficient to prove the ... charges beyond a reasonable doubt,' Magistrate Sweeney said.

She asked Sef whether he had anything to say to the court, to which he replied: 'No, Your Worship.'

Every day of the committal so far, Father Cahill had sat behind Sef in the dock offering him encouraging smiles whenever he turned around. This day, however, he was absent, on the understanding of Sef's legal counsel that the court would be closed all day to hear the evidence of the undercover police officer, 'Leo'. Massey had not expected the hearing to wrap up so quickly.

Only a few media representatives filled the seats behind the dock. So Sef turned around and gave the media a nod and a brief smile, before he was led from the court.

Chapter 39

Sef on trial

On Monday, 5 April 2004, seven months after his committal, the trial of Sef Gonzales on three murder counts finaly began.

Sef was brought into the courtroom promptly for the 10 am start, wearing a grey suit, white shirt and blue tie. He appeared withdrawn and shaken. Dwarfed by the large dock, which could comfortably accommodate about a dozen defendants, he looked towards the ceiling and his lips moved rapidly. What he said could not be heard but his mouth shaped the words 'Our Father'. In his small hands he clutched a white strand of rosary beads. Sef Gonzales was praying.

In the very back of the public gallery sat his long-time supporter Father Paul Cahill, the Catholic priest from Killara parish who had visited Sef in custody every week since his incarceration to offer him spiritual support.

Justice Bruce James entered the stuffy, wood-panelled courtroom in his wig and scarlet robes, seating himself on the bench before the bar table. On the left of the bar table sat Mark Tedeschi, QC, and his junior, barrister Sarah Huggett, and behind them their instructing solicitor, Fiona Rowbotham. To the right of the bar table sat Winston Terracini, SC, and his junior, Philip Massey. Their instructing solicitor was Paul

Townsend, from Legal Aid, and his legal clerk was Melini Pillay, also of Legal Aid. Rowbotham, Townsend and Pillay were to do most of the heavy legwork for the trial.

Sitting in the back of the court was a raggle-taggle group of more than 30 potential jurors picked at random from the electoral roles of Sydney's Eastern Suburbs, Inner West, North Shore and Northern Beaches. Before the jury selection began Sef was asked to rise while the indictment was read to him. He stood, his shoulders hunched, blinking rapidly — a trait that betrayed his nervousness — as the charges were read out to him by the judge's associate. Sef was asked to answer the charge that he, Sef Gonzales, did murder Clodine Gonzales at North Ryde on 10 July 2001:

'I plead not guilty — not guilty,' Sef replied.

Next he was accused of killing his mother Mary.

'Not guilty.'

Then his father Teddy.

'Not guilty, not guilty.'

After his formal pleas, the jury was empanelled.

Sef looked on with interest during these proceedings. His fate was in the hands of a jury that consisted of six women and six men. Three were middle-aged or elderly, and the rest appeared to be aged from the early 20s to the late 30s. There was only one of apparent Asian ethnicity, a man who seemed to be of either Indian or Pakistani background.

During his 27 years as a barrister — 21 as a Crown Prosecutor — Tedeschi had perfected the art of addressing a jury. In the Crown's opening address, he had to summarise the evidence that would be put before the jury, and the implications the Crown believed the jury could draw from this evidence. The Crown evidence was lengthy, intricate and complicated. Tedeschi's opening address to the jury had to make it understandable. He likened the pieces of evidence to pieces of a jigsaw puzzle that the jury would be asked to put together. He adopted the attitude of storyteller, emphasising his tale with his characteristic frequent hand gesticulations. Metaphorically, he aimed to take the jury away from the stuffy courtroom, to have a 'fireside chat' with them.

Tedeschi wove a story about a man who had been a lawyer in the Philippines and done very well financially, before he and his family decided to come to Australia in 1991. He told the jury how, once in Australia, Teddy quickly requalified as a solicitor and opened the law firm T Gonzales & Associates in Blacktown, where Mary (Loiva) also worked as office manager. By 2001, Teddy and Mary had amassed considerable wealth, he said.

He told the jury how Sef's parents bought him the green Ford Festiva, and how Sef had put accessories on the vehicle and 'zipped it up'. Sef was very fond of the car and was rarely seen without it, Tedeschi said.

He then told how Teddy and Mary were 'very demanding' of their children, particularly of Sef. 'They believed Sef was very intelligent and had the capacity to become either a doctor or a lawyer,' Tedeschi told the jury.

However, Sef had done very poorly in his Higher School Certificate and in his tertiary studies at the University of New South Wales and Macquarie University. By June 2001 he was in deep trouble in his Macquarie University pre-law course. 'He was staring failure in the face … he was risking expulsion from the course,' Tedeschi said.

Around that time, he met Kathy Wu and 'decided he liked the looks of her'. They developed a fondness for each other, despite his mother's disapproval. Even though Kathy broke up with Sef after they had sex, he seemed to disregard her wish to end their relationship. 'From Sef's point of view this was just a minor hurdle in the pursuit of his girl ... he had decided that he loved the girl,' Tedeschi told the court.

Sef, Tedeschi argued, was more concerned about his parents' threats, due to his poor grades, to imposing a series of sanctions, from taking away his car and withdrawing his allowance, to 'disowning' him.

'The Crown case is that by late June 2001 Sef's life was unravelling, and the prospect of his whole life coming apart was looming large,' Tedeschi said. Faced with this, Tedeschi told the court, Sef set in train a plan to murder his parents and his sister. There were two purposes to this plan: the first to rid himself of the impediments to his privileged lifestyle, and the second to get his hands on their wealth. During the course of the trial, Tedeschi would rely heavily on evidence from Sef's friends and family, particularly Emily Luna and Amelita Claridades, about the growing friction between Sef and his parents. Emily would also repeat what she saw at the house on the night of the murders.

The three things the Crown had to prove for Sef to be convicted of the murder charges were: that each of the three family members died, that it was Sef's actions that caused their deaths, and that Sef had intended to kill them.

The proof of intent to kill did not just lie with the 'overkill' — the frenzied stabbing — of Teddy and Loiva, to which forensic pathologist Allan Cala would attest at the trial. Proving not only that Sef intended to kill his family the day of the murders but that the murders had also been planned months in advance would rely heavily on the admission of the 'poison plot' scenario into evidence. This evidence was allowed, even though Sef's trial was purely for murder. The charge of threatening product contamination had been put on hold pending the outcome of the murder verdict, as it carried a lesser penalty and a hearing was unlikely to proceed if Sef was found guilty of killing his family.

JASON BECKETT, the police computer expert, was the first Crown witness to take the stand. Tedeschi led Beckett painstakingly through the complicated evidence found on the Gonzales' home computer and the laptop seized from Sef's bedroom. Beckett told the court how he had recovered from these computers the searches on the Internet about poisons and methods of killing, the drafts of the threatening letter sent to the food and beverage company, as well as the letters to the Australian Federal Police and Australian Quarantine and Inspection Service, alerting these bodies to the poisoning threat. Evidence was produced that Sef, on 13 February and 19 and 20 June 2001, placed e-mail orders for two types of poisonous seeds. Two of the orders were placed with suppliers in the United States and one was with a supplier in Australia. He stressed the urgency in his orders and gave his home address for delivery. One of these deliveries from a US supplier was intercepted by the Australian Quarantine and Inspection Service. On 25 June he placed another e-mail order for poisonous seeds from a supplier on the New South Wales North Coast, stressing that they were needed urgently for his mother's 60th birthday. (Loiva was actually 43 when she died.) The supplier gave a statement to police that he did actually send the seeds, and this statement was read out to the court.

A police fingerprint expert testified that a fingerprint had been left on the envelope of the letter sent to the Australian Federal police and stated that it was a very good match with Sef's fingerprint. The jurors also heard about the film canister filled with clear liquid seized from Sef's bedroom, and heard that he had told Linda Pham it contained one of the two poisons, which he had derived from the seed himself.

Dr Corey Cunningham, a doctor who treated Loiva during her admission to Sydney Adventist Hospital on 3 July 2001, testified that despite blood, urine and faeces tests on Loiva, he could find nothing to truly account for her symptoms. She had presented to the hospital, he said, with a three-day history of abdominal pains and diarrhoea. In the day leading up to her admission her symptoms became more acute, as she developed fever, cramps and bloody diarrhoea. She had told the doctor she had eaten out four nights earlier, and Dr Cunningham had concluded she was suffering inflammation of the large bowel, probably due to food poisoning.

Dr Cunningham said that at the time he never considered Loiva had been deliberately poisoned, and indeed he had never heard of the two poisons derived from the seeds Sef had allegedly ordered. Certainly the hospital did not test for the presence of such poisons, only for the microbes that commonly cause food poisoning. The tests found nothing that could fully explain Loiva's symptoms. However, the tests did find that her white cell count was high, indicating some sort of inflammation in her body.

Terracini then cross-examined Dr Cunningham.

TERRACINI: You have seen a lot of people who have had food poisoning?

CUNNINGHAM: I have.

TERRACINI: Did you see anything on this lady in her tests, on your physical inspection, taking a history from her, and analysing all of the information that came your way, back from pathology to indicate that there was anything wrong with her other than the fact that she had a dose of food poisoning?

CUNNINGHAM: No, that was my clinical impression.

After Terracini sat down, Tedeschi had an important question to put to Dr Cunningham about the course food poisoning usually took, considering that Loiva's symptoms worsened dramatically on day three of her illness and she took a turn for the better on day four.

TEDESCHI: What is the normal progression of gastroenteritis from an infection?

CUNNINGHAM: One would expect onset of symptoms between eight to twenty-four hours.

TEDESCHI: So the symptoms are worse between eight and twenty-four hours?

CUNNINGHAM: Symptoms [at] onset are often worse over the first one to two days and then settle. But not in all cases.

After Cunningham was excused from the stand, Tedeschi called the Crown's big gun. Major Mike Rowell was a senior medical officer from the Incident Response Regiment of the Australian Defence Force. He was well versed in the effects of biological weapons, including the two poisons made from the two types of seeds Sef Gonzales allegedly ordered over the Internet.

Major Rowell told the jury he was not aware of anyone being diagnosed as having been poisoned with either substance in either Australia or the United States. In fact, the only case he was aware of was that of a defector from an Eastern European country.

The two poisons, he said, had similar effects, although one substance was more toxic than the other. The symptoms that occurred within hours of consuming either of the poisons were nausea, vomiting, diarrhoea, and possibly abdominal pain and a low-grade fever. The symptoms could then worsen to include severe diarrhoea, which might be bloody. The low-grade fever would persist, and the victim's white cell count would be elevated. If a strong enough dose were administered, the poison would affect the liver, spleen and lymph nodes, causing dehydration. At worst, it would bring about failure of the organs and circulatory system, and death.

> **TEDESCHI:** And in a mild degree of intoxication by [either poison] how soon does death occur if there is a sufficient dose to cause death?
>
> **ROWELL:** If a sufficient dose is taken then generally not prior to three days and generally in the order of three to seven days.
>
> **TEDESCHI:** If a person receives a low dose of [either poison] not leading to death, are you able to say [within] what period of time recovery would take place?
>
> **ROWELL:** Generally over three, four days. The physiological process is still the same, tissue damage is the same. And low-grade symptoms for a number of days followed by recovery at the three- to four-day mark.

Tedeschi quizzed Major Rowell as to whether, on examining Loiva's hospital record, he found her symptoms to be consistent with poisoning by either of these two toxins. Rowell replied that they were consistent with being caused by either, as both worked in the same way, but he went on to qualify this, referring to the tests done on Loiva in hospital: 'none of these tests alone or together would lead me to make the diagnosis of [one type] or [the other type of] poisoning ... There are multiple other diagnoses which could provide the same clinical syndrome and provide the same test results.'

As he had with Dr Cunningham, Terracini led Major Rowell to state in cross-examination that the symptoms Loiva suffered could have been caused by food poisoning. He said he wanted Major Rowell to assume that there had been no sign of damage to Loiva's organs consistent with poisoning from either type of seed during autopsy. Rowell responded, 'I did not see an autopsy report so, no, I cannot comment on that.'

At this point it was important for Tedeschi to explain to the jury why forensic pathologist Dr Cala had not found such damage during Loiva's autopsy.

TEDESCHI: Major, you were asked questions about what you would expect to find in relation to changes to organs during a postmortem examination. Did you mean by that where the person has died from [either type of] poisoning that you would expect to see those organ changes?

ROWELL: Yes.

TEDESCHI: If a person had had a low dose of [either type of poison], which caused the kinds of symptoms that Mary Gonzales had, but had then recovered, do you know whether you would expect to see organ changes if she died of completely unrelated causes about a week later?

ROWELL: I would not claim to be an expert in that area in particular, but I would expect that she wouldn't show those changes.

TEDESCHI: That she ... ?

ROWELL: Would not show those changes in her organ systems if she had recovered. That the damage to each of those organs was not sufficient to cause her death and may have resolved within the subsequent week or two.

Despite its complicated nature, the jury seemed to be following the poisons evidence closely, as was shown when they visited the Gonzales house on day three of the evidence to get an idea of its layout and where the bodies and particular evidence were found. In the rear of the yard, at least one juror noted a large tree. The jury passed a note to the judge, asking if it was a particular sort of tree, which produced one of the two types of seeds that Sef had allegedly ordered. Tawas detectives were taken by surprise at this sudden turn; they had not really taken much notice of the plant, which had not been there at the time of the murders. They would quickly arrange for horticulturist and botanist Patrick Houlcroft, from Sydney's Royal Botanic Gardens, to come out and view the plant. His statement would later be admitted as evidence in the trial.

Houlcroft had instantly identified the plant. It was, he said, the plant that produced one of the two seeds Sef had allegedly ordered. He estimated the tree to be older than 18 months. Houlcroft stated the plant was an 'introduced weed' that was prevalent in Sydney. However, in inspecting rear yards of adjoining residential properties, and taking a drive around the immediate vicinity, he could not see any other trees of the same variety.

'The ... plant is not spread by birds and tends to germinate adjoining parent plants, normally in moist soil conditions. In view of this it is highly unlikely that the ... plant that I inspected germinated by natural distribution. For this reason I believe that the plant ... was deliberately planted or at least seed discarded by human activity.'

The jury's question was answered, but jurors were left to wonder whether Sef had deliberately planted seeds in the back yard, or whether seeds had been discarded by Sef and took hold in the fertile soil. And if he deliberately planted them, for what purpose?

THE POISONS EVIDENCE was important in proving premeditation, as was the evidence of the 'false trails' that showed Sef was trying to cover up for his alleged guilt — the threatening e-mails, the attempted break-in at his Chatswood apartment, and the alleged abduction. However, this evidence would mean little if the Crown could not link Sef to the scene of the murders, at the time of the murders, beyond reasonable doubt. Of all the evidence introduced to the trial, the forensic evidence obtained from the house, along with the sighting of Sef's car there during the murders, were most crucial to gaining a conviction.

To set the scene for this forensic evidence, it is important to note that the jury watched Sef's videotaped interview with Sheehy and Sim held on 3 August 2001. In the interview, Sef tells the officers two key things about himself. Firstly, that he writes with his left hand. Secondly, that the shoe size he normally wears is between a 6 and 7 (although he is not asked and does not elaborate in the interview on whether this is a United States or United Kingdom shoe size, as they vary according to country of manufacture or sale). Sef also denied in the interview that he ever owned a pair of the Human brand shoes, but said his father may have had a pair and that his father did buy his cousin Monica a pair when she visited the family from the Philippines in April to May 2001. He told the officers Monica left her shoebox behind when she packed to leave and that he then stored his hair clippers inside it. The box was marked size 7, the same size as the shoe prints found at the murder scene.

Crime-scene officer Detective Sergeant Robert Gibbs, who had completed a university course on detection and identification of footwear impressions, was called to the witness box.

Gibbs described how bloodied shoe prints were found around Teddy's body and briefcase, in the hallway leading from the front foyer towards the back family room–kitchen area, on the stairs to the upstairs level, and leading into Clodine's bedroom. One partial shoe print had been found underneath Loiva's bag and its scattered contents, and blood had also been found underneath Teddy's briefcase.

TEDESCHI: So were you of the view that that blood, which had a shoe print in it, had been shed before the handbag and its contents [were] put on the ground?

GIBBS: Yes.

TEDESCHI: Did you come to any general conclusion about the items in the vicinity of Teddy and [Loiva] Gonzales?

GIBBS: It didn't look like they'd fallen out as a result of the attack. It looked like the bag had been emptied and placed onto the ground [after the blood was shed]. And so did the briefcase.

Gibbs described how police had treated the bloody prints with Leuco Crystal Violet, a chemical that reacts with the protein in blood, to make the prints turn a deep purple colour that would stand out. The officer told the court how he had conducted an experiment with six different pairs of Human brand shoes, both men's and women's and of varying sizes. He told the jury the bloody prints appeared to have been made by the sole of men's Human brand shoes size UK 7/US 8. None of the bloody prints had been made by the size UK 7 Brahma brand hiking boots that Sef had been wearing at the time of his 'discovery' of the bodies, Gibbs said.

Monica Gonzales, Teddy's niece, was called to give evidence on whether Teddy had actually bought her a pair of laceless Human brand shoes, as Sef had stated. Monica had some extremely interesting additional information for the jury. She revealed how, during her visit to Sydney in early 2001, she and Teddy had gone shopping at Birkenhead Point, where Teddy bought her a pair of white Human brand shoes, size 6, the shoebox for which she said she left in Clodine's closet when she returned to the Philippines.

TEDESCHI: Was there any particular reason why he [Teddy] bought you those shoes on that day?

MONICA: I was just browsing around and I liked the shoe. Unfortunately it wasn't available in the ladies' line, so I decided to buy the smallest size for the men's. And, him being a generous man, he decided to purchase it for me.

TEDESCHI: After he got you those shoes did you notice something about his shoes in the days following when you were at 6 Collins Street?

MONICA: Yes.

TEDESCHI: What did you notice?

MONICA: A day or two after that we were at home and I noticed him wearing the exact same brand of shoe, except that his was in a different colour. It was in grey and it was in suede instead of being in leather.

TEDESCHI: Did you try his shoes on?

MONICA: No I didn't, but we did have a conversation about the size being the smallest in men's as well, because he had small feet. And he did indicate that he chose the smallest size.

TEDESCHI: So what did you discover about your shoe size in men's shoes and his shoe size?

MONICA: They were similar. They were the smallest size.

TEDESCHI: Similar or the same?

MONICA: Well, I noticed here [in the photo Tedeschi showed her of the shoebox for white Human brand Rhythm model shoes, priced $79.95, from Insport, in Sef's room] that it actually says UK 7 and I think that from memory I just recall it being 6, because the attendant said that the smallest size is 6. But this is definitely the box which contained my pair of shoes.

A statement from an Insport employee informed the court that a cash sale for a pair of Human brand, Rhythm model shoes had been made at Birkenhead Point, Drummoyne, on 29 April 2001. They were a size UK 7/US 8 and cost $79.95. This backed up the purchase by Teddy of Monica's shoes.

More importantly, though, Monica, in her evidence, confirmed that Teddy had his own pair of Human brand shoes, which he wore on weekends to run errands, and otherwise kept in the shoe closet under the stairs. Teddy's were the same style and size as the shoes he had bought her at Birkenhead Point: men's, size UK 7/US 8. The only difference was in the colour and material. However, Teddy's shoes were never found inside the house.

DETECTIVE SERGEANT ROBERT GIBBS had some other crucial evidence to give about the crime scene — in particular about the racist scrawl 'FUCK OFF ASIANS KKK' spray-painted in blue on a section of Gyprock wall in the back family room. Gibbs told Tedeschi that he took samples of the paint from the wall. Later, these were sent off for analysis at the University of Technology (UTS), Sydney.

Police had also seized a number of cans of spray paint from the Gonzales' shed, he said. Evidence was later given by

Detective Sergeant Brian O'Donoghue that these cans contained silver, chrome, matte black and gold paint, of the Australian Export brand. Police had then purchased two shades of blue spray paint, Sky Blue and Ocean Blue, in the same brand, for comparison with the paint on the wall.

Gibbs had been keenly observant, enough to notice, on the jumper Sef wore on the night of the murders, discolouration on the left-hand sleeve, just above the cuff. He took a photo of it under a microscope at a Westmead laboratory.

Dr Philip Maynard, a paint expert employed at UTS's Department of Chemistry, Materials and Forensic Science, was provided by police with the two blue comparison paint cans of the paint brand Australian Export, and five additional ones: White Knight brand Bermuda Blue, Royal Blue and Metallic Blue, 5 Star brand Ocean Blue, and Polycraft brand Ocean Blue. He was asked to compare these with the discolouration on Sef's jumper using microspectrophotometry, which determines colour, and Raman microspectroscopy, to determine chemical composition.

Giving evidence in court, Dr Maynard said he compared the two Australian Export shades of blue with the paint on the wall and on the jumper.

TEDESCHI: Is this correct, that you found both in terms of colour and composition that the blue on the wall and the jumper was indistinguishable from the Ocean Blue spray paint?

MAYNARD: That's correct. The paint was the darker of the two Export brand paints.

TEDESCHI: Could I summarise your position in this way: so far as colour and composition are concerned, the blue on the wall was identical with the blue on the jumper, and in turn that was

identical with the dark blue can of spray paint that
you have got there? [Tedeschi had presented
Maynard with the Australian Export spray paint
during evidence.]

MAYNARD: That's correct.

TEDESCHI: Did you then compare the same Ocean
Blue colour with other types of ocean blue spray
paint?

MAYNARD: That's correct. From other brands.

TEDESCHI: And those brands were White Knight,
Bermuda Blue; White Knight, Royal Blue; White
Knight, Metallic Blue; 5 Star, Ocean Blue; and
Polycraft, Ocean Blue?

MAYNARD: That's correct.

TEDESCHI: Is this what you found, that you were not
able to distinguish between different brands of the
same colour?

MAYNARD: Yes, the three Ocean Blue paints that I
examined were all indistinguishable.

So any of the three Ocean Blue paints could have left the
scrawl on the wall and the mark on Sef's jumper sleeve.

Terracini set about finding out whether the paint on Sef's
sleeve could have been left by the blue woodchips in the
Gonzales' yard, as Sef had claimed in a police interview.

MAYNARD: I examined them by
microspectrophotometry as well, and they were
different.

TERRACINI: Are they, like, demonstrably different, or are
they still bluish in colour, or what?

MAYNARD: They are blue, but they were easily
distinguishable.

The next thing for Terracini to pin down was the time it would take for the paint on the wall to dry. This would be relevant if Sef had come home, found his family dead and accidentally rubbed his sleeve against the racist scrawl. (However, Sef had denied to police that he ever saw the racist scrawl that night.)

TERRACINI: And the studies that you made about spray paint, assume that it is spray paint somewhere on this jumper, can you get it when you rub your arm, or anything like that, up against an object that has got spray paint on it?

MAYNARD: It's possible. Spray paint dries very quickly.

TERRACINI: But lasts for an hour or so?

MAYNARD: Yes, about an hour before it sets.

Dr Paul Westwood, a handwriting expert, was asked to testify to comparisons he made between samples of Sef's handwriting and the 'FUCK OFF ASIANS KKK' scrawl. The section of Gyprock that contained this writing had been removed from the house by police and was laid out before the jury in three pieces. It was confronting.

Dr Westwood stated that there were numerous similarities between Sef's handwriting and that on the wall: the 'A's, 'C's, 'F's, 'K's and 'S's had similar characteristics. However, the differences between the 'N's and 'O's caused him to qualify his opinion. He could only offer 'moderate support' for the claim that the writing was Sef's, but he said the differences could be attributable to the different motor skills involved in handwriting, as opposed to the action of spray painting.

TEDESCHI: So would you expect to find differences between the same person writing with a pen and the same person writing with a spray can?

WESTWOOD: I would expect that there would be some features you wouldn't be able to account for. But, regardless of what instrument or what mode that you're writing in, you're still writing from a practised image, if you like, that's stored, that has been stored in the mind as a result of many years of practice. And writing is to a large extent a subconscious act. You don't necessarily give a lot of thought to the way you actually construct your writing.

Westwood said the person who wrote the scrawl would likely be left handed (as Sef was), due to the 'O's being written in a clockwise direction (right-handed people write 'O's anticlockwise).

TEDESCHI: Finally, Mr Westwood, if a person is trying to disguise their writing do you still tend to find some features of their normal handwriting that come through?

MAYNARD: Well, it's a case-by-case situation. But normally you do expect people to still manifest some characteristics of their writing, even when they're attempting to disguise.

Terracini, in cross-examination, summarised Westwood's testimony.

TERRACINI: Based on all the material that you have got, your best opinion is that you wouldn't rely on your opinion to satisfy anybody even on the balance of probabilities, would you?

MAYNARD: As I say, my evidence alone certainly
    wouldn't establish a case against somebody. I'm saying
    it is a qualified view, but it's very low on the scale.

Robert Gibbs described how the family's cordless phone —
the one that had a cut cable — was discovered on the upstairs
floor near the top of the staircase, close to Clodine's room. Sef
had claimed that the phone had not worked when he tried to
use it downstairs, after discovering his father's body, so he had
used his mobile instead.

Gibbs also explained the deductions he had made about
the strange marks on the wall in Clodine's bedroom above
where her body was found. He described the experiments he
had performed: striking a piece of Gyprock with various
items, including baseball and T-ball bats, an axe handle and a
spade handle. He had found that a black-painted T-ball bat
caused the most similar marks. A comparison chart of the
marks Gibbs made on the Gyprock and the marks made on
Clodine's wall was displayed to the jury. Gibbs said that
nothing was found inside Clodine's room or in the rest of
the house that could have caused similar marks, although in
other evidence the jury was told about the baseball bat that
Sef admitted once owning and that he said had gone
missing. Gibbs readily admitted under cross-examination,
however, that the Gyprock had been lying on carpet when
he struck it with the various items, and that it had by no
means been a scientific experiment.

OF COURSE, THE Crown also had to prove beyond
reasonable doubt that Sef had not been elsewhere during the
murders. He had already admitted the Raf De Leon alibi was
false and given police a fresh alibi, saying that he was with the
prostitute Latisha on the evening of the murders.

Latisha, a woman of around 30 with a hardened face and slim figure, clad in denim and black leggings, took the stand. She maintained she had just been trying to get Sef off her back when she said she thought she may have been with him on the night of the murders, but had told Sef to check the brothel records. She maintained she had taken that week off to spend with her son because he was on school holidays. Unfortunately for the defence, Latisha's story was shored up by the tendering of La Petite Aroma's work records, including a roster on which she was listed to work but her name had been crossed out with the notation: '[Latisha], one week off, don't ring'. Her name was certainly crossed off for the Tuesday evening of the murders, and the only night that week she may have decided to work after all was the Friday night, where there was a tick beside her name.

Terracini delivered a stinging, lengthy cross-examination, accusing the prostitute of being a person who lied about her income and support benefits, and a person of dishonesty. In the face of his questions, Latisha grew very vague and uncertain about the subject of her income but maintained she considered herself a person of honesty.

Had there been no brothel records to back up her claims, perhaps the trial may have had a totally different result, as she was Sef's alibi. The defence had done its best to discredit Latisha in the eyes of the jurors, and may have succeeded — but in the end it was shadow-boxing.

Chapter 40

Trial: the conclusion

Sef's 'Latisha' alibi may have been in tatters, but his defence team was handed a gift during the six-week trial. It came in the form of evidence from Clodine's best friend and Sam Dacillo's little sister, Michelle Dacillo. This evidence revolved around a number of calls she made to Clodine's mobile telephone, which police found on Clodine's desk in her bedroom, hooked up to a phone charger, after the murders. Michelle made the calls while — according to the Crown — Clodine lay dead in her bedroom.

The evidence, in this writer's opinion, was the only aspect of the trial that implanted a niggling doubt in the minds of those who had sat through the whole proceedings. The question would be: was it enough to create reasonable doubt in the jurors' minds for them to acquit Sef?

Robert Gibbs told the court how, when he entered Clodine's bedroom, he examined her mobile telephone. On the screen he saw a message that there were eight missed calls.

Detective Senior Constable Darren Murphy told the jury how he had obtained phone records for all the Gonzales family members for the day of the murders. These records showed that the last text message Clodine had sent from her mobile phone was at 4.04 pm, to a phone used by Clodine's Melbourne friend Vanessa O'Mera.

Tedeschi questioned Murphy about Clodine's eight missed calls, six of which were made by a telephone service in the name of Michelle Dacillo on the night of the murders. Michelle had made the calls while Sef was out on the town with her brother Sam, the only alibi of Sef's that was rock-solid, Sam having testified to their movements — that they went to Planet Hollywood for dinner.

> **TEDESCHI:** And in fact are there six calls which have been attempted by Michelle Dacillo's mobile phone number to Clodine Gonzales' mobile phone number with a duration of zero seconds?
>
> **MURPHY:** That's correct.
>
> **TEDESCHI:** And they are at these times: 9.01 pm, 9.04 pm, 9.20 pm, 9.26 pm, 10.45 pm and 11.04 pm?
>
> **MURPHY:** That's correct.

The person making the calls took the stand. Michelle Dacillo, now twenty, was well-spoken with a cheerful face. Her family had known the Gonzales family since Michelle was seven years old, and she had maintained her close friendship with Clodine even though they attended different schools in different cities.

Michelle said she had organised to meet up with Clodine some time after 1 pm on 10 July 2001, but they never ended up doing this.

> **TEDESCHI:** Why was that?
>
> **MICHELLE:** She sent me a text message, between, like, around 10 o'clock [am], saying that she had to break our plans because she had to do something with her

mum that afternoon, and that we'd organise to meet
again maybe in the next few days.

Michelle said that she tried to call Clodine around 7 pm but
could not get through to her, and she persisted throughout
the night, including the period when Sef was out with Sam.
Her next statement would make the ears of Sef's defence
lawyers prick up.

> **TEDESCHI:** What happened when you tried to ring her?
> **MICHELLE:** Well, I tried to ring her house, that was
> busy, tried her mobile and just, she didn't pick up.
> I alternated between the house phone and the
> mobile, and at one point I called her mobile and
> after about three rings it, like, the call was rejected.
> I tried again and after one ring it was rejected. Tried
> again and it just kept ringing. And kind of carried
> on like that.
> **TEDESCHI:** So you carried on till when, trying to ring
> her?
> **MICHELLE:** Probably stopped trying to call her about
> ten o'clock.

Michelle had used the term 'rejected', which in mobile
phone users' parlance typically means someone does not wish
to take the call and presses the 'End' or 'No' button. For a call
to be rejected, it means someone is physically pressing a
button on the phone. The Crown case was that all the
Gonzales family members were dead at this point, and Sef was
the killer. If Sef was with Sam, as he had been, then who was
pressing the button on the phone? Was it the killer?

Michelle may have simply used the wrong term; it may
have been a slip of the tongue. However, no-one would find

out, because Tedeschi skipped on to his next line of questioning, rather than probing further.

> **TEDESCHI:** At some stage did you ring your brother
>   that night?
> **MICHELLE:** No, he called me.
> **TEDESCHI:** He called you?
> **MICHELLE:** Yeah.
> **TEDESCHI:** Did you tell him about your attempts to
>   contact Clodine?
> **MICHELLE:** Yes.

Michelle continued with her evidence, describing how Sef had come to the Dacillos' house at about 8 pm on the night of the murders. She said she was still up when her brother returned home that night, around 11.40 pm.

Terracini's cross-examination of Michelle was meandering, revolving mostly around how Michelle and Clodine usually communicated by phone. He certainly did not ask her about the 'rejected' calls. Had he asked her, she may have made some clarifications or changes to her terminology.

Optus support liaison officer David Finlay was called later in the trial to explain the meaning of the 'eight missed calls' message on Clodine's mobile telephone. (Her phone provider had been Optus.) Tedeschi kept his questioning brief, showing Finlay the missed call records.

> **TEDESCHI:** A missed call is a call which is not answered,
>   is that right?
> **FINLAY:** That is correct.

Terracini took considerably longer. There was a lot of importance in this for the defence.

TERRACINI: Just on that note, sir, I want you to assume we have heard evidence in this case where the word 'rejected' has been used. In terms of your field does that have any meaning that is peculiar to mobile phones?

FINLAY: It's not what we would say a technical term. But our — when we are — it is mentioned to us through customer service, about calls being rejected. To us that would indicate a call when it is ringing and someone hitting the end button or the reject button on their phone, 'cause they don't want to take a particular call.

TERRACINI: Can it also mean that it's dropped out?

FINLAY: Not the word 'rejected', 'cause to us that would indicate someone not wanting to take a call. For a drop-out call it would be just that, dropped out.

TERRACINI: In terms of the person who is on the other end of the phone, the person making the call, does something flash up on the screen of the Optus mobile phone service that tells you what's happened?

FINLAY: Different handsets have different characteristics. I'm not an expert in what every handset would be able to show. My own particular handset doesn't show anything at all if I make a call and the call drops out or is rejected. It just goes back to its ready state for another call.

Finlay agreed that North Ryde was not an area where Optus had any significant reception problems, limiting the likelihood of repeat call drop-outs.

TERRACINI: So we can basically eliminate, can we, almost every example of how a phone would appear to be rejected, excepting the one that somebody's actually pressed a rejection button, that is, the disengaged button?

FINLAY: Yes, it's a bit hard for me to say that's what's happened to any particular call, because I do not have records that would be able to indicate that for any call. If someone pushes the reject button or just lets the call ring out and it's not answered, the results would show the same, a non-answered call, to us.

TERRACINI: But certainly if someone said they ring a number of times and it was rejected, that would normally mean at least that somebody's been physically in control of the handset and pressed the reject or the disengage button?

FINLAY: That is a possibility. But, again, as I said, from the records I have I would not be able to indicate whether that happened or if the phone rung out to its maximum number of rings and then just terminated because the call itself wasn't answered.

TERRACINI: I want you to assume we have heard evidence that a person by the name of Dacillo rang the relevant mobile, rang about three times, the call was rejected, and then she tried again and then after one ring it was rejected, and then she tried again, it was rejected. Obviously assuming that she is accurately recording what took place, the only rational interpretation of that is that somebody has the handset and is pressing the disengaged or —

Tedeschi objected to the line of questioning, saying Finlay could not be asked to interpret what another witness had meant when she referred to a 'rejected' call. Terracini said he would withdraw the reference to Michelle Dacillo, and continued his questioning.

TERRACINI: If you ring on a mobile phone and it rings three times and the call is stopped, that is consistent with somebody disengaging?

FINLAY: It is. That, or someone could just have a very short ring time on their phone.

TERRACINI: And if it only rings once and the same thing happens again, the most likely result of that is that somebody's disengaging the call?

FINLAY: That's a possibility, yes.

TERRACINI: If they ring back only moments later and the same thing happens on the same number, and it rings and it's disengaged, the most likely reason for that is that somebody's disengaging the call?

FINLAY: That is correct.

TERRACINI: Other than a dropped-out call, whatever, any other reasonable explanations?

FINLAY: There could be any reason why the call has terminated. It would depend on the number of calls, how many rings the customer has their phone set up to ring for.

Tedeschi rose to re-examine Finlay.

TEDESCHI: Is this the case, have you conducted an experiment to see what different records are created at the Optus exchange between a missed call — that is, a call that rings out without being answered — and a call which is rejected because somebody has pressed the no button?

FINLAY: There are no physical records as such, but I have, in conjunction with one of my colleagues in my office, had him ring my mobile and then let it, one,

ring out, and then again have him ring the number
and I then push the reject button.

TEDESCHI: When you say the reject button you mean
the no button?

FINLAY: The no button. And what he got was the same
response of beeps as if the phone you normally get if
you make a phone call and the other person hangs up
before you and you hear a couple of beeps. That's
what he received both times.

Finlay described how his colleague rang his mobile from a
landline to see what would come up on his phone screen if
he rejected the call.

TEDESCHI: Did it come up on your phone as a missed
call?

FINLAY: No, not when I pushed the end button.

TEDESCHI: When you pressed the —

It was Terracini's turn to object, but Tedeschi pressed the point.

TEDESCHI: My friend [Terracini] is attempting to create
some sort of impression that these calls on Clodine
Gonzales' mobile might have been calls that
somebody pressed the no button.

TERRACINI: Because the witness has given evidence
about it.

TEDESCHI: And I am attempting to demonstrate in my
re-examination that that is not the case. I press the
line, Your Honour.

Tedeschi was given leave to continue this line, and showed a
police photograph of Clodine's phone found at the crime

scene to Finlay. Finlay agreed that the screen showed eight missed calls.

TEDESCHI: Could I clarify it this way. The experiment you conducted where you pressed the end or no button to terminate the call, did that come up as a missed call on your phone, that is the receiver's phone?

FINLAY: No, it did not. But also as I stated earlier not all handsets respond the same way to different things, so —

Terracini pressed the issue further.

TERRACINI: The experiment — I am not being critical of you, Mr Finlay — was conducted with another bloke on a landline?

FINLAY: That is correct, yes.

Terracini went on to question the nature of Finlay's 'experiment'.

TERRACINI: And to use a landline to compare what shows up on the landline as opposed to what shows up on the mobile, what significance is that?

FINLAY: I was only really doing it to see what was on my phone. Not from the person making the call.

TERRACINI: In fact, from the point of view of the person making the call, no assistance whatsoever?

FINLAY: That is correct.

TERRACINI: What is going to show up on his landline phone?

FINLAY: Nothing would show up on that.

Terracini probed the call rejection scenario once more.

> **TERRACINI:** I suggest that laymen have got experience in this as well, in that most people use telephones. When you are ringing somebody and it just goes ring once and it stops, that tends to suggest that somebody stopped the call, doesn't it?
>
> **FINLAY:** From personal experience that's what I would believe, yes.
>
> **TERRACINI:** And if you tried again a second or two later and exactly the same thing happens, that's what you'd think as well, wouldn't you?
>
> **FINLAY:** Yes, it would.
>
> **TERRACINI:** And if you kept on trying eight times and exactly the same thing happens, consistent with somebody stopping the call?
>
> **FINLAY:** It would. I'd probably start worrying they might have had a faulty handset too.
>
> **TERRACINI:** I assume the police never asked you anything about a faulty handset?
>
> **FINLAY:** Well, I wasn't asked anything about any particular handset.

Terracini had proven that the police never got Finlay to actually examine either Clodine's or Michelle's actual handsets to see how they worked, and sat down, his job done. The rejected call scenario had not been resolved one way or the other. It was up to the jury to decide whether this question would be enough to outweigh the mass of incriminating evidence presented against Sef in the trial.

SEF GONZALES HAD been sitting in the dock listening intently to each piece of evidence — sometimes studiously taking notes, sometimes scowling and shaking his head as witnesses gave particularly unfavourable evidence, and sometimes resting his head on his hands dramatically, as if overwhelmed with sadness. Now he wanted his say in court.

The young man who had seemingly manipulated people so well in the past backed his own ability to sway the jury. He was the defence's only witness.

On 10 May, after all the other evidence had been presented, Terracini began his opening address outlining the case for the defence. Terracini reminded the jury that Sef did not have to take the stand, and in doing so was exposing himself to a grilling on a vast range of evidence. He said Sef would tell the jury he had told lies about a number of matters. The question for the jury to decide was: was he telling the truth now, in this, his murder trial?

'Please don't impose a burden on him that perhaps you could not bear yourselves. In this way, there probably — I emphasise "probably" because some of you may have standards of integrity and honesty far beyond that of mortal men. But I bet that all of you perhaps have told at least a white lie or fudged the truth at least once in your life.

'So when you assess that perhaps — and it is up to you ultimately to assess the evidence for yourselves. It is not what I say or what the Crown says, or indeed — and I don't expect he's going to — but even if the learned trial judge said he had a view. It is your view that counts and only your view.

'But when you come for instance to the somewhat amateurish bragging to young women and things like that, or trying to make out as if you're a strong fellow or a wealthy man or a genius or a tae kwon do expert or you went to the Olympics or you're flying to meet somebody in New York because you've got a multimillionaire business. Even if you find that a lot of that was just nonsense, that doesn't mean that he's guilty of killing his parents and his sister. Not more complex than that.

'You have to be satisfied beyond reasonable doubt that he did those things. Not because you're suspicious. Because reasonable doubt does not mean I don't like the look of someone. It does not mean why can't he prove his alibi? It does not mean he's told lies repeatedly about a whole range of things in the past.'

Terracini, in his deep, rumbling voice, sombrely reminded the jury of the great responsibility resting upon their shoulders. They must reach their verdicts within the confines of the law, and must be unanimous in their belief of Sef's guilt if they were to convict him of these three murders.

'And having said that, I will call the accused,' he finished.

Tedeschi watched keen-eyed as, 23 minutes before court was due to finish for the day, Sef was released from the dock and walked to the stand. He watched as Sef swore an oath before God to tell the truth, the whole truth and nothing but the truth. Tedeschi was eager for the chance to cross-examine, to expose Sef's character to the jury, to give them a first-hand glimpse of Sef's dishonesty. It was one thing to hear about Sef's lies in court; it was quite another actually to witness the lies spilling from his mouth.

Sef took the stand and his evidence in chief was extremely brief.

Terracini had Sef state his full name then launched into the key questions.

TERRACINI: Mr Gonzales, did you murder your
mother?

SEF: No, sir, I did not.

TERRACINI: Did you murder your father?

SEF: No, sir, I did not.

TERRACINI: Did you murder your sister?

SEF: No, sir, I did not.

Terracini led Sef through his version of the day of 10 July 2001, starting with Sef's microwaving a meal for lunch at home around midday. Sef then left for his father's Blacktown office, arriving about 1.30 pm, and leaving before 4 pm. He headed home to North Ryde, parked his car in the carport, walked to the service station on Wicks Road and caught a taxi to Chatswood railway station. From there he walked to La Petite Aroma brothel where, after having to wait for a period of time, he selected the prostitute Latisha. He said he had never met her before. After leaving the brothel he walked back to Chatswood station and caught a cab home, arriving back in North Ryde about 7.45 pm. From there, he got in his car and drove to Sam Dacillo's house and they drove together into the city, arriving just before 9 pm.

> **TERRACINI:** What time, then, did you arrive home back at North Ryde and find that your family had been killed?
>
> **SEF:** I think it was some time after 11.30, sir.

Sef's evidence-in-chief only took a couple of minutes. Terracini sat down, and Tedeschi rose from his seat.

Tedeschi was skilled at picking up visual clues from witnesses that indicate they are nervous and may be lying. With Sef, Tedeschi observed, it was the rapid blinking. It was a dead giveaway. Tedeschi would soon have Sef blinking frantically.

Tedeschi began, his manner abrupt, his voice hard.

TEDESCHI: Mr Gonzales, were you distressed on the night of 10 July that your parents and sister had been murdered?

SEF: After finding them, sir?

TEDESCHI: Yes?

SEF: Yes, sir.

TEDESCHI: Were you anxious to assist the police as much as you could to help them catch those who were responsible?

SEF: Sorry, sir, could you repeat the question?

TEDESCHI: Were you anxious to assist the police as much as you could to help them to catch those who were responsible for the deaths of your family members?

SEF: Very much, sir.

TEDESCHI: Yet you remained sufficiently composed, did you not, to tell the police a litany of lies about your movements for the period between 4 pm and 8 pm that evening, did you not?

SEF: Sorry, sir, could you repeat the question?

TEDESCHI: You remained sufficiently composed when you were interviewed by the police to tell the police a litany of lies about where you had been between 4 pm and 8 pm on the night of the deaths of your family members, did you not?

SEF: No, sir, I was not composed, I was crying in the first interview.

TEDESCHI: You were sufficiently together, were you not, to tell them an intricate story about where you had been?

SEF: No, sir.

Asked whether his first statement to police was 'all lies', Sef replied he had been panicking.

> **TEDESCHI:** Well, you did tell them a whole series of lies, didn't you?
>
> **SEF:** Sorry, I did, sir.
>
> **TEDESCHI:** You told the police a whole series of lies, didn't you, that night?
>
> **SEF:** Yes, sir.
>
> **TEDESCHI:** That very night, the night of the deaths of your family members, you told them a litany of lies, did you not?
>
> **SEF:** Sir, it wasn't a litany, it was one lie that I said in that statement.
>
> **TEDESCHI:** Let's just have a look at how many lies you told. Would you have a look at a copy of your first statement to the police dated 11 July 2001.

With ruthless persistence, Tedeschi went through the statement, outlining the false Raf De Leon alibi, pointing out untruth after untruth, followed by the question: 'That was a lie, wasn't it?' Sef's response to most of these questions was a meek 'Yes, sir.'

> **TEDESCHI:** You identified 20 or 21 lies that you've told the police in this first statement. You agree that they're all lies?
>
> **SEF:** Yes, sir, but it was all regarding the same account.

Sef said he had lied to protect himself from 'embarrassment'.

He then admitted that in his videotaped interviews, shown to the court, he had lied about not knowing who had researched and ordered poisonous seeds on the computers seized by police. Sef said he placed several orders but only ever received one batch of seeds.

> **TEDESCHI:** I suggest to you that you told those lies that we saw on the videos unhesitatingly, without hesitating. What do you say to that?
>
> **SEF:** In my mind, sir, I was hesitating.
>
> **TEDESCHI:** In your mind you were hesitating?
>
> **SEF:** Yes, sir.

Sef agreed he had lied about both big things and small things.

> **TEDESCHI:** I suggest to you that you kept up these same lies repeatedly for at least six months during your police interviews and during numerous conversations that you had with family and other people.
>
> **SEF:** Yes, sir.
>
> **TEDESCHI:** And you tell the court, do you, that you are telling the truth now?
>
> **SEF:** Yes, sir.

The clock struck 4 pm and Sef was returned to the jail, where, on the advice of police that he might be a suicide risk, he was put in a 'dry' cell with the light on and a video camera monitoring his movements throughout the night. Sef complained he could not sleep, and that he was without his asthma medication and the freshly painted cell was inflaming his illness.

The next morning in court, Sef appeared pale and drawn and Sef's defence team hit the roof. Terracini saw the dry cell incident not as showing the police's concern for Sef's life, but as an attempt to break the young man down and disorientate him for what was to be a lengthy day of cross-examination.

Justice Bruce James agreed it would be entirely inappropriate to put Sef in the stand considering the circumstances, and sent the jury home for the day. The jury was not told the reason, as the argument was held in closed court.

THE DAY AFTER, 12 May, Sef was back in the stand. If his first fifteen minutes of cross-examination two days earlier had discredited him severely, by the end of this day he was left without a shred of credibility. By the time the court adjourned, jury members were rolling their eyes or stifling giggles at Sef's answers and explanations, which was never a good sign for an accused.

Among the more unbelievable highlights of that day was when Sef explained that he gave his first false alibi to police because of the potential embarrassment if his extended family found out he had been with a prostitute. He explained it as a complete moral violation which, if his mother had still been alive and found out about it, would have broken her heart.

TEDESCHI: You preferred to be considered a suspect for the murders of your parents and sister rather than for it to be generally known that you had been with a prostitute; is that what you are saying?

SEF: I don't think I have a preference, sir. I think, I think the best way to say it is that they're just both as bad.

TEDESCHI: So they are equally as bad, are they?

SEF: I don't know how to rate them, sir.

TEDESCHI: You can't rate them?

[Sef doesn't answer.]

TEDESCHI: You don't know which one is worse, is that what you are saying?

SEF: They were both bad, sir.

TEDESCHI: Are they both equally bad?

SEF: I'm not sure, sir.

TEDESCHI: You are not sure which is worse, that is what you're saying?

SEF: It's hard to explain the feelings, sir. I can't put my feelings into words.

Sef was struggling.

TEDESCHI: I'm asking you now, do you have difficulty saying which is worse, being a suspect for the murder of your parents and sister, or it being generally known that you were with a prostitute?

SEF: Well, to fully answer that question, sir, I guess back then it was worse, that I was with a prostitute, but after what I'd been through in the past three years I've realised that this is worse.

TEDESCHI: So you have only just worked out in the last two years, have you, that it's worse to be suspected of the deaths of your family members; is that what, are you saying, that you only worked that out recently?

SEF: No, sir.

TEDESCHI: You have been with prostitutes on numerous occasions, have you not?

SEF: No, sir.

Sef, surprisingly, did admit to faking the 3 August 2001 e-mail in which he was told about the wealthy Filipino businessman's alleged involvement in the murder. Sef said that while he created the e-mail on his own computer, the content was information that he had been informed of shortly after his family's funeral. It is unclear why Sef confessed to doing this of all things — it may have been due to the overwhelming computer evidence at the trial that pointed to his having created it, together with the businessman's evidence at the trial that he had never even met the Gonzales family.

Sef admitted he knew it was illegal to create false evidence but he felt he 'had no choice'.

> **TEDESCHI:** So you created some false evidence?
> **SEF:** It's false in the sense that —
> **TEDESCHI:** Just answer my question. You created some false evidence, didn't you?
> **SEF:** Yes, sir.
> **TEDESCHI:** To try and divert suspicion away from yourself and onto [the wealthy businessman] or his organisation?
> **SEF:** That's not true, sir.

Quizzed about the 'image' he claimed he chased down the street from the house on the night of the murders, after he heard the side gate slam shut, Sef maintained this was the truth.

> **TEDESCHI:** And you chased after him, or them?
> **SEF:** I said it was an image that I chased after.
> **TEDESCHI:** An image of what?
> **SEF:** I assume it was a person.
> **TEDESCHI:** It was not an image of an antelope?
> **SEF:** No, sir.
> **TEDESCHI:** It was not an image of . . . a dog or a horse or a unicorn, it was an image of a person?
> **SEF:** I can't recall, describe, what I saw, but as I was tilting my head up, I don't know if I was oversensitive, but I saw an image moving in that direction.

Tedeschi asked if Sef felt any fear for himself while he was in the house with his dead family members.

TEDESCHI: Why did you assume it [the gate shutting]
was someone leaving? Why didn't you think it might
be the killers coming in to get you?

SEF: I don't know, sir. That's what I assumed.

TEDESCHI: That was a real possibility, based on your
version?

SEF: It is equally possible.

Sef said he did feel fear but did not alert the emergency
operator to the fact the killers might still be in the vicinity. He
was more concerned about his family than himself, he said.

TEDESCHI: Because that thought never entered your
head, that the killers might be coming in to get you?

SEF: I never thought of it, sir.

TEDESCHI: And the reason why you never thought of it
was because there was no person there, because you
were the killer?

SEF: No, sir.

Tedeschi set about proving just how preposterous it was for
Sef to claim he made the fast-acting poison in his bedroom
not to kill his mother but to commit suicide, which Sef said
he had tried to mask by telling friends he had cancer the year
before the deaths. Sef admitted he had never had tests for
cancer.

TEDESCHI: Cancer doesn't kill in three days, does it?

SEF: No, it doesn't. I told them months before.

Asked by Tedeschi whether he thought his mother had
slipped up to his bedroom and sipped his poison, Sef said he
did not think so.

TEDESCHI: Have you got any explanation for why she
  got the symptoms which are consistent with [the two
  types of] poisoning?
SEF: Sir, I did not poison my mother.

Regarding motive, Sef said his parents were not as demanding
on him as they were made out to be. 'My mother and father
were to some degree strict in their own way but not the way
that they have been unfairly portrayed in this court.' He went
on to say his parents were 'not here to defend themselves'.

For Tedeschi, it was too good an opportunity to pass up,
and his voice rose with accusation.

TEDESCHI: They're not here to defend themselves
  because you killed them.
SEF: That's not true, sir.

Tedeschi wrapped up the cross-examination by putting to Sef
a series of 'coincidences' that all pointed to Sef's guilt.

TEDESCHI: Mr Gonzales, there's been a lot of
  coincidences and sheer coincidences, hasn't there?
SEF: Yes, sir, that's probably why I was arrested.

Tedeschi asked Sef if he believed he was a 'very unlucky man'.
  Sef replied, 'Yes, sir.'

THE CROSS-EXAMINATION was continued into a third
day, and was devastating to Sef's case. Then, all that was left
for Tedeschi was the formalities.

TEDESCHI: Finally, did you kill your parents and your sister?
SEF: No, sir, I did not.

Sef then turned to the judge and asked to say something. He said it was 'important on the oath that I made and the evidence that I have given'.

Tedeschi objected, saying it was not the accused's role in a trial to make speeches. Terracini, obviously concerned by this unusual request by his client, rose to his feet and managed to cut it short.

> **TERRACINI:** Does it go to whether you murdered your mother and father and sister?
> **SEF:** No, sir, it relates to the oath that I have given and —
> **TERRACINI:** Well, you say you have been telling the truth?
> **SEF:** Yes, sir.

The uncomfortable moment passed, and Sef Gonzales left the stand and returned to the dock. He was unable to make the dramatic speech he had obviously prepared in advance to sway the jury. One could assume he was going to tell the jurors how important God was to him, and how seriously he took his oath before God to tell the truth.

AFTER LENGTHY CLOSING addresses and the judge's summing up, the jury retired to deliberate at 12.55 pm on Wednesday, 19 May. Those hoping for a verdict that afternoon were disappointed.

The jury left the court at 4 pm and came back the next morning at 10 am to resume deliberation. A flurry of activity soon arose outside the court when the lawyers were called back in, but it was for a question from the jury. Being particularly observant, the jurors were querying which mobile telephone numbers were used by Michelle Dacillo. (The list of eight missed calls to Clodine's phone included six from Michelle Dacillo's mobile number, one from Clodine's friend Vanessa O'Mera's number, and one from a different number which, it turned out, was also used by Michelle to call Clodine, meaning she had actually made seven calls to Clodine's mobile phone on the night of the murders.)

Sef appeared heartened, smiling and nodding as he talked to his defence team, and hope could be seen in his eyes. Journalists who had covered every day of the entire six-week trial exchanged shocked glances. Perhaps the jury was buying the rejected call scenario. If so, the jury could not possibly convict.

It was not to be. A little after 11 am, the jury came back and the foreman, a serious-looking man in his 50s, was asked whether the jury had found that Sef murdered his sister, mother and father. 'Guilty', 'Guilty', 'Guilty', the foreman replied softly for each count.

The first conviction came like a physical blow to Sef, who was standing for the jury's verdict. He gasped and collapsed into his seat, his head resting on his hands. But by the time the jury was ushered from the court to resume their regular daily routines, Sef Gonzales seemed to have collected himself. Already he was planning an appeal.

THE GONZALES' EXTENDED family were relieved but still shattered by the guilty verdicts. Emily, who had watched the evidence in court for almost every day of the trial, remained calm as she chatted to the cops, who were jovial and relieved that their worst fear — acquittal — had not come to pass. Emily felt that somehow her fight for justice, her persistence in spite of her pain and fear, had been rewarded with these convictions. Justice has been served, she thought, and she felt she had been part of that process.

However, other relatives, Annie Paraan in particular, could not stop the flow of tears. It may have been hard for others to understand, but the family, Emily included, still loved Sef despite the terrible crimes they now knew he had committed. Outside the court, Annie would try to explain it to the media pack. With the convictions, she said, they had just lost a fourth member of their family.

Father Paul Cahill visited Sef in custody following the convictions. He could see young Sef was devastated. As far as Father Cahill was concerned, Sef was still the lovely boy he had known at the Chatswood parish years ago, so full of life. Father Cahill was impressed by the way Sef, since the murders, had carried his own cross with dignity, like the Lord, who had also been disbelieved and persecuted.

But after the verdicts, even Father Cahill needed his faith in Sef reaffirmed. He had invested so much time in supporting Sef while he was in jail, and needed to hear from Sef once again on the subject of his guilt or innocence. Father Cahill would support him no matter what Sef's answer was, as the Lord had not died just for saints, but for saints and sinners alike.

'You've got to tell me the truth now,' Father Cahill told Sef. 'I've stuck by you and I don't like to think you'd leave me hanging on a limb.'

Sef looked Father Cahill straight in the eye and told him: 'Father, I would never do that.'

For Father Cahill, this was enough. He believed him.

Chapter 41

Life times three

In June 2004, while Sef was awaiting his sentencing, Detective Mick Sheehy received a curious two-page letter. It was addressed 'Dear Detective Sheehy', and was handwritten, and signed, by Sef Gonzales.

Sef had written the letter from jail, where, almost immediately after the verdicts, he had been placed in segregation. The segregation of inmates at greatest threat involves their being put into a cell on their own. Their movements within the prison are severely restricted. Sef was assessed as being in danger of violence from other prisoners.

Indeed, not long after his arrest, police had foiled a plot by two murder suspects at Sef's jail to kill him. The plan was to stab him with a 'shiv' — a makeshift jail knife — but a bug in the inmates' cell picked up their conversation. The following day, the inmates' cell was raided by prison staff, who seized several 'shivs'.

Suffice it to say that convictions for killing your family members, particularly your defenceless mother and teenage sister, do not endear you to many among the hardened prison population. According to the unofficial code among prisoners, people like Sef fell into the same category as child molesters and police informers.

The letter to Sheehy showed that Sef was again reaching out to the one Tawas officer with whom he seemed to think he had some sort of bond. It was disturbingly personal in nature. Sef, the master manipulator, was at work once again.

It read:

I know what you must think of me, so I won't continue to plead my innocence to you. I know that you have made up your mind about me and I don't blame you. It was my shortcomings, imaturity [sic], and weakness as a young person, which you were able to point out that convicted me.

Maybe I do deserve all of this because although I am no murderer, I should've taken greater care of my relationships specially as a son, or as a friend. I should have been a better person.

Through all of this experience, information has come to light which may provide us all with answers. Since no one would believe me, I was hoping to first gain some credibility, then pursue this after I was acquitted. I may never get that chance.

I believe that deep within each person is goodness. So I write this with faith and hope. We both know that despite the verdicts there are many questions left unanswered. Again, I don't blame you if you just wish to throw away the key and forget about me. But I know that many years down the track, those unanswered questions will continue to haunt any good police officer.

Please don't turn away from these doors which I hope by now have been brought to your attention. Doors which may answer those questions. It may turn out that we were both wrong about our suspicions. Please don't let that stop you.

Whatever happens to me. Where I am or continue to be, I leave that to fate. I now believe that things do happen for a reason. If not for what we have been through, we wouldn't know what we know now. These few weeks have been the longest I have been in segregation, yet this is the closest I have ever been to God.

I have not understood my faith as much as I do now. Understanding leads to forgiveness. And forgiveness is such a powerful thing. For the first time I have no blame, anger, or hate in my heart. It's a liberating feeling.

Please do your best to find the answers to those remaining questions. If not for me or for you do it for my Father, mother, and sister.

P.S. If you are able to, please tell my relatives and friends that I do understand them, love them, miss them, and always pray for them. Thank you.

The meaning of this letter — the references to the unanswered questions and the 'doors' that might answer them — became apparent with a letter Father Paul Cahill sent to the office of the Director of Public Prosecutions, dated 2 July 2004.

Father Cahill made some startling revelations. He referred to the alleged confession of another jail inmate to the murders of the Gonzales family. The inmate concerned had allegedly made this confession to his former cellmate. Father Cahill supplied the inmate's name — given to him on a scrap of paper by Sef — and criticised Sef's defence counsel for not bringing up the matter in the trial. (However, if it had been brought up at the trial and turned out to be another of Sef's creations, the Crown could have used it as further evidence of Sef's 'false trails'. As it is, statements made by prison informers are viewed as inherently unreliable in the courts.)

The DPP forwarded the letter to Tawas officers. Under the direction of Detective Inspector Geoff Leonard, the matter would be investigated over the course of the next few weeks. Despite the detectives' strong faith in the proof against Sef, they could not very well ignore this new turn of events and hope it would go away.

The police went to interview the alleged confessor, who was incarcerated in a country New South Wales prison. The inmate was in his late teens when, in the company of his younger girlfriend, he stabbed a man to death in Sydney's Northern Beaches. He had pleaded guilty to the murder, which occurred only two weeks after the Gonzales killings.

When detectives visited the convicted killer, who was serving a lengthy prison sentence, he claimed he had only just become aware of the allegation of the confession from a friend, who had read the newspapers and told him about it during a prison visit.

The killer told Tawas detectives he had never known Sef or the Gonzales family members and that he had only recently learned of the matter through the news media. He denied making the confession. The prisoner's male visitor, a decent sort of guy, later informed detectives the killer had told him the very same thing during the visit.

The police tracked down the former cellmate of the young killer. The confession took place in December 2001, when they shared a cell in a suburban Sydney jail. At the time, the cellmate was on remand for break-and-enter charges and the killer was still on remand for murder.

The cellmate was twice the young killer's age and the young man seemed to look up to him as a kind of father figure. The killer was not terribly bright but was eager to impress the older man, boasting to him and referring to himself as 'Johnny one murder one'. He made out that he was tough, and told the older man not to worry, if anyone tried to attack him in jail, he'd look after him.

Referring to the murder on the Northern Beaches, the killer said: 'It's not the first murder I've done. I did the Gonzales murders. I went there to get Sef but the family turned up and I stabbed the fuck out of them.'

The older inmate did not probe the killer for further information. In fact, he sat on it for some two years, until a chance meeting in late 2003 with an inmate from the Silverwater MRRC, where Sef was on remand. They were both in the holding cells of a suburban Sydney court, which they were attending for court appearances, and got to chatting.

The MRRC inmate mentioned to the other man that he knew Sef Gonzales. It sparked a memory in the man's mind. He decided he might as well reveal the confession made to him by the killer about the Gonzales murders. He wrote down the killer's name on a piece of paper and handed it to the MRRC inmate.

The MRRC inmate wasted no time in passing the information and the scrap of paper to Sef, back at the MRRC. Sef would dig out this scrap of paper for Father Cahill, who would send a photocopy of it along with his letter to the DPP following Sef's murder conviction. Why Sef failed to alert authorities sooner remains a mystery.

TAWAS DETECTIVES HAD several problems with the alleged confession.

First was the obvious problem that the killer had said he went there to kill Sef but the family turned up and he stabbed them all. This was at odds with the evidence, which showed the Gonzales killer had waited for long periods of time between murdering Clodine, then Loiva, then Teddy, but that Sef was not attacked when he arrived home.

Equally troubling was the nature of the Northern Beaches killing as opposed to the Gonzales killings. They were poles apart. While the Gonzales killings were extremely well organised — the evidence having been staged by someone intent on evading detection — the Northern Beaches one was absolutely disorganised. It was planned in as much as the killer invited his victim to pick up his girlfriend and him in the victim's car, on the pretext of going to buy some drugs. The killer believed the man had sexually assaulted his girlfriend. The killer and the girlfriend, sitting in the back seat, set upon the driver with knives and the man fled from the car into the street. They chased him and continued the attack, despite the fact it was broad daylight in a busy area. Then they stole their victim's car and, covered in blood, stopped off at a service station with CCTV cameras. Not only that, but the killer then phoned a friend and confessed to the murder, as well as subsequently pleading guilty in court.

The third discrepancy was the clincher. The detectives examined the size of the lanky killer's feet. They were four to five sizes bigger than the bloody footprints left by the Gonzales killer, who had worn size UK 7/US 8 Human brand shoes.

The police notified the DPP of their investigation and findings and their belief that the alleged confession just did not check out. The DPP wrote back to Father Cahill, letting him know the matter had been put to rest.

ON FRIDAY, 27 AUGUST, the old St James Road courtroom in central Sydney was packed for the sentencing of Sef Gonzales. Sef, who had beefed up considerably in jail, sat awaiting his sentence, his face puffy. He was wearing his green prison jumpsuit, and his eyes appeared cold and hard and his mouth set.

Emily Luna and Amelita Claridades were there but Annie Paraan had returned to the Philippines. Emily was accompanied by her grief counsellor, Kate Friis, from the Department of Forensic Medicine. Kate was a kind woman with a patient, gentle manner. She had seen Emily through the years of pain since the killing of her sister, niece and brother-in-law, and Emily relied heavily on Kate's emotional support. Emily was having a bad day; she felt particularly stressed and emotional and was glad to have Kate and her mother by her side.

Shane Hanley, who had testified at the trial about entering the murder house with Sef, sat at the back of the court, sending Sef filthy looks, hoping to let Sef know with his eyes just how much he resented having been used, that he knew Sef was guilty, and that he deserved everything he got. The detectives from Tawas were packed into benches at the side of the court and the media were there in force.

Father Cahill was present too, of course. Sitting next to him were a slovenly-looking man and woman. According to police, the man, a government contractor who had helped remove the bodies from the Gonzales home after the murders, somehow thought he had a secret insight into the evidence because of this. It appeared that, due to the force of the attacks, he believed Sef could not have been the killer. Journalists watched, appalled, as the man refused to give up his seat at the front of the court for the arrival of the Gonzales relatives.

Sentencing submissions were made by both the prosecution and defence, and previous ranges of murder sentences were cited as guides. Tedeschi told the court Sef had no prior criminal convictions and tendered a copy of a pre-sentence report, carried out on Sef in jail. Tedeschi asked that, at the request of the Gonzales' relatives, three victim impact statements be read aloud in court. Terracini objected, saying it was unnecessarily emotionally for all concerned. However, the judge allowed Kate Friis to take the stand and read the statements of Emily Luna, Annie Paraan and Amelita Claridades.

Emily Luna's long-held composure broke as Kate read her statement. She mopped her tears with tissues. Her nephew Sef stared at her with a hard expression as Kate outlined the very personal effects of the case on Emily.

The statement described Emily's fears and insecurities following the murders, and the fact that the tension and strain had seriously affected her relationship with her husband. 'Our marriage had been through difficult times before but my sister, Loiva, had always helped us work through our differences and stay together. I no longer had my sister to support and help me as she had always done before and [my husband] and I just drifted apart', it said.

The statement spoke about how her son Gerard had begun misbehaving, being surrounded by so much tension, and how she had to get him counselling on numerous occasions.

By Easter of 2003, she realised just how depressed she had become. 'I had been pushing my family and friends away without realising it, as all I could think of was about the trial', she stated.

She saw a doctor in April who prescribed antidepressants, which she feared taking but felt she had no choice. 'I experienced quite bad side effects — trembling hands, drowsiness, low energy levels and very severe mood changes — and so my medication was changed. Fifteen months on, I am still taking antidepressants ... my general health has undoubtedly been affected and I have had a number of hospital confinements. I have lost a significant amount of weight over the last three years.'

Annie's statement was shorter, and almost poetic. It spoke about the pain, heartache, grief and loss caused by the murders, and the mixed emotions caused by the fact that Sef carried them out. 'The mixed feelings I have experienced were just too much to bear that up to now I am clouded with profound sadness. Our cry for justice was answered and given to us wrapped in sorrow and tears ... I never knew justice could be this cruel.'

She described how, at the trial, as she listened to the evidence about how the crimes were staged, she felt blood rushing to her face. 'My hands, tightly clasped on my lap, were cold and sweating. I was trembling with fear and tears were rolling down my cheeks. I found the act so horrible and heinous that there were times after the trial I was having nightmares about my own death and each time I wake up moaning and struggling for breath.'

Amelita's statement was the saddest of all. Maybe it was because she had shunned any and all publicity, retreating into the protective shell of her family. Finally, Amelita's deepest thoughts and feelings were being spoken by Kate in open court, while she sat with her face composed and still. They were the thoughts of a grandmother who just wanted her family around her, but had been robbed of this simple and all-important joy.

She spoke about how the love, concern, attention and support she had constantly received from Loiva and Teddy over the years had been 'more than any mother could ask for'.

'They were always genuinely concerned and protective, and sensitive to the fact that I was now living on my own, my husband deceased and all my children married and living further away. I was never lonely.'

She told how her daughter and son-in-law always made her feel safe and tried to make things easier for her. 'Whether it was a trip to my doctor's appointment, a trip to and from the airport, an operation that I was scheduled for, or simply moving my furniture from house to house, I could always count on their support.

'They gave me strength and peace of mind. I felt safe and secure that nothing would go wrong because they were a strong, loving, and reliable couple I could always depend on.'

She spoke of how, before their deaths, she had planned to move to Queensland with Teddy and Loiva for their retirement, once Sef and Clodine finished university. She stated that she and Clodine, a talented cook, dreamed of teaming up one day to run a small bed and breakfast, where Amelita could sell her arts and crafts.

'To this day, I am struggling to cope with the emotional pain and trauma of what has happened. I miss all of them every day. And the depression is something that prevails and visits constantly. I miss them in small yet familiar incidents, and in the faces of strangers who resemble them.

'I still live on my own today, with my remaining children concerned and also coping with the loss. However, the love of Clodine, and the love and presence which Teddy and Loiva selflessly provided and shared with me when they were alive is something I find irreplaceable.'

The woman who had prepared Sef's pre-sentence report, probation and parole officer Karen Langdon, was asked to read a particularly important section of her report from the stand.

According to Langdon, while holding discussions with Sef in jail to prepare the report, Sef had vigorously maintained his innocence but stated he felt he could have prevented the murders if he had been a better son, continued studying medicine or listened more attentively to his father's concerns about threats that had been made against Teddy.

Then Sef had told her of information he possessed that differed from that he had previously provided. He admitted that it was he who had cut the cable to the family's downstairs telephone.

'The offender stated that upon entering the house on the night of the offences he had discovered his father's body and did not call for assistance immediately. He stated he had found his mother's and then his sister's body before attempting to call for help. Mr Gonzales stated he attempted to use the portable home phone but thought that it did not work and then called for assistance on his mobile phone.

'He stated that he cut the line to the home phone in an attempt to conceal the fact that he had not called for assistance immediately upon finding his father's body. He stated that in hindsight his behaviour in that regard was not rational or reasonable.' Langdon stated Sef had told her that upon entering the house that night that he felt 'like a suspect'.

Langdon said Sef had also admitted to her that he now believed he did not see an 'image' fleeing the house that night. 'Mr Gonzales stated he now believed that he told the police he saw the "image" because he feared there could have been a person in the house on that night.'

These admissions raised the question: why would Sef be saying these things now, if he planned to appeal against his conviction? Was he edging closer to admitting he killed his family, and just testing the reaction from others by making a few confessions peripheral to the actual killings? Or was he trying to manipulate Ms Langdon, take her into his confidence so she would write a favourable report for him? Only Sef would ever really know.

However, in cross-examination, Terracini at least had Ms Landgon attest to the fact that since Sef had been in custody, jail staff had described him as 'polite and unproblematic'.

SEF GONZALES, OF course, wanted to have his say in court that day. Winston Terracini, SC, called him to the stand.

When Sef first began speaking, it seemed he was leading up to a public confession. 'I will be the first to admit that nothing I say will really hold any weight,' Sef began in a breathy, halting voice. 'Although three years seems like a long time, I look back at my life before the murders and before I was arrested and I accept that there are so many things I've done that I am not proud of, so much that I wish I could take back. So much I wish that I could do differently but I can't.'

Questioned by Terracini as to whether he still protested his innocence, Sef maintained that he did. He said he did not blame people for looking at him the way they did, for 'judging' him the way they did. He said he had constantly been told that if he pleaded guilty he could receive a lesser sentence, that if he showed remorse he could still be released from prison. He said he was sorry to all the people he had ever hurt or lied to. 'I believe I was put on trial for being a bad person and not for murder,' Sef said.

He said when he looked back at the trial, if he had been on the jury he probably would have convicted himself. 'But I'm not going to plead guilty for something I didn't do, just to make people happy ... but I believe that in time things will make more sense.'

By this stage, Emily was outside collecting herself, while Amelita sat by herself in the court in a front seat. Sef looked at his grandmother and dealt a sickening blow. He said he wanted to tell his relatives, particularly his grandmother, that when they 'abandoned' him he had felt angry for a long time, but that anger had enabled him to get through this ordeal. He said people had accused him of being cold-blooded but that he had 'run out of tears to cry'.

Still addressing Amelita, Sef said: 'If you don't think I am feeling any pain then you are wrong. I want you to know that any pain that you are feeling, I'm feeling it much worse than you.'

Tedeschi, who had pulled Sef apart on the stand during his trial, rose for his cross-examination.

Tedeschi asked Sef if he felt sorry for killing his sister, mother and father. Sef replied that he did not kill them.

Then Tedeschi launched into the new Karen Langdon evidence. Sef immediately began to deny that he had made the admissions about not having seeing the image, and about cutting the phone wire, saying Ms Langdon had misunderstood him.

He said he had gone over and over in his mind the image he thought he had seen run from the house that night. 'I said that after the trial and all the evidence I accept it is possible it was just my fear playing with my imagination.'

TEDESCHI: Did you tell Ms Langdon that it was you that had cut the telephone line downstairs in your house?

SEF: No, that's not what I said.

Tedeschi continued his attack, and Sef retreated further into denial. He denied saying that he had found all three bodies before attempting to call for help, or that he had cut the line. 'I told her it was suggested to me so many times that I cut the phone line ... and I go back to that night and I start to doubt myself.'

On the subject of feeling like a suspect immediately upon entering the house, Sef explained, 'I told her that I felt there was something wrong straightaway.'

Tedeschi, in an exasperated tone, concluded his cross-examination.

TEDESCHI: Mr Gonzales, I suggest to you that you would just as easily tell a lie as to tell the truth.

SEF: That's not true. You are forcing me to say something that I don't want to say.

In his submissions, Tedeschi told the judge it was hard to imagine a more heinous crime than killing one's parents — except for killing one's little sister so as not to have to share one's inheritance. He said there were a number of aggravating factors associated with the murders, including the fact there were three killed, the relationship of the killer to the victims, the brutality, the clear premeditation, the fact he lay in wait between each of the murders, and the numerous steps he took to hide his involvement in the crimes.

There was a lack of contrition that would reflect on his chances of rehabilitation and likelihood of reoffending. The report submitted for the defence, by forensic psychiatrist Dr David Greenberg, who analysed Sef, found no evidence of any significant psychiatric condition that could mitigate his deeds. On the objective facts of the case, the crime fell into the most serious category of murder and a life sentence was warranted, Tedeschi concluded.

Sef's young age was the only subjective factor that might be to his advantage, and was something the judge had to consider, Tedeschi said. 'But there are some crimes so heinous, so callous, that the youthful age of the offender does not have any significant mitigating effect,' he continued.

He added that the evidence of Ms Langdon was only consistent with Sef's guilt and could be seen as exhibiting 'a desperate need to confess' to the murders. By making the admissions and then lying about them, he was almost demonstrating a wish to punish himself, Tedeschi argued. 'To use the vernacular, one could conclude the accused has just lost the plot by making confessions like that.'

Terracini then made his submissions for the defence, saying a maximum sentence of 30 years would be appropriate in such a case. 'I am not going to retreat from the fact that this is, on its facts, an extremely wicked offence. But the time spent wasting one's life away [in jail] doing nothing is a very very serious punishment indeed.'

He said the sentence, by law, must be approached on the basis of the jury's verdicts, despite the fact Sef maintained his innocence. '[But] he doesn't have the benefit of a plea of guilty, he doesn't have the benefit of expressing his sorrow.'

He said Sef would not have been the first person to tell lies in court. And Dr Greenberg's report on Sef was not about to enlighten anyone as to why Sef committed the murders. 'We're in a position where we're able to explain nothing. We are able to put before the court little if any explanation that would give some glimmer of . . . what has moved this young man to do what he did.'

Terracini argued that Sef was from a good background and had had a reasonably bright future, but had now lost everything. He pointed out that Sef was only 23 and there was at least some prospect of rehabilitation during such a lengthy prison term. If the judge chose to give a determinate sentence, it would mean Sef would eventually be released and given another chance to make something of his life.

Justice Bruce James wanted time to ponder both arguments. He reserved his judgment.

ON 17 SEPTEMBER 2004, Sef Gonzales received three life sentences, one for each murder, to be served concurrently, of course. This meant Sef would die in jail. According to New South Wales law, life *means* life.

Justice Bruce James delivered his reasons for sentencing to the court. While the jury had delivered their verdicts, they had never had the opportunity to explain why they reached their verdicts; which evidence they accepted as true and which they rejected as being false. Indeed, each member of the jury did not need to rely on the same evidence as the others to reach their verdict. However, Justice James had presided over the whole trial, heard all the evidence, and by law, had to make findings of fact.

It was chilling to hear the judge describe what he found had happened that day when Sef arrived home from his father's work, while the prisoner himself, in his regulation green tracksuit, scowled.

'At approximately 4.30 pm the prisoner entered Clodine's bedroom, where she was studying,' Justice James said. 'The prisoner was armed with a baseball bat or a bat similar to a baseball bat and with one or two kitchen knives which the prisoner had taken from a knife block in the kitchen of the house. These two knives were the longest knives in the set of knives in the block.

'Inside Clodine's bedroom the prisoner, not necessarily in this order, compressed Clodine's neck endeavouring to strangle her, struck her at least six separate blows to the head with the bat and stabbed her many times with one or both knives.'

He described Loiva arriving home at about 5.30 pm. 'Very shortly after Mrs Gonzales entered the house, the prisoner attacked her with one of the kitchen knives, while Mrs Gonzales was in the living room of the house.'

He said the multiple stab wounds resulted in her windpipe being completely severed, and the fact she was stabbed very soon after her entry to the house was shown by the fact she was still wearing the shoes she had worn to work and that her handbag was found close to her body. Her usual practice was to stow these items upon her entry to the house.

The judge said that Sef had remained in the house. 'A few minutes after 6 pm the prisoner's aunt Emily Luna came to 6 Collins Street. She saw the prisoner's car parked in the carport. She rang the front doorbell of the house but no-one answered and she left. Although no-one answered the front doorbell, the prisoner was still inside the house.'

Justice James said Teddy arrived home about 6.50 pm. 'Very shortly after [Teddy's] entering the house the prisoner attacked Mr Gonzales with one of the kitchen knives, while Mr Gonzales was still close to the front door … vastly more force was used by the prisoner than was necessary to kill Mr Gonzales.'

The judge found that Teddy had just arrived home because he was dressed in the clothing and shoes he had worn to work, and his briefcase was near his body.

Justice James found that, at some time during the evening, Sef had spray-painted the words 'FUCK OFF ASIANS KKK' on the family room wall.

'After killing the three victims the prisoner disposed of the knife or knives he had used in stabbing the victims, the bat he had used in striking Clodine and the shoes and clothing he had been wearing at the time of committing the murders. The shoes and clothing had become bloodstained. None of these items have ever been found.'

The judge also found that, based on the trial evidence, Sef had indeed poisoned his mother, which indicated premeditation in the killings of his family members. She did not die, due to the fact that Sef's attempt to extract poison from the seeds was only 'partly successful'.

'I am satisfied to the requisite standard that Mrs Gonzales' illness was not due to food poisoning but was due to the administration to her by the prisoner of poison he had extracted from the seeds he had received by the supplier.' He said he rejected the suggestion that Sef had made the Internet searches about poisons and ordered the poisonous seeds in order to commit suicide.

As to the motive for the murders, Justice James found it was a mixture of Sef's fear of sanctions from his parents and his greed. 'I find that the motives for the prisoner committing the murders were that he was fearful that, because of his poor performance in his university studies, his parents might take his car away from him and might withdraw other privileges which had been granted to him and that he wishes to succeed, without delay and as sole heir, to his parents' property.'

The judge then spoke of Sef's mental state. He referred to Dr Greenberg's report in some detail. He said Dr Greenberg had been instructed to assume Sef was guilty in making his assessment for the sentencing.

He said Dr Greenberg reported Sef as saying that in the six months prior to his family's murders he felt suicidal and depressed. Yet Sef told the psychiatrist that during this period he had not stopped attending uni classes, or going out with friends or dating young women. There was no reported loss of weight or appetite, although Sef complained of some loss of energy and poor concentration. The doctor reported he thought Sef was in a 'depressed mood' around the time of the murders but could not diagnose a major depressive illness.

As for personality disorders, Dr Greenberg found: 'There is insufficient evidence to diagnose Mr Gonzales as suffering from a personality disorder at this time.'

Dr Greenberg also found that following the 1990 Baguio earthquake Sef may well have been suffering post-traumatic stress disorder, but Sef denied suffering PTSD symptoms just before the murders, or afterwards.

Dr Greenberg found that Sef's repeated 'flu-like' illnesses were possibly linked to an 'undifferentiated somataform disorder' (in which psychological conditions cause symptoms of illness that have no physiological cause) or incipient schizophrenia (a personality disorder that warps perception, thought and behaviour, but is not as severe as schizophrenia). But Dr Greenberg found both these possibilities unlikely.

After presenting these findings from the psychiatric assessment, the judge concluded: 'Having regard to Professor Greenberg's report, I do not make any finding that at the time of committing the murders the prisoner had any delusional beliefs or suffered from any psychiatric illness or personality disorder or from post-traumatic stress disorder, or from some as yet undiagnosed mental condition or any undifferentiated somataform disorder or incipient schizophrenia ... I do not accept that the prisoner seriously contemplated suicide or that he was seriously depressed in the period leading up to the murders.

'I find that at the time of committing the murders the prisoner was not suffering from any mental illness or any mental disorder or any mental abnormality which might, to some degree, mitigate his objective criminality.'

The judge found the murders to be of 'very great heinousness', not mitigated by any of the objective facts. In relation to Sef's personal circumstances, he took into account Sef's age, but found that Sef had misled investigating authorities and that he posed a risk of reoffending and 'future dangerousness'. The murders fell into the 'worst case category' of common law.

In the final sentence of the judgment, Sef was told he was to serve life imprisonment. There were no histrionics this time. Sef showed absolutely no emotion when confronted with his fate.

BY MID-SEPTEMBER 2004, Sef had lodged his notice of intention to appeal, in a form he filled out from jail. It appeared he was already laying the groundwork for lodging his grounds of appeal, which would be the next step in the appeal process.

In an interview with the *Daily Telegraph*, Father Cahill stated that Sef had told him he had suffered from memory 'blackouts' since he was a child, in fact from the moment of the earthquake. He claimed his father knew of these blackouts, and that his father would ask Sef if he was cognisant during these periods. Father Cahill explains that it wās not a split personality disorder. It was not as if Sef did not know what he was doing during these periods, it was more that he could not remember what he had said, that he was in another world.

If Sef told lies during these blackouts and was informed of the lies he had told afterwards, Sef would continue to affirm the lies to cover up for the fact he did not remember.

'I think with the earthquake ... he thought he was going to die, and I don't think he had any trauma treatment,' Father Cahill says. 'Perhaps there's some element that causes some mental amnesia sometimes. There might be blackouts — not loss of consciousness, but things happen and you don't remember them.'

Father Cahill said Sef had not made these 'blackouts' public previously because he did not want people to think he was confessing to committing the murders. Father Cahill said Sef clearly remembered what he had been doing during the period of the murders — that he was with the prostitute Latisha. According to Father Cahill Sef was to undergo a fresh psychiatric assessment in jail.

What Father Cahill described could very well have been the grounds Sef planned to lodge for his appeal.

Chapter 42

Moving on

Within two months of his sentencing in September 2004, Sef began casting about for a new legal team to handle his appeal. At the time, he was still at Silverwater's MRRC, from which he would be transferred to maximum-security Goulburn jail — known for housing 'lifers' — in southern New South Wales.

Sef rang solicitor Dennis Miralis and asked him to visit Silverwater to discuss Sef's case. Miralis works for the respected law firm Nyman Gibson Stewart, which specialises in defending those accused of serious organised crime or violent crime. 'He picked me because he had heard my name from other inmates in jail,' Miralis says.

Miralis had previously acted in a triple murder case, albeit briefly. He represented former Adelaide soccer star Adrian Michelon, who was accused of bludgeoning his wife Indis and two sons, Darian, thirteen, and Ramon, ten, with a hammer in their Chifley home in February 2002. Michelon then stabbed and slashed himself and set fire to the family home before being rescued. He committed suicide in Long Bay jail the following month.

From the beginning, there was one particular man who topped Moralis's wish list of barristers to act for Sef on appeal. Paul Byrne, SC, is one of the most eminent appellate barristers in criminal work in Australia. Fortunately for Sef, Byrne had already taken a keen intellectual interest in the Gonzales case, having followed it closely in the media and read the sentencing judgment of Justice Bruce James of his own volition. Byrne agreed to take on the case.

But first, the issue of whether Sef would get Legal Aid for his appeal needed to be addressed. In deciding this, the Legal Aid Commission had to determine whether there was merit in Sef's appeal against his conviction and sentence — in other words, whether Sef had any chance on appeal or whether he had no chance and would just be wasting taxpayers' money. Sef was never going to appeal just his sentence; he still strongly maintained his innocence. Legal Aid referred the case to a public defender, Robert Hulme, SC, to review and report on whether there was merit.

Hulme immersed himself in the case and was nearing completion when he was appointed as a District Court judge. The case was then handed to another public defender, Chris Craigie, SC, who had to start all over again so he could get his mind around the complexities. What he eventually reported back to Legal Aid is unknown — except that it caused the Legal Aid Commission to reject public funding for Sef's appeal.

Time dragged on until, as of mid-February 2006, one year and nine months after his conviction, Sef had still not lodged his grounds for appeal. But because of the unforeseen delays in assessing his case, the Court of Criminal Appeal could not refuse to grant Sef extension after extension for lodging his grounds.

Byrne completed his own review of whether Sef's conviction and sentence were appellable. As a result, all indications are that Sef will appeal against both, and that he may well be granted Legal Aid after all. What the grounds will be are yet to be seen.

Like Miralis, it will not be Byrne's first time in acting for a triple family murderer, but Byrne had acted on appeal. In 2000, before the Court of Crimnal Appeal, he represented a killer whose case bore some startling parallels to Sef's. In March 1996, Matthew Wayne De Gruchy murdered his mother and two siblings at his parents' home in Albion Park Rail, near Wollongong, south of Sydney. De Gruchy was eighteen at the time. He bludgeoned his mother Jennifer, his fifteen-year-old brother Adrian and his thirteen-year-old sister Sarah. His father had been staying in Sydney overnight for work. De Gruchy left the bodies inside the home and went to stay the night at his girlfriend's place. He returned the next morning, 'discovered' the bodies and, sobbing, went to the home of a neighbour directly across the street to tell him something was wrong with his mother and sister.

Dr Allan Cala, who performed the Gonzales autopsies, also performed the autopsies on the De Gruchy family members. He found the fatal injuries could have been caused by the wheel brace or jack handle that had been missing from Jennifer De Gruchy's hatchback, which her killer son had been allowed to drive. Also, De Gruchy tried to cover his tracks by telling others his mother had received prank phone calls, with the caller saying that three family members would die. He also staged evidence to point to an intruder, disposing of several household items to point to robbery as a motive. Like Sef, De Gruchy had no prior criminal record, and pleaded not guilty, thereby showing no remorse. It is interesting to note that, largely due to his youth and prospects for rehabilitation, De Gruchy did not get life. He was sentenced to a maximum 28-year jail term, with a minimum non-parole period of 21 years.

The De Gruchy case, like the Gonzales case, was entirely circumstantial — that is, no-one had witnessed the killings take place. However, of course no two cases are the same, and there were some marked differences between the De Gruchy and Gonzales murders. For one, De Gruchy had been stupid enough write a note, obviously in his own handwriting and later recovered by police, that included the names of his victims. It was clearly a list relating to the murders and instructions of what to do afterwards, such as 'have shower' and 'hit arm with pole'. De Gruchy's appeals against his convictions to the Court of Criminal Appeal, then to the High Court of Australia, were both rejected.

FROM LATE 2004, Sef's appeal faded into insignificance in the public eye, compared with the controversy of the sale of the Gonzales house.

In mid-2004, Amelita, as executrix of the estate, put the house on the market through LJ Hooker North Ryde. It was always going to be difficult job selling the house, due to what had taken place there. After all she had gone through, Amelita would be brought into a windstorm of publicity surrounding its sale. And she would not even financially benefit from the sale, with the proceeds to go to Teddy's parents in the Philippines.

According to Emily, LJ Hooker requested that the house be emptied and cleaned out before buyers moved in. Emily let a family friend, Vicky Bugayong, into the house and showed her what needed to be done. All the family's remaining belongings were to be gathered and assembled in the garage for collection by a charity, St Vincent de Paul. Vicky and one of her girlfriends would then clean the house.

It was not a pleasant task, no doubt. Emily says that while Vicky's friend was cleaning the upstairs area, she became aware that a tap was running in the en suite bathroom of the master bedroom. Vicky's friend was sure that the taps had been turned off in there. Vicky herself was not in there; she was cleaning the common bathroom on the other side of the upper floor. Vicky's friend dropped to her knees and began to pray to Loiva, whom she had known, begging that Loiva not scare her.

Whether her imagination was in overdrive or not, this is a good indication of the challenge faced by the real estate agency tasked with selling the place. The mind can sometimes conjure up things far more terrifying than reality, if you are superstitious and believe in things that go bump in the night. But there would, of course, be other buyers who would not be put off. In fact, if they felt they could comfortably live in the house, they could score a bargain.

Ellen Lin and her husband Derek Kwok, of Carlingford, a suburb about 6 kilometres from North Ryde, definitely fell into the former category. They got more than they bargained for when they made an offer on behalf of Ms Lin's parents, who agreed to buy the home for Mr Kwok and Ms Lin to live in. Ms Lin's parents handed over an $80,000 deposit for the house, as part of a total $800,000 sale price. Ms Lin and Mr Kwok claimed that they were oblivious to the fact the murders had occurred there, and that LJ Hooker owner Peter Hinton and his daughter Ereca Hinton, a sales representative at the agency, did nothing to enlighten them. They only became aware of it after handing over the deposit, when a local newspaper ran a story about the house and the murders.

Ellen Lin and her husband had planned to raise their three-year-old son at 6 Collins Street. But their strong Buddhist beliefs and superstitions meant living in a house where murder had occurred was impossible.

The Hintons were eventually fined $20,900 by the New South Wales Commissioner of Fair Trading for failing to disclose the history of the home to the couple. The Hintons responded by appealing the decision in the Administrative Decisions Tribunal. The Tribunal, at the time of writing, has yet to make a ruling. The Gonzales estate kept the $80,000 deposit, but the LJ Hooker organisation made a special payment of $80,000 to Lin and Kwok to recoup their losses, following the bad publicity.

Peter Hinton told the Tribunal in February 2006 that he felt it was adequate that he had instructed his staff to market the home as a deceased estate, and told buyers it had been vacant for three years and that the Filipino owners no longer had need of it. 'What I intended to convey was that somebody had died in the property and give them [potential buyers] an opportunity to ask questions,' Mr Hinton said.

He also argued that publicity of the murders and of the house's whereabouts was so widespread that it was hard to believe anyone was unaware of the home's history. 'As far as I'm concerned there wouldn't have been a human being within a 5-kilometre radius of that property that wouldn't know about the murders at 6 Collins Street,' he said.

Hinton described how the property had become the biggest 'tourist attraction' in town, besides Sydney Harbour.

The fascination with the morbid is an unfortunate fact of human nature. The same curiosity that urges rubber-necked motorists to slow down when passing a car accident, to better view the scene, made many people drive past 6 Collins Street to get a first-hand look at the site of the killings.

Those who did so must have been disappointed. All they would have seen was two storeys of bricks and mortar standing empty, the blinds drawn, and a garden that was going to seed.

Fortunately, according to Shane Hanley, who still lives in Collins Street, the traffic flow in his little side street has begun to abate since the new owners of number 6, an Anglo-Saxon couple and their teenage son, moved into the home in time for Christmas 2005. The family bought the home via private treaty in late 2005 for $720,000, after it failed to sell at an auction earlier that year. The highest bid had been $715,000.

The family is understandably reluctant to talk about the purchase. They just want to be left alone to get on with their lives. Obviously, to them, 6 Collins Street is not a 'house of horrors' as it is labelled in the media, but their home. The neat lawn shows their pride in it. But the closed blinds there are still a sign that the flow of sightseers has not dropped off entirely.

Emily is grateful that the new owners did not wish to buy for the wrong reasons, like a British man, Craig Gill, who in October 2004 told any media outlet who would listen that he wanted to buy it and turn it into a tourist attraction. The insult of that to the memories of Teddy, Loiva and Clodine was, for the Claridades family, almost too much to be borne.

'At least it's a family that's moved in there. I'm happy for that,' Emily says.

Shane Hanley agrees, saying the fact the new owners are regretful about what happened there, but do not let it unduly perturb them, is a good sign that the street may move on and heal.

Shane's mother has met the new neighbours. 'They're quite nice, from what I gather,' says Shane. But he has no plans to drop in and say hello, given his role in the Gonzales murder case. One reason is consideration for the new owners. He does not wish to burden them with any details of what he saw inside their house on the night of the murders.

'I don't want to be the cloud that rained on their parade,' Shane says.

But mostly, it is because the memories are still too fresh. Time is slowly relegating them to the back of his mind, and Shane doesn't want his memory jogged. Even now, on the odd occasion, the images he saw inside 6 Collins Street on that cloudy winter night can blindside him with terrible vividness.

'I'm not in any great hurry to go in there,' he says.

Epilogue

It is just after the guilty verdicts have been given on 20 May 2004, and I am among the throng of journalists waiting outside Darlinghurst's Supreme Court for the Gonzales relatives and police to emerge and comment.

Throughout this whole saga — from my several meetings with Sef, to getting to know the investigators and the prosecution and defence teams in the trial — I have tried to maintain objectivity, as all journalists must in their reporting. Crime reporting has the capacity to harden someone, to the point where other people's misery becomes simply fodder for a story. You sympathise, but if you dwell too much on it, become too personally involved, you will not be able to perform your job properly.

But I cannot deny this case has affected me like few others. To write this book, I have let so much evil into my thoughts, in an attempt to truly understand these crimes. And I am convinced today that the verdicts are correct, that on any objective analysis of the facts, Sef Gonzales cruelly and calculatedly killed his three family members. There are others who will remain convinced of his innocence, as is their right. An obviously disappointed Father Paul Cahill, for example, who slips out a side door of the court after the verdict, and is chased by the media down the road. The only comment the Catholic priest will make on the verdict is this: 'What I think doesn't matter.'

As the media pack gives up the chase of Father Cahill and returns to the court steps, I think of how many people have become victims of Sef Gonzales and his manipulation. I think of Teddy, Loiva and Clodine Gonzales, whose graves I have visited while writing this book. Feeling very out of place and almost ashamed of doing so, I silently paid my respects to three people I never knew, but have heard described so often by relatives and friends, to the point where I hope I can see into their characters. I went there to remind myself this is not just about the story. I make a promise that I will not varnish the truth about their lives. I will try to portray them in all their goodness, their strengths and achievements, as well as their human foibles.

Above all, I want to let the world know it is a little bit poorer for their loss.

I have realised that while Teddy, Loiva and Clodine Gonzales lost their lives, there are so many others who have also become victims. Firstly, there are the extended family members on both sides, who have had the shame and publicity brought upon them, not by their own doing. I have learned more than ever about strength and dignity from them, in particular from Emily Luna, who put her trust in me and allowed me into her home, sharing her personal thoughts and fears with me, as well as the occasional light-hearted moment. I hope her trust was not misplaced. I have come to know her as a friend, as well as one of the most courageous people I have ever met.

Then there are the countless other victims, those unwittingly caught up as pawns in Sef Gonzales' machinations. The list is long: Shane Hanley and John Atamian, Sam Dacillo, Kathy Wu,

Latisha, Don McGregor, Alan, Amanda, and their mother, Belinda, to name a few. Even me. Much as it pains me to realise it, while I thought I was getting the exclusive story on Sef, he was using me to achieve his ends, to set up a smokescreen for his staged abduction.

As I wait, I decide on impulse to head into the victims' room adjoining the court. It is a room I have deliberately not entered during the six-week trial, preferring to give the family its privacy, although I have chatted to relatives outside the court. I go to the door. Emily and her sister Annie Paraan are there, as is their brother Joseph Claridades, who was formerly married to Monica Gonzales. On a seat is the elderly Amelita Claridades. I put one arm around Emily's shoulders and she turns and gives me a hug. 'I just wanted to say thank you for everything,' I tell her, at a loss for any more words. Then I thank Annie, the woman I met in the Philippines long before the trial began, the woman who generously gave her time, crying freely as she told me about her family, then tried to insist on paying for our coffees. I give her a hug as well and quickly leave the room.

The tears don't hit me until I reach the steps of the court again. I am standing with two other female journalists and Mick Sheehy is approaching us. I feel bewildered and embarrassed by my reaction, particularly in front of this senior cop who has been so professional and so very helpful to me. But, to his credit, Sheehy doesn't raise an eyebrow or even comment on it as he talks to us.

Not long afterwards, I am chatting to the defence team in another section of the court, with a couple of other print journos, away from the hubbub of the television media. After keeping my distance from the defence for most of the trial — I was always highly suspicious of defence lawyers — I have realised they were simply doing their job to the best of their

ability, and doing it with the same integrity as the police who
investigated the murders. As the saying goes, it's a thankless
job, but someone has to do it.

That night, everyone goes out to blow off some steam at a
local pub, and a few newspaper journos, myself included, turn
up late after frenetically filing stories on the verdicts. Copious
amounts of alcohol flow as people throw off the emotional
burden and stress of the experience. Back at Silverwater jail,
Sef will shortly be assessed as at risk of violence from other
inmates and placed in segregation. No celebrating or
companionship for him.

FOUR MONTHS LATER, a day after his 24th birthday, Sef
is sentenced to spend his life in jail. Still he continues to
create more fiction and protest his innocence. The trouble is,
not many people are interested in listening to Sef Gonzales
any more. That, in the end, is his problem. He pulls you in
with his charm, uses you, then discards you when you are of
no further use. With his fanciful tales, he is like the boy who
cried wolf. Eventually, it is he who loses out and ends up
alone. It is almost sad.

Sometimes I wonder what made Sef the way he is. Was he
born like this? If not, when did he lose his way? If there is
any lesson in the Gonzales tragedy, it would be from this. If
Sef could tell us what could have been changed, how it went
so wrong, such tragedies could possibly be averted in the
future.

Emily Luna is still hoping Sef will show some sign of
remorse, and is concerned that if he doesn't come clean, even
to himself, he will not join his family in Heaven when he
dies. His life sentence means he will have all the time in the
world to come to grips with the enormity of his crimes. Yet
somehow, I think no-one but Sef Gonzales will ever truly

know the reason behind the triple murder at 6 Collins Street, North Ryde, on 10 July 2001. To explain it, Sef will have to confess his guilt. It may even be that he has convinced himself of his innocence, that the truth is too ghastly for him to face. I, for one, won't be holding my breath.

I think Sef will take the truth with him to his grave.

Author's note

This book has been written without the use of footnotes, for the sake of uninterrupted reading. I do not propose to list of every source of information I have used during the more than three years I have been researching and writing this book. However, I do wish to list some key source material. A significant part of the book has been written from coverage of court proceedings, including Sef's preliminary court hearings, the committal hearing, the murder trial, the sentencing, and the court proceedings regarding the estate. I covered these extensively for the *Daily Telegraph*, and have looked through reams of transcript material as well as court judgments. I have also viewed court records for the matter of Teddy's immigration fraud charges, and accessed the Administrative Appeals Tribunal judgment regarding *Gaculais and Minister for Immigration and Multicultural Affairs*. Lastly, I have cited findings from the Baguio court judgment regarding Peter Ng and Teddy Gonzales' stabbing in 1978.

Much of the court evidence I have referred to is in the committal and trial chapters, and it is unnecessary to reiterate here the names of the witnesses involved. However, in some earlier sections of the book I have used evidence introduced at trial where the chronology calls for it. For example, when referring to the observations and thoughts of emergency uniformed personnel who first arrived at the murder scene, I have mostly used information obtained from their evidence at the trial. The mentions of the discovery of the poisons material on Sef's computer and the post mortems by Dr Allan Cala are also good examples of where I have used trial evidence in earlier chapters of the book.

I have also relied on numerous police witness statements and police interviews. The statement of 'Kathy Wu' and her evidence at the committal hearing have formed the basis for the 'Kathy Wu' chapter. A police interview of 'Linda Pham' and her evidence at trial were key sources of information about her relationship with Sef, and Tawas police have helped me fill in the gaps. Information about Chris Fernstat's experiences with Clodine came from his police statement. Statements from family members, including Emily Luna and Amelita Claridades, were also of use, as were Sef's statements and transcripts of Sef's police-recorded interviews. Other sources include the website Sef set up, supposedly by 'Daisy Diaz', and letters written by Sef to the *Daily Telegraph* and Mick Sheehy.

I have also conducted my own interviews — sometimes too many to count — with a number of people in both Sydney and Baguio. These form the basis for a large proportion of the book, in relation to both the family history and the investigation. In alphabetical order, those I interviewed are:

Attorney Bensheen Apolinar
Sue Atamian (John's wife)
Paul Auglys (now out of the force)
Madeleine Azcona
Senior Sergeant Bob Betts
Father Janusz Bieniek
Father Paul Cahill

Attorney Rickson Chiong (Cordillera Regional Director,
   National Bureau of Investigation, the Philippines)
Father Rex Curry
Father Kevin Dadswell
Bernado David
Jess Diaz
Dr Amado Dizon
Freddie Gonzales
Sef Gonzales
Annie Gonzales–Tesoro
Shane Hanley
'Jane' (Loiva's friend)
'Jane's' daughter
Detective Inspector Geoff Leonard
Emily Luna
Dennis Miralis
Peter Ng (who stabbed Teddy in 1978)
Annie Paraan
'Amanda Pedro'
'Belinda Pedro'
Harry Potter
Mick Sheehy (now Detective Inspector)
Darren Sly (now Detective Sergeant)
Mark Tedeschi, QC
Winston Terracini, SC

As a last note, I must add that Mark Tedeschi, Winston
Terracini and Dennis Miralis, as lawyers involved in Sef's case,
were restricted both professionally and legally in what they
could divulge about it. However, they could and did advise me
on matters of legislation and case law, their legal careers and
backgrounds, and how they came to be involved in the case.

Acknowledgments

There are many people without whose time and assistance I could not have completed this project.

First and foremost I extend sincere thanks to each and every person who allowed me to interview them for this book. In particular, I wish to acknowledge Emily Luna, Annie Paraan, Freddie Gonzales and Annie Gonzales-Tesoro, for sharing their family memories with me, and Amelita Claridades, who gave me access to the Gonzales' extensive photo albums.

To the police on the case, including Mick Sheehy, Paul Auglys and Geoff Leonard, I appreciate your time, assistance and limitless patience.

I wish to thank Mark Tedeschi, QC, for your advice on matters of law, and DPP solicitors Nicole Paul and Fiona Rowbotham, for the legwork you both put into chasing up transcripts and exhibits. I thank Winston Terracini, SC, Philip Massey and Paul Townsend, for assisting me where you could.

To Attorney Rickson Chiong and Dr Amado Dizon, of the Philippines, you made my Baguio trip so much easier. I also wish to acknowledge the New South Wales Police and the Office of the Director of Public Prosecutions for giving me access to in-depth information on the investigation, as well as allowing me to access court transcripts, and crime-scene photographs taken by the police and tendered as evidence during the trial, for publication. I must also thank both the New South Wales and Commonwealth government agencies that allowed me to reproduce copyright transcript material.

To my *Daily Telegraph* colleagues Charles Miranda and Letitia Rowlands, who covered early aspects of the case for the paper, thank you for sharing your insights. On that note, I also thank those friends and colleagues who provided a listening ear, encouragement and advice. I must also thank the *Telegraph*'s former editor Campbell Reid for allowing me to pursue this project, and former *Telegraph* news editor Andy Byrne for providing the original inspiration.

Thank you to my agent Bill Tikos, and the HarperCollins team, especially my editor Emma Kelso, who helped turn inspiration into reality.

David Sylvester, thank you for your support, and for generously lending me a car and computer in those early research stages.

Last but not least, I thank my family, in particular my sisters Angie and Michelle (the great brain-stormers), for your encouragement and belief in this project.

Kara Lawrence
2006